Governance and Democracy in Asia

MODERNITY AND IDENTITY IN ASIA SERIES

MODERNITY AND IDENTITY IN ASIA SERIES

Globalization, Culture and Inequality in Asia
Timothy S. Scrase, Todd Miles Joseph Holden and Scott Baum

Looking for Money: Capitalism and Modernity
in an Orang Asli Village
Alberto Gomes

Governance and Democracy in Asia
Takashi Inoguchi and Matthew Carlson

JAPANESE SOCIETY SERIES
General Editor: Yoshio Sugimoto

Lives of Young Koreans in Japan
Yasunori Fukuoka

Globalization and Social Change in Contemporary Japan
J.S. Eades, Tom Gill and Harumi Befu

Coming Out in Japan: The Story of Satoru and Ryuta
Satoru Ito and Ryuta Yanase

Japan and Its Others:
Globalization, Difference and the Critique of Modernity
John Clammer

Hegemony of Homogeneity:
An Anthropological Analysis of Nihonjinron
Harumi Befu

Foreign Migrants in Contemporary Japan
Hiroshi Komai

A Social History of Science and Technology in
Contempory Japan, Volume 1
Shigeru Nakayama

Farewell to Nippon: Japanese Lifestyle Migrants in Australia
Machiko Sato

The Peripheral Centre:
Essays on Japanese History and Civilization
Johann P. Arnason

A Genealogy of 'Japanese' Self-images
Eiji Oguma

Class Structure in Contemporary Japan
Kenji Hashimoto

An Ecological View of History
Tadao Umesao

Nationalism and Gender
Chizuko Ueno

Native Anthropology: The Japanese Challenge
to Western Academic Hegemony
Takami Kuwayama

Youth Deviance in Japan: Class Reproduction of Non-Conformity
Robert Stuart Yoder

Japanese Companies: Theories and Realities
Masami Nomura and Yoshihiko Kamii

From Salvation to Spirituality:
Popular Religious Movements in Modern Japan
Susumu Shimazono

The 'Big Bang' in Japanese Higher Education:
The 2004 Reforms and the Dynamics of Change
J.S. Eades, Roger Goodman and Yumiko Hada

Japanese Politics: An Introduction
Takashi Inoguchi

A Social History of Science and Technology in
Contempory Japan, Volume 2
Shigeru Nakayama

Gender and Japanese Management
Kimiko Kimoto

Philosophy of Agricultural Science: A Japanese Perspective
Osamu Soda

A Social History of Science and Technology in
Contempory Japan, Volume 3
Shigeru Nakayama and Kunio Goto

Japan's Underclass: Day Laborers and the Homeless
Hideo Aoki

A Social History of Science and Technology
in Contemporary Japan, Volume 4
Shigeru Nakayama and Hitoshi Yoshioka

Escape from Work: A Lifestyle Choice of Japanese Youth
Reiko Koike

Social Welfare in Japan: Principles and Applications
Kojun Furukawa

Toyota's Assembly Line: A Sociological Participant Observation
Ryoji Ihara

Social Stratification and Inequality Series

Inequality amid Affluence: Social Stratification in Japan
Junsuke Hara and Kazuo Seiyama

Intentional Social Change: A Rational Choice Theory
Yoshimichi Sato

Constructing Civil Society in Japan:
Voices of Environmental Movements
Koichi Hasegawa

Deciphering Stratification and Inequality: Japan and beyond
Yoshimichi Sato

Social Justice in Japan: Concepts, Theories and Paradigms
Ken-ichi Ohbuchi

Advanced Social Research Series

A Sociology of Happiness
Kenji Kosaka

Frontiers of Social Research: Japan and beyond
Akira Furukawa

MODERNITY AND IDENTITY IN ASIA SERIES

Governance and Democracy in Asia

Edited by

Takashi Inoguchi

and

Matthew Carlson

This English edition first published in 2006 by
Trans Pacific Press, PO Box 120, Rosanna, Melbourne, Victoria 3084, Australia
Telephone: +61 3 9459 3021 Fax: +61 3 9457 5923
Email: info@transpacificpress.com
Web: http://www.transpacificpress.com

Copyright © Trans Pacific Press 2006

Designed and set by digital environs, Melbourne. www.digitalenvirons.com

Printed by BPA Print Group, Burwood, Victoria, Australia

Distributors

Asia and the Pacific
Kinokuniya Company Ltd.

Head office:
Shin-Mizonokuchi Bldg. 2F
5-7, Hisamoto 3-chome
Takatsu-ku, Kawasaki 213-8506
Japan
Telephone: +81 (0) 44-874-9642
Fax: +81 (0) 44-829-1025
Email: bkimp@kinokuniya.co.jp
Web: http://www.kinokuniya.co.jp

Asia-Pacific office:
Kinokuniya Book Stores of Singapore Pte., Ltd.
391B Orchard Road #13-06/07/08
Ngee Ann City Tower B
Singapore 238874
Telephone: +65 6276 5558
Fax: +65 6276 5570
Email: SSO@kinokuniya.co.jp

Australia and New Zealand
UNIREPS
University of New South Wales
Sydney, NSW 2052
Australia
Telephone: +61(0)2-9664-0999
Fax: +61(0)2-9664-5420
Email: info.press@unsw.edu.au
Web: http://www.unireps.com.au

USA and Canada
International Specialized Book
Services (ISBS)
920 NE 58th Avenue, Suite 300
Portland, Oregon 97213-3786
USA
Telephone: (800) 944-6190
Fax: (503) 280-8832
Email: orders@isbs.com
Web: http://www.isbs.com

All rights reserved. No production of any part of this book may take place without the written permission of Trans Pacific Press.

ISBN 978-1-876843-37-3 (Hardback)
ISBN 978-1-876843-38-0 (Paperback)

Contents

Figures	viii
Tables	ix
List of Contributors	xi
Acknowledgements	xv

1	Introduction *Takashi Inoguchi and Matthew Carlson*	1
2	Support for Democracy and Freedom in Japan *Matthew Carlson and Taku Sugawara*	20
3	Trust and Confidence in the Government of South Korea *Chung-Si Ahn and Won-Taek Kang*	44
4	The Social Foundation of Taiwan's New Democracy *Hsin-Huang Michael Hsiao*	70
5	A New Era of Politics in Malaysia: Ferment and Fragmentation *Francis Loh Kok Wah*	86
6	Political Participation and Governance in Thailand *Chaiwat Khamchoo*	107
7	Democratic Developments and Changing Values in China *Guo Dingping*	131
8	India's Maturing Democracy *Sanjay Kumar*	163

Appendix	185
Index	196

Figures

2.1	Freedom House scores and per capita GDP	23
2.2	Governance by the will of the people by age group	27
2.3	Selection of freedom and per capita GDP	34
2.4	Selection of freedom by age	36
3.1	Democratic representation and government responsiveness	48
3.2	Perceptions of government as efficient and just	50
3.3	Perceptions of government as bureaucratic and corrupt	51
3.4	Human rights are fully respected	52
3.5	Right to freedom of speech respected	53
3.6	Equality before the law and equal pay for equal work	54
3.7	Perceptions of equality between women and men	55
8.1	Turnout rates in India's lower house, 1952–2004	165
8.2	Voting rates in rural and urban areas	166
8.3	Interest in election campaigns	168
8.4	Preference for political system	169
8.5	Believe that the individual vote matters	171
8.6	Increasing belief that political parties are important	172
8.7	Change in economic conditions among different segments of population	175
8.8	Overall satisfaction of people with their present economic conditions	179
8.9	Future expectations about economic conditions	181

Tables

1.1	Support for political, economic, and human rights questions	11
1.2	Political rights and civil liberties ratings	14
2.1	Governance by the will of the people by country	25
2.2	What matters most in life	31
2.3	Logistic regression for selection of freedom	39
3.1	Changes in political efficacy and system responsiveness in South Korea, 1994–1996	58
4.1	Democracy and trust in Taiwan	72
4.2	Human rights in Taiwan	75
4.3	Discrimination in Taiwan	77
4.4	Attitudes toward environmental problems in Taiwan	79
4.5	Attitudes toward public safety and crime in Taiwan	81
5.1	Perception of the government	97
5.2	Attitudes toward procedural democracy	97
5.3	Attitudes toward democracy by education level	98
6.1	Perceptions of the Thai government	111
7.1	How Shanghai youth view independence	139
7.2	Level of political interest among Beijing urban residents	142
7.3	Selected democratic values	146
7.4	The United Nations' most important future aim	150
7.5	Level of trust in political principles among Shanghai youth	151
7.6	Attitudes toward democratization among Shanghai youth	153
8.1	Turnout among social communities, 1996–2004	167
8.2	Preference for political system by age, education, and class	170
8.3	Importance of vote and parties	173
8.4	Present living conditions	177
8.5	Sufficiency of income by economic class	178
8.6	Perception of future economic conditions	182

Contributors

Chung-Si Ahn is professor of political science at Seoul National University. He has held visiting appointments at Princeton University, the National University of Singapore, and the University of Tokyo. His former academic positions include the chairman of the Department of Political Science at Seoul National University (1991–1993), Director of the Institute of Social Sciences (1994–1996), and the Institute for Korean Political Studies (2000–2002). He served as the 2004 President of the Korean Association of International Studies, and was instrumental in founding the Asian Consortium for Political Research (ACPR) in 2004. His recent publications include: *Democracy in Asia and Europe: Toward a Universal Definition* (co-editor, Marshall Cavendish Academic, 2006), *New Development of Local Democracy in Asia* (Seoul National University Press, 2005). He earned a Ph.D. in 1977 at the University of Hawaii.

Matthew Carlson is assistant professor of political science at the University of Vermont. He has been a lecturer at the University of California, Davis and a research associate at the Norwegian University of Science and Technology. He specializes in Asian politics, public opinion, electoral systems, and human rights. His recent publications include: 'The evolution of informal norms in Japan' (*Asian Survey*, 2006), 'Electoral reform and the costs of personal support in Japan' (*Journal of East Asian Studies*, 2006), and 'Citizens' evaluations of political rights in Asia' (in *Human Beliefs and Values in Striding Asia,* Akashi Shoten, 2006). He earned his Ph.D. at the University of California, Davis and M.A. in international studies from the University of Washington.

Dingping Guo is professor of political science at the School of International Relations and Public Affairs and Vice-Director of the Center for Japanese Studies, Fudan University (Shanghai). His research interests focus on comparative politics, especially comparative East Asian politics. His publications include: *Development Model and*

Regional Cooperation in East Asia (co-editor, Fudan University Press, 2005), *Governance and Democracy in Shanghai* (Chongqing Press, 2005), *Study of Political Transition in Korea* (Chinese Social Science Press, 2000), *Political Party and Government* (Zhejiang Renmin Press, 1998), and *Political Pluralism* (San Lian Book Store Ltd., 1994), as well as many articles in Chinese, English, and Japanese. He earned his Ph.D. from Fudan University in 1999, and another Ph.D. from the University of Tokyo in 2002.

Hsin-Huang Michael Hsiao is the executive director of the Center for Asia–Pacific Area Studies (CAPAS) at Academia Sinica in Taipei. He has been a research fellow at the Institute for Sociology at Academia Sinica since 1983 and a professor of sociology at the National Taiwan University since 1984. He was national policy advisor to the President of Taiwan between 1996 and 2006. Dr. Hsiao's most recent publications include: *The Changing Faces of the Middle Classes in Asia–Pacific* (editor, Academia Sinica, 2006), *Taiwan's New Paradigms* (co-author, Taiwan Advocates, 2006), and *Asian New Democracies: The Philippines, South Korea and Taiwan Compared* (Taiwan Foundation for Democracy, forthcoming). He earned his M.A. in 1976 and Ph.D. and 1979, both at the State University of New York at Buffalo.

Takashi Inoguchi is professor of political science, Chuo University, Tokyo and professor emeritus of the University of Tokyo. He specializes in comparative politics and international relations, especially in East and Southeast Asia. His recent publications include: *Political Cultures in Asia and Europe* (coauthor, Routledge, forthcoming), *The Uses of Institutions* (coeditor, Palgrave, forthcoming), *Federalism in Asia* (coeditor, Edward Elgar, forthcoming), *Human Beliefs and Values in Striding Asia* (principal coeditor, Akashi Shoten, 2006), *Japanese Politics: An Introduction* (Trans Pacific Press, 2005), *Values and Lifestyles in Urban Asia* (principal coeditor, Siglo XXI Editores, 2004), *Japan's Asian Policy* (editor, Palgrave, 2004), *American Democracy Promotion* (coeditor, Oxford University Press, 2000), and *Japanese Foreign Policy Today* (coeditor, Palgrave, 2000). He is President of the Asian Consortium for Political Research and former president of the Japan Association of International Relations. He is the founding editor of two journals, *Japanese Journal of Political Science* (Cambridge University Press) and *International Relations of the Asia–Pacific* (Oxford University Press).

Won-Taek Kang is currently teaching at Soongsil University in Seoul, Korea. His academic interests include elections, party politics and legislative studies. He has published articles in journals including *Electoral Studies, Journal of Theoretical Politics*, and *Public Administration*. His recent work is about effects of the Internet on party politics. He received his Ph.D. at the London School of Economics and Political Science in 1997.

Chaiwat Khamchoo is professor of political science at Chulalongkorn's Department of International Relations and former dean of the Faculty of Political Science. His latest publications include: 'Thailand: the primacy of prosperity in democracy' in *Values and Life Styles in Urban Asia* (coedited, Siglo XXI Editores, 2005) and 'Thailand: democracy and the power of a popular leader' in *Human Beliefs and Values in Striding Asia* (coedited, Akashi Shoten, 2006). He holds a Ph.D. from the University of Washington.

Sanjay Kumar is a fellow at the Centre for the Study of Developing Societies (CSDS), Delhi specializing in survey research and electoral politics. He was their National Coordinator of National Election Studies for 1998, 1999 and 2004. He also directed various other CSDS national and state-level studies, and participated in a pioneering study on assessing election expenses during the 1999 Lok Sabha elections. He has contributed more than 125 articles to national dailies, news magazines, academic journals, and edited books.

Francis Loh Kok Wah is professor of politics at the Universiti Sains Malaysia in Penang. His latest publications are *Southeast Asian Responses to Globalization: Restructuring Governance and Deepening Democracy* (co-editor, NIAS Press, 2005), *New Politics in Malaysia* (co-editor, Institute of Southeast Asian Studies, 2003), and *Democracy in Malaysia: Discourse and Practices* (co-editor, Routledge, 2002). He is the secretary of Aliran, a multi-ethnic Malaysian NGO advocating human rights and justice for all, and a member of the editorial collective of Aliran Monthly. He is a fellow of the Asian Regional Exchange for New Alternatives (ARENA, Seoul) and was a member of the Global Security and Cooperation Committee, SSRC (New York), from 1999–2003. He received his Ph.D. from Cornell University.

Taku Sugawara is project researcher of political science at the University of Tokyo. His recent publications include contributions to *Sangiin no Kenkyu* [Japan's Upper House: Members and their Activities, 1947–2002] (co-editor), *Senkyo Poster no Kenkyu* [Political Posters in Japan: Slogans and Images], *Gendai Nihon no Seijikazo* [Members of the Japanese Diet: An Analysis of their Political Activities, 1990–1998] (all published by Bokutakusha), as well as other works. He received his M.A. in law from the University of Tokyo and is completing his Ph.D. at the same institution.

Acknowledgements

We would like to acknowledge the indispensable support and encouragement from many individuals and institutions in completing this multinational project. Emiko Tomiie, Nippon Research Center, alerted us of the Gallup Millennium Survey even before the results were publicized. With her suggestion, the initial seeds of this project were planted. The project benefited from the help of Chung-Si Ahn at Seoul National University. We are grateful to Professor Ahn and the Seoul National University's Center for Korean Political Studies for holding a conference where scholars presented papers that eventually formed many of the chapters of this book. A second conference was hosted by the Institute of Oriental Culture at the University of Tokyo. We are thankful to the Institute for their generous support as well as to all of the participants in these conferences. A special thanks to Tanya Casperson for helping us to edit and proofread each and every sentence. We are also appreciative to Japan's Ministry of Education and Science for the financial support provided to Professor Inoguchi (grant #11102001, #15203005, and #17002001). Thanks are due to the Shizuoka Forum that enabled Sanjay Kuman to present his paper in Shizuoka in 2005. We owe a large debt to Yoshio Sugimoto, Director of Trans Pacific Press, for his unswerving belief in our manuscript.

Each of us has several specific institutions and individuals we would like to acknowledge. Takashi Inoguchi thanks Chuo University and his staff members. Kimiko Goko and Ken Firmalino are worthy of special mention. He also acknowledges the helpful comments provided by Gregory Noble and Satomi Tani at the annual convention of the Japanese Politics Study Association in 2003. Matthew Carlson expresses gratitude to the Department of Political Science and Asian Studies Program at the University of Vermont for providing research support and an excellent working environment. He also thanks the authors of each chapter for their hard work and patience in bringing this volume to completion.

July 2006
Takashi Inoguchi & Matthew Carlson

Chapter One
Introduction
Takashi Inoguchi and Matthew Carlson

Asia is one of the most dynamic and divergent parts of the world. Divergence is a fundamental factor in a region that contains countries that range from poverty-stricken to affluent, from complete dictatorships to full-fledged democracies, and from communist to capitalist systems. Dynamism is no less basic, with many countries rising from the nadir of devastation of war and colonialism in 1945 to affluence and the object of envy in recent times. In this book we examine how the divergence and dynamism of this region interacts with citizens' understanding of governance and democracy. A deeper understanding of mass attitudes in Asia is imperative, necessitating elaboration and explication.

This book signifies one of the latest efforts of scholars to investigate what citizens think about national governance and democracy in Asia. What do people think about the state of democracy in their country? Are elections free and fair? Are human rights respected? The purpose of this study is to investigate patterns of national governance in seven countries located in East, Southeast, and South Asia: Japan, South Korea, Taiwan, Thailand, Malaysia, China, and India. The authors of each chapter analyze aspects of governance and democracy on the basis of public opinion surveys and other evidence, and draw their own conclusions. Most of the authors make frequent use of the Gallup International Millennium Survey (1999) (henceforth referred to as the Gallup survey), a public opinion poll conducted in a broad range of countries that asks respondents many pertinent, governance and democracy-related questions.[1]

This scholarly endeavor contributes to our broader understanding of the Asian region in several ways. From a theoretical standpoint, what citizens think about issues of national governance and democracy contributes to existing studies of public opinion in countries at various stages of political and economic development. An examination into what citizens think about government, human rights, and democracy in these countries contributes to knowledge about public opinion, political attitudes, as well as the specific political and socioeconomic context of individual countries. From a policy standpoint, Asia accounts for approximately three-fifths of the world's population. How citizens in different parts of Asia think about governance and democracy is an important issue for policymakers, educators, and scholars alike.

As a lead-up to the country chapters, let us take inventory of some of the major theoretical debates in the study of Asian politics. Although we could mention many debates, we opt to focus more narrowly on three broader concepts used in the literature: Asian values, the developmental state, and third-wave democracy. We consider to what extent these debates can help characterize national governance for countries in East, Southeast, and South Asia on the basis of the Gallup survey and use of democracy measures from the Freedom House organization. We begin by situating these three concepts in a broader global context during the last quarter of the twentieth century.

Global trends in the region

Francis Fukuyama (1992) argues that the end of the Cold War marked the end of history. What he meant by this was that the Western model of liberal democratic capitalism had triumphed. In the long run, he believed that all societies would be organized along liberal democratic lines, because this model had proved itself to be superior to all other forms of government. Fukuyama's convergence thesis had an element of truth as suggested by the new tide of democratization and the increased integration of global markets. However, it is also the case that stark disparities exist among the types of political and economic systems utilized around the world. The rise of hybrid regimes that combine democratic and authoritarian elements, for example, challenges the thesis that liberal democracy will prevail (Diamond 2002).

Given the passage of time since Fukuyama made this argument in the 1990s, it is instructive to qualify the original convergence thesis somewhat, as these disparities have become clearer, or have simply refused to go away. When convergence is achieved in one dimension, it does not necessarily follow that convergence will ensue in every dimension. This recognition led the former World Trade Organization director, Renato Ruggeiro, to remark that the integrated world is proving more difficult to govern than the divided world ever was. In a similar vein, the multinational company Shell created a catch phrase that specified that as markets become more globalized, consumption patterns become more fragmented. It is mistaken to assume that inexorable convergence is taking place. Moreover, even where convergence does occur, we should not assume that it will proceed uniformly across all dimensions of political, economic, and social life.

Taking these caveats into consideration, some favorable signs can be detected that suggest that some of the broad convergence, along the lines Fukuyama mentioned, took place in parts of Asia at the close of the twentieth century. In countries such as Thailand, Taiwan, and South Korea, rapid economic development has lead to democratic transition (Laotamatos 1997: 15). The process of the late-marketization in the economies of China and Vietnam, which started nearly two decades ago, is becoming more similar to the late industrialization experienced in South Korea and Japan (Lee et al. 2000: 5). Additionally, the process of marketization often appears to be accompanied by the unleashing of other social forces that can help to propel a society toward democratization. In November 2002, for example, the Sixteenth Congress of the Chinese Communist Party adopted an inclusive doctrine that allows bourgeois capitalists to be admitted as party members. This willingness to accept bourgeois capitalists as a legitimate element of Chinese society constitutes a significant concession to the forces of capitalism.

Convergence in Asia can also be discerned in political and economic realms. For many countries in Asia, the reconfiguration and liberalization of state-market links in the region appear to steadily undermine the powers of the government. The interconnectedness of Asian economies was nowhere more evident than in the case of the Asian financial crisis (Hagaard 1999; Pempel 1999; Noble and Ravenhill 2000). In an overview of this crisis, one scholar suggests that in Asia a complicated multilevel dynamic exists in which politics and economics are locked in '...an ongoing dance in which actions by one partner are matched by responses from the other' (Pempel 1999: 4). It therefore seems meaningful to speak of a broad convergence along several political and economic axes. This does not mean, however, that scholars should neglect areas of divergence within and across Asia. The areas where the political and economic dimensions do not converge perfectly warrant our attention and explanation.

A major purpose of the authors involved in this book is to reveal some of the divergence within and across Asia by investigating the values and opinions of ordinary people as expressed in the Gallup survey and other surveys. The Gallup survey was available for most of the country chapters in this volume with primary exception of India; the survey was conducted in China, but only some of the questions were asked.[2] The Gallup survey not only contains many relevant questions on governance and democracy, but it asks the same questions across different countries, which enables the authors of the country chapters to make cross-national comparisons. In the next section, we discuss the three larger concepts used in the literature that can help us better characterize the civil, economic, and political features of governance in the Asian region: Asian values, the developmental state, and third-wave democracy.

Asian values, the developmental state, and third-wave democracy

The term Asian values refers to a set of norms and values that are communitarian, collectivist, hierarchical, and often associated with Confucianism. Some of the key values identified as being Asian include respect for one's family, deference to authority, and selfless diligence. The former prime minister of Singapore, Lee Kuan Yew, was an eloquent exponent of Asian values in the early 1990s, and suggested that if Asians were to adopt the American conception of freedom, then chaos and a decline in competitiveness would likely ensue.[3] Likewise, the former prime minister of Malaysia, Mahathir bin Mohamad, has been no less eloquent in advocating his 'look East' policy centered on the construction of Asian values that he claimed were responsible for the success and stability of Asia (Khoo 2003: 25)

To better understand the Asian values debate, it is essential to place it in an appropriate political and historical context. What has been called the Asian values offensive took place in the early and mid-1990s in the ideological vacuum that the end of the Cold War created (Thompson 2001; Bell 2000). At the heart of the controversy is the claim that because Asia is fundamentally different from the West, it must construct political systems that fit the unique conditions of its cultures (Hood 1998: 1). It was, therefore, necessary for some Asian governments to intervene in the economy or to curb such liberties as free speech to support communitarian and other admired values. Some Asian leaders could thus make the case that authoritarian practices can co-exist in countries that are highly developed.

Viewed retrospectively, in the first half of the 1990s, East Asia was booming and the East Asian miracle was at its zenith (World Bank 1993). East Asia at that time was also experiencing a mini-domino democratization effect, starting in the Philippines, and spreading through Taiwan, South Korea, China, Thailand, and Cambodia (Laotamatos 1995; Marsh, Blondel, and Inoguchi 2000; Case 2002; Marsh 2006). In the security sphere, both Koreas temporarily experimented with the idea of a nuclear free Korea in the early 1990s. In the Philippines, the United States withdrew the last of its military bases at the end of 1992. In Taiwan, Lee Denghui, a native Taiwanese, served as chairman of the Kuomintang and was elected president. Vietnam mended fences with China and then with the United States.

After the shackles of the Cold War and the associated regional dominance of the United States were cast off, some parts of Asia appeared to change and even prosper. Most of the economies in East Asia experienced booms and heightened trading with each other. The scale of Asian intraregional transactions came to surpass the scale of its regional transactions with the United States. The Japanese invested in East Asian manufacturing so heavily that it looked at one time as if the idea of 'Asia in Japan's embrace' was a reality (Hatch and Yamamura 1996). In the political sphere, the dons of developmental authoritarianism, Ferdinand Marcos of the Philippines, Park Chung Hee of South Korea, Chiang Ching Kuo of Taiwan, and the Thai military, all fell one after the other in this heyday of high economic performance.

At this time the post-Cold War prospects of East Asia were not clear. The end of the U.S.–Soviet rivalry made it likely that U.S. hegemonic unipolarity would permeate East Asia. The deepening of financial globalization meant the likely intrusion of market forces into highly regulated domestic markets. East and Southeast Asia, bastions of developmental authoritarianism and communism, were apprehensive of the further diffusion of democracy. The Asian values offensive should be understood within this larger historical and political context.

In addition to the debate over Asian values, the literature on the developmental state is relevant and useful for characterizing patterns of governance in the broader Asian region. A developmental state is one that focuses utmost attention and efforts on economic development. Developmental states are able to take advantage of their comparative backwardness to develop in a twentieth-century context. Such states are characterized by a concern to raise living standards, a pro-active strategy toward the market, and a small but intrusive bureaucracy that controls society. Instead of allowing the free market to govern, governments in such states actively intervene through such actions as deciding industrial policy or setting the foreign exchange rate.

The Japanese state in the third-quarter of the twentieth century is often said to provide the paradigmatic example of the developmental state (Johnson 1982). The primary feature of the developmental state, as far as production is concerned, is the massive mobilization of capital and labor. In other words, the significance of technological innovation and the information revolution are not stressed. In the next chapter on Japan, the authors discuss some of the history of the Japanese developmental state, which they then relate to their analysis of public opinion.

In twentieth-century East and Southeast Asia, the developmental strategy has attracted many adherents (Woo-Cumings 1999). Many of the states that have pursued a developmental strategy at one time or another were even less developed than Japan was when it decided to adopt the model. One reason for the popularity of the developmental model, which should not be underestimated, is that many states in the region view Japan as a paradigm case of developmental success and seek to emulate it (Hatch and Yamamura 1996). Despite the more recent rise and influence of China (Lardy 2002), many still regard Japan as a regional role model. The country chapters on the Philippines, Malaysia, South Korea, Thailand, Taiwan, and India offer useful contrasts to the paradigmatic example of Japan's developmental state.

The last concept we wish to introduce is third-wave democracy, which refers to countries that democratized in the fourth quarter of the twentieth century (Huntington 1991; Vanhanen 1997; Rose and Shin 2001). The first wave of democratization occurred after World War I and the second wave after World War II. Several types of democratic development can be discerned.[4] The first type is classical democracy, which developed among a small number of privileged elites. This type of democracy is said to be characterized by societal liberalism and political democracy (Lipset 1998; Rose and Shin 2001). Societal liberalism refers to the generally high levels of civic liberty enjoyed by citizens, whereas political democracy refers to the generally high levels of political entitlement granted to everyone above a certain age.

The second type is the twentieth-century development of democracy under state-led economic development and war mobilization. The development of democracy in Japan is characteristic of this type. In contrast to classical democracy, restrictions on the freedom of speech and the press often coincide with the consolidation of democracy (Banno 1995). Like Japan, similar trends can be discerned in such polities as South Korea and Malaysia as suggested in their respective country chapters. Here the process of democratization has deepened in terms of levels of political participation and contestation, although societal liberalism has remained weaker, in part because of the retention of internal security acts from nondemocratic or colonial days.

The last type is the development of third-wave democratization in the fourth quarter of the twentieth century. According to Huntington (1991: 21), democratic regimes replaced authoritarian ones in approximately thirty countries in Europe, Asia, and Latin America between 1974 and 1989. In Asia, the wave began with India's return to the democratic path in 1977, Turkey (1983), the Philippines (1986), South Korea (1987), Taiwan (1987), and, finally, Pakistan in 1988. In a brief span of fifteen years, the third wave rolled across southern Europe, moved through Latin America, moved on to Asia, and ushered an end to dictatorship in the Soviet bloc (Huntington 1991: 25).

The shift of these countries from authoritarian to democratic regimes, however, has often been problematic. This is because many of the countries have introduced competitive elections before establishing basic institutions of a modern state such as the rule of law and institutions of civil society (Rose and Shin 2001: 331). For this reason, many of the third-wave countries are democracies only in the minimalist or procedural sense. As one scholar notes, many of these countries are developing a form of government that mixes a substantial degree of democracy with a substantial degree of illiberalism (Zakaria 1997: 22). These countries do not represent the notion of a liberal democracy with such characteristics as free and fair elections, rule of law, and protection of civil liberties. The significance of the so-called third-wave democracies has been central to existing characterizations of governance and democracy in broader Asia.

Patterns of governance in Asia

In this introduction we have used the concepts of Asian values, the developmental state, and third-wave democracy to frame our discussion of East and Southeast Asian governance in the 1990s. But it is important to note that we are not necessarily suggesting that these three concepts provide the most accurate representation of contemporary governance in parts of Asia. The phrase 'Asian values,' for example, no longer appears in newspaper headlines. The popularity of the Asian values movement peaked in the early and mid-1990s in the wake of the end of the Cold War. The withering of this debate can be related to specific historical events such as the end of the East Asian economic miracle, accelerated by the Asian financial crisis in 1997 (Thompson 2001). Additionally, few proponents of Asian values have raised their voice in wake of the 9/11 events of 2001 and the subsequent U.S.-led military actions in Afghanistan and Iraq.

Like Asian values, the concept of the developmental state has undergone transformation. Instead of discussing the virtues of the developmental state, much of the debate has shifted to considering ways in which states might adapt and cope with globalization (Jayasuriya 2000). Indeed, it is often suggested that the very nature of the developmental state makes it unsuitable as an agent of rapid and effective response to globalization (Schaede and Grimes 2003). Moves to reconfigure developmental state-led economies in an era of globalization have been underway for some time in parts of Asia.

Finally, the optimism for the so-called third-wave of democracies may prove to be short-lived, especially as many have stagnated or even regressed in the direction of authoritarian practices. As one scholar observed, the almost automatic assumption of democracy promoters during the peak years of the third wave that any country moving away from dictatorship was in transition to democracy has usually been misleading or inaccurate (Carothers 2002: 14). In the twenty-first century, many of the third-wave democracies have started to manifest some symptoms of destabilization and degeneration (Jayasuriya 2000). Asian values, the promotion of the developmental state, and the celebration of the third wave of democratization, are all phenomena that belong to a period that may be passing. The 9/11 terrorist attacks, the war on terrorism, and the emerging prospect of worldwide recession all provide evidence that what might be referred to as a post-Cold War interregnum may be ending.

Yet these three concepts—Asian values, the developmental state, and third-wave democracy—have been widely used in various discussions of regional governance in Asia for the last decade or so. It is, therefore, reasonable to assume that these concepts are still relevant in considering the features of governance in the region. The task we undertake is to use these concepts to examine patterns of governance in Asia at the turn of the twenty-first century. To do so, we choose to use these concepts in conjunction with the Gallup survey and measures of political rights and civil liberties derived from the Freedom House organization.

In the proceeding analysis, we have selected three particular questions to analyze from the Gallup survey that will help us characterize patterns of Asian governance and democracy given our discussion of Asian values, the developmental state, and third-wave democracy. Although the Gallup survey contains a variety of questions that may help us make sense of different components of governance, we focus on questions that reflect citizens' perceptions of political, economic, and civil aspects of society. This task is necessary to examine the debates over Asian values, the developmental state, and third-wave democracy through the lens of mass public attitudes.

The first question we examine taps political aspects of the Asian countries. In the Gallup survey, respondents are asked: 'Do you think that elections in [this country] are free and fair?' The responses to this question are relevant to the debate over third-wave democracies. For the countries we examine that democratized in the third wave, the larger debate suggests that many of these countries may be democracies in only the minimalist or procedural sense. If this characterization contains a kernel of truth, to what extent do respondents in these countries think elections are free and fair?

The second question we chose from the Gallup survey reflects economic aspects of society: 'What would you say matters most in life?' Respondents are asked to select two responses from a list of nine choices that range from having good health to living in freedom. Here we examine the percentage of respondents who selected having a good standard of living as one of the things that matters most in life. How important, exactly, is having a good standard of living in different parts of Asia? Understanding the ways in which citizens think about economic issues can help us make better sense of debates surrounding developmental states, third-wave democracies, and Asian values.

The third and final question from the Gallup survey that we analyze taps civil aspects of society or specifically what citizens think about the human rights condition in their country: 'In general do you think that human rights are being fully respected, partially respected, or are they not being respected at all in [your country]?' Unlike the questions that involve more explicit political or economic evaluations, the responses for this question reflect the extent that human rights are respected. The literature suggests that developmental states and third-wave democracies often repress civil and political rights at the expense of economic development. By analyzing and comparing the responses of these questions, we can consider whether this characterization extends to the dynamics of mass public attitudes in Asia.

The analysis we offer serves as a springboard to introduce many of the country chapters in this book. The countries included in this study represent only parts of Asia rather than the entire whole, although all may face similar economic forces as part of the larger global society. Yet the countries also differ considerably in terms of their history, economic, and political system, and experience with democracy. By commissioning authors to write individual country chapters, the authors are able to compare and contrast their assigned country in order to draw their own conclusions for how issues of governance and democracy should be approached.

In addition to the use of the Gallup and other public opinion surveys, many of the authors make use of the political rights and civil liberties scores published annually by the Freedom House organization. Since 1972, this non-governmental organization has published an annual report, entitled *Freedom in the World*, which is a comparative assessment of the state of political rights and civil liberties around the world. Each year a team of experts rate individual countries using a checklist of questions derived primarily from the Universal Declaration of Human Rights.[5] Using this checklist, Freedom House compiles and publishes a political rights and civil liberties rating for each country.

The Freedom House ratings are commonly used by scholars in comparative research. Some criticize the Freedom House ratings on theoretical or methodological grounds (Onuma 1999; McCormick and Mitchell 1997). However, the Freedom House measures are available for multiple countries and years, which allow us to make cross-national comparisons. As there are shortcomings with any sort of measure, it is important to look beyond the numbers to consider the broader political and socioeconomic context of each country.

Governance, democracy, and public opinion

To examine the dynamics of public opinion toward governance and democracy, the responses for the three questions, which shed light on political, economic and human rights, are summarized in Table 1.1. The figures reported are the percentage of respondents who responded to each of the answer categories. The responses for free and fair elections are listed first, good standard of living second, and the responses to the human rights question last. An examination of the response patterns suggests three general groupings of countries:

1) Japan, Korea, and Taiwan; 2) Malaysia; and 3) Thailand. It remains for China and India to be placed among these countries on the basis of their Freedom House ratings.

The countries in the first group demonstrate fairly low enthusiasm on the political and economic dimensions compared to the other countries but a more moderate position on human rights. On the political dimension, only 40 percent of respondents in Japan, Korea, and Taiwan feel that elections are free and fair. In Taiwan, 56.5 percent of respondents think that elections are not free and fair, whereas the corresponding number for Korea is 53.3 percent. In Japan, approximately 23.5 percent do not know if elections are free or fair. On the economic dimension, approximately 98.2 percent of the respondents in Japan and 90.5 percent in Taiwan do not mention a good standard of living as one of the aspects that matters most in life. In Korea, the corresponding figure is slightly lower at 78.9 percent.

For countries in the first group, the percentage that agrees that human rights are fully respected is less than 4 percent in Japan and Korea but higher in Taiwan at 16.5 percent. The largest percentages of respondents, however, feel that human rights are at least partially respected: Korea has the highest percentage of 80.7 percent, followed by Taiwan (80%) and Japan (74.7%). At the same time, the highest percentages of respondents who feel that human rights are not respected are from Korea (13.8%) and Japan (7.3%). Similar to the

Table 1.1: Support for political, economic, and human rights questions (%)

	Japan	Korea	Taiwan	Malaysia	Thailand
Free & Fair Elections					
Yes	42.2	40.8	39.7	71.3	31.0
No	34.2	53.3	56.5	18.3	66.3
Don't know	23.5	6.0	3.8	10.4	2.8
Good Standard Living					
Mentioned	1.8	21.1	9.5	13.9	26.9
Not mentioned	98.2	78.9	90.5	86.1	73.1
Respect Human Rights					
Fully respected	3.0	3.7	16.5	33.0	10.0
Partially respected	74.7	80.7	80.0	60.3	84.7
Not respected	7.3	13.8	2.1	3.9	4.7
Don't know	15.1	1.8	1.3	2.9	0.6

Source: Gallup survey, questions 6, 22, and 26.

political question, many respondents from Japan do not know if human rights are respected.

Malaysia composes its own distinct group. On the political dimension, approximately 71.3 percent in Malaysia answered that elections are free and fair. This is the highest percentage across all of the countries surveyed in this book. For the economic dimension, 86.1 percent of respondents in Malaysia did not mention a good standard of living as one of the most important aspects of life. Among the five countries, this was neither the lowest nor the highest percentage but rather somewhere in the middle. Finally, on the human rights question, 33 percent of respondents in Malaysia feel that human rights are fully respected in their country. This is the highest percentage among the included countries.

The case of Thailand differs from the first group and the case of Malaysia, and thus we place it in its own category. On the political dimension, Thailand has the smallest percentage of respondents who believe that elections are free and fair. On the economic dimension, Thailand stands out again for having the highest percentage of respondents who selected a good standard of living as one of the things that matters the most in life. Finally, the pattern of responses for the human rights question places Thailand somewhat in the middle of both groups. Approximately 10 percent believe that human rights are respected, which is a considerably lower figure than Malaysia, but higher than the countries in the first group with the exception of Taiwan.

The results of this analysis highlight both areas of convergence and divergence within the Asian countries selected in this volume. On the basis of the three survey questions, Japan, South Korea, and Taiwan form one group, and Malaysia and Thailand compose their own group. Although countries in the first group share similar characteristics, there is ample evidence to suggest considerable divergence as well. The high percentage of 'don't know' responses in Japan, for example, sets this country apart from South Korea, Taiwan and even from Malaysia and Thailand. The analysis presented here needs further analysis and explanation to discern additional areas of divergence and convergence. This is a task carried out in many of the country chapters that follow this introduction.

Freedom House ratings versus public perceptions

Having discussed some of the broader patterns in the responses across these countries, we can further examine these results in light of the

Freedom House ratings for political and civil rights. This is one way to examine whether public perceptions correspond to the Freedom House's rating scheme. As most literature suggest, a large disparity between the Gallup survey and Freedom House might be expected for some illiberal third-wave democracies. It is possible that citizens may view the realities within their country with a more positive evaluation than it deserves because of the strong hand of the state in the political and economic system. Alternatively, some disjuncture may exist between public opinion and 'reality' in countries at high levels of economic development. Few respondents, for example, may be likely to select having a high standard of living as one of the most important things in life if the standard of living is already extremely high.

The Freedom House publishes scores for both political rights and civil liberties, which we compare separately with the results of the Gallup survey. The political rights scores are roughly compared to the survey responses on free and fair elections, whereas the civil rights scores reflect citizens' assessments of human rights. These scores are measured on a one-to-seven scale, with one representing the highest degree of freedom and seven the lowest. In Table 1.2, we report the 2000–2004 scores for all seven countries. For both political rights and civil liberties, the countries with the highest degree of freedom are listed first.

The Freedom House scores indicate that the first group of countries (Japan, Korea, and Taiwan) is ranked very high for political rights and civil liberties with all three countries at the top of each category. The high scores for these three countries stand in contrast to their intermediate position among the Asian countries examined in the Gallup survey for free and fair elections. Moreover, their high and favorable ratings for civil liberties seem to contradict the fairly critical perceptions captured in the Gallup survey.

In contrast, Malaysia is near the bottom of the table for both political rights and civil liberties despite the higher levels of enthusiasm for elections and human rights on the survey questions. At the same time, the case of Thailand occupies a middle position across all of the countries. Unlike the other four countries, the match between the Freedom House scores and results of the Gallup survey appears to be the closest in this country.

Although answers from the Gallup survey are not available for India and China, we are able to situate them among the five other countries surveyed in this book on the basis of the Freedom House scores. China received the least favorable ratings for both political rights and civil liberties. Indeed, the score it received on political rights is the lowest

Table 1.2: Political rights and civil liberties ratings

	2000	2001	2002	2003	2004	Average 2000–2004
Political Rights						
Japan	1	1	1	1	1	1.0
Taiwan	1	1	2	2	2	1.6
Korea	2	2	2	2	2	2.0
India	2	2	2	2	2	2.0
Thailand	3	3	3	3	3	3.0
Malaysia	5	5	5	5	4	4.8
China	7	7	7	7	7	7.0
Civil Liberties						
Taiwan	2	2	2	2	1	1.8
Japan	2	2	2	2	2	2.0
Korea	2	2	2	2	2	2.0
Thailand	3	3	3	3	3	3.0
India	3	3	3	3	3	3.0
Malaysia	5	5	5	4	4	4.6
China	6	6	6	6	6	6.0

Source: Freedom House available at http://www.freedomhouse.org/ratings/index.htm.
Note: Political rights and civil liberties are measured on a one-to-seven scale, with one representing the highest level of freedom and seven the lowest. Countries with the highest scores are listed first under each category.

level of freedom possible in the Freedom House survey. In contrast to China, Freedom House ranks India at the same level as Korea on political rights and at the same level as Thailand on civil liberties. The author of the China chapter make use of public opinion surveys conducted in Beijing and Shanghai to examine perceptions toward issues of governance and democracy; the author of the India chapter uses a national survey to place these results in context.

The disparities captured between the public opinion responses and the Freedom House ratings for political and civil rights suggest that considerable gaps can exist in any assessment of governance and democracy in Asia. To better understand the survey responses, we need to take into full account the political contexts and cultural proclivities from which these responses derive. We caution readers now that we are unable to render an easy verdict. Each author uses a variety of approaches and methods to examine the themes of governance and democracy. Not all of us agreed on which tools and concepts should be used or discarded. We hope, however, that our diverse insights and perspectives are a valuable asset to readers and inspire future thoughts. We now turn to the final section to present a brief overview of the country chapters as they appear in the book.

Japan

In this chapter, Matthew Carlson and Taku Sugawara analyze two main survey questions from the Gallup survey to examine and compare Japan with other countries in the region and other developed economies in the world. First, to what extent do Japanese respondents believe that the country is governed by the will of the people? Second, what sorts of things matter the most in life? For the first question, the authors find that Japan ranks second to last from other Asian countries. For the second question, they find that respondents value things such as health and family. Carlson and Sugawara also find different levels of generational support for the selection of freedom as one of the most valued qualities of life. The authors emphasize the importance of Japan's historical and political context to explain these results.

Korea

In the second country chapter, Chung-Si Ahn and Won-Taek Kang demonstrate that although by many standards Korea is free and democratic, the gap between what people expect and what the government delivers creates some discontent. Although the authors argue that Korea is a fully-fledged democracy, the country exhibits key features of third-wave democracies such as a 'critical' citizenry. Freedom House gives Korea relatively high ratings for political rights and civil liberties. Also, the people, more than ever, feel that the electoral process is legitimate, even though more than half of the citizens do not believe that the system is free or fair. Large numbers of citizens also feel that the government is corrupt and bureaucratic. Koreans question the human rights record and the justice system of their country. Yet Koreans still feel democracy is the best form of political organization, and do not agree that it is alien to Asian thinking.

Taiwan

Hsin-Huang Michael Hsiao examines Taiwan's third-wave democracy, which has made a successful transition from one-party dictatorship to democracy. It has also been successful as a developmental state.

Although Freedom House gives Taiwan high marks for democratic governance, Hsiao's analysis uncovers that its people still tend to be highly critical. Few Taiwanese believe that the government is just; fewer believe that it is efficient; and most believe that it is too bureaucratic. Only a small majority feels that the government answers to the will of the people. The Taiwanese still feel, however, that a democratic system is preferable. They believe that they are able to influence politics and that if they exert enough pressure, Taiwanese society and government can be changed for the better.

Malaysia

Francis Loh Kok Wah considers why Malaysia has experienced rapid economic growth but also a lack of real democratic reform. There has been strong state control since independence. In recent years the growth of multi-ethnic political parties has lead to an increased sense of national solidarity and cooperation among various religious, ethnic, and language groups. With greater significance attached to economics, political reforms have tended to take a back seat. Although wide sections of Malaysian society have called for reform in the areas of human rights, the rule of law, and greater accountability, citizens are relatively satisfied with their government, when compared with other Asian countries in the Gallup survey. Wah attributes these results as a product of 'developmentalism,' which he argues now impose limits on Malaysia's democratization.

Thailand

In his analysis of Thailand, Chaiwat Khamchoo shows that despite high levels of discontent with the quality and actions of elected officials, Thais tend to be more complacent about the slow pace of political reform, when compared to their East Asian counterparts. A factor that may play a role is that with an improved standard of living, successful Thais are not as interested in politics as they are in economic growth.

Open debates do not take place regularly, and people may fear reprisals if they voice discontent in public even though the situation has greatly improved since the overthrow of the military government in the early 1970s. Khamchoo notes that a variety of factors have contributed to the slow progress of democracy in Thailand, and that without widespread public support and mobilization, reforms will prove difficult to consolidate.

China

The communist regime in China places many restrictions on the media, and genuine freedom of the press does not exist. Guo Dingping claims that the people themselves place more value on stability than on freedom, and they tend to be satisfied with the leadership. He argues that the Confucian legacy does not predetermine the desires of the Chinese people, and that this can be seen in many areas of present-day Chinese society. Economics plays a more significant role than before for many people. It is now considered acceptable for one part of society to become wealthy when other parts do not. This has created a growing gap between the rich and the poor, and the gap between urban and rural incomes is particularly wide. Guo concludes that although China's values have traditionally been very Asian, changes in Chinese society have created a change in priorities. Even though economic advances have not really led to widespread democratic reforms, various aspects of contemporary society are moving in that direction, whether the leaders like it or not.

India

As one of the world's largest democracies, India is marked by diversities in terms of language, culture, caste, ethnicity, and religion. India has also experienced significant socioeconomic changes as a result of modernization. Sanjay Kumar questions to what extent the perceptions of people have changed in face of the economic changes. His analysis of public opinion surveys conducted in India suggest that although the upper and middle class feel they live a more dignified life than their parents, few from the lower class believe the same. However, Kumar also finds that people's faith in democracy is generally strong. More than 70 percent of the people polled expressed a high-level of satisfaction for democracy compared to other forms of government, and this view was shared relatively equally among people of different social backgrounds.

Notes

1 See the Appendix for the Gallup survey questionnaire and information about its methodology. This survey was not conducted in India, and thus the author of this chapter uses an alternative survey.
2 The Gallup survey for China did not include any of the survey answers to questions pertaining to such topics as democracy and human rights, which we presume were too sensitive for the authorities to allow. To remedy this

shortcoming, the author of the China chapter makes use of two surveys conducted in Beijing and Shanghai.
3 See Lee (2000: 491) for his interpretation of this debate as well as his distinction between Confucian and Asian values.
4 See Potter (1997) and Feng (2003) for a broader discussion of democratization in history, and Wood (2004) for a discussion of democracy in Asia.
5 See Freedom House's website for the list of these questions and more information about their methodology, available online at *www.freedomhouse. org/ratings/index.htm*

Bibliography

Banno, Junji (1995), *Establishment of the Japanese System*, London and New York: Routledge.
Bell, Daniel A. (2000), *East Meets West: Human Rights and Democracy in East Asia*, Princeton, N.J.: Princeton University Press.
Carothers, Thomas (2002), 'The end of the transition paradigm', *Journal of Democracy,* 13 (1), pp. 5–21.
Case, William (2002), *Politics in Southeast Asia: Democracy and Less*, Richmond, Surrey, UK: Curzon Press.
Diamond, Larry (2002), 'Thinking about hybrid regimes', *Journal of Democracy*, 13 (2), pp. 21–35.
Feng, Yi (2003), *Democracy, Governance, and Economic Performance: Theory and Evidence*, Cambridge: MIT Press.
Fukuyama, Francis (1992), *The End of History and the Last Man*, New York: Free Press.
Hagaard, Stephan (1999), *The Political Economy of the Asian Financial Crisis*, Washington, D.C.: Institute of International Economics.
Hatch, Walter and Kozo Yamamura (1996), *Asia in Japan's Embrace: Building a Regional Production Alliance*, Melbourne: Cambridge University Press.
Hood, Steven (1998), 'The Myth of Asian-Style Democracy,' *Asian Survey* 38 (9), pp. 853–866.
Huntington, Samuel (1991), *Third Wave: Democratization in the Late Twentieth Century*, Norman: University of Oklahoma Press.
Jayasuriya, Kanishka (2000), 'Authoritarian liberalism, governance and the emergence of the regulatory state in post-crisis East Asia', in Richard Robison, Mark Beeson, Kanishka Jayasuriya and Hyuk-Rae Kim (eds.), *Politics and Markets in the Wake of the Asian Crisis*, London: Routledge, pp. 283–296.
Khoo, Boo Teik (2003), *Beyond Mahathir: Malaysian Politics and Its Discontents*, London and New York: Zed Books.
Laothamatas, Anek (1997), 'Development and democratization: a theoretical introduction with reference to the Southeast Asian and East Asian cases', in Anek Laothamatas (ed.), *Democratization in Southeast and East Asia*, New York: Palgrave, pp. 1–20.
Lardy, Nicholas (2002), *Integrating China into the Global Economy*, Washington, D.C.: The Brookings Institution.

Lee, Keun, Justin Y. Lin, and Ha-Joon Chang (2000), 'Late marketization versus late industrialization in East Asia: convergence and divergence among Japan, Korea, Taiwan, China, Vietnam, and Mongolia', paper, Institute of Economic Research, Seoul National University.

Lee, Kuan Yew (2000), *From Third World to First: The Singapore Story: 1965–2000*, New York: HarperCollins.

Lipset, Seymour Martin (ed.) (1998), *Democracy in Europe and the Americas*, Washington, D.C.: Congressional Quarterly.

Marsh, Ian (ed.) (2006), *Democratization, Governance and Regionalism in East and Southeast Asia: A Comparative Study*, London: Routledge.

Marsh, Ian, Jean Blondel and Takashi Inoguchi (2000), *Democracy, Governance and Economic Performance*, New York and Tokyo: United Nations University Press.

McCormick, James and Neil Mitchell (1997), 'Human rights violations, umbrella concepts, and empirical analysis', *World Politics*, 49 (4), pp. 510–525.

Noble, Gregory and John Ravenhill (eds.) (2000), *Asian Financial Crisis and the Architecture of Global Finance*, Cambridge: Cambridge University Press.

Onuma, Yasuaki (1999), 'Toward an intercivilizational approach to human rights', in Joanne Bauer and Daniel Bell (eds.), *The East Asian Challenge for Human Rights*, Cambridge: Cambridge University Press, pp. 103–123.

Pempel, T. J. (1999), 'Introduction,' in T. J. Pempel (ed.), *The Politics of the Asian Economic Crisis*, Ithaca: Cornell University Press, pp. 4–14.

Pharr, Susan and Robert Putnam (eds.) (1999), *Disaffected Democracies*, Princeton: Princeton University Press.

Potter, David, David Goldblatt, Margaret Kiloh and Paul Lewis (eds.) (2000), *Democratization*, Cambridge: Polity Press.

Rose, Richard and Doh Chul Shin (2001), 'Democratization backwards: the problem of third wave democracies', *British Journal of Political Science*, 31 (2), pp. 303–329.

Samuels, Richard (1996), *Rich Country, Strong Army: National Security and Technological Transformation of Japan*, Ithaca: Cornell University Press.

Schaede, Ulrike and William Grimes (2003), *Japan's Managed Globalization: Adapting to the Twenty-First Century*, Armonk: M. E. Sharpe.

Thompson, Mark (2001), 'Whatever happened to "Asian Values"?' *Journal of Democracy*, 12 (4), pp. 154–165.

Vanhanen, Tatu (1997), *Prospects of Democracy: A Study of 172 Countries*, London: Routledge.

Woo-Cumings, Meredith (ed.) (1999), *The Developmental State*, Ithaca, N.Y.: Cornell University Press.

Wood, Alan (2004), *Asian Democracy in World History*, New York: Routledge.

World Bank (1993), *The East Asian Miracle: Economic Growth and Public Policy*, New York: Oxford University Press.

Zakaria, Fareed (1997), 'The Rise of Illiberal Democracy', *Foreign Affairs*, 76 (6), pp. 22–43.

Chapter Two
Support for Democracy and Freedom in Japan
Matthew Carlson and Taku Sugawara

Introduction

Japan's postwar period of tremendous economic growth is heralded as an 'economic miracle,' which few countries have matched in modern times.[1] The concept of a strong, developmental state where the government intervenes in the economy is frequently mentioned as an explanation for Japan's rise to an economic giant (Johnson 1982). Despite the extensive attention in the literature devoted to Japan's postwar political economy, it is unfortunate that less effort has been exerted to understand the broader context of this growth on the perceptions of Japanese citizens.[2] What do citizens think about specific aspects of democratic governance? What sorts of things matter most in life to Japanese respondents? These questions are important to better comprehend what citizens think about issues that pertain to governance and democracy in one of the world's major economies.

Japan, along with several other Asian countries including Hong Kong, Taiwan, and Singapore, have made up some of the most rapidly developing parts of the world economy in the latter half of the twentieth century. From the early 1950s, Japanese modernization took off at a rapid pace and helped push the country into the ranks of a developed economy by the mid-1970s. In this chapter, we analyze the Gallup International Millennium Survey (henceforth, referred to as the Gallup survey) to discern whether any indirect effects of its economic take-off might be registered in the values and preferences of Japanese citizens. Secondly, we are interested to assess how the responses from Japan compare to those of other countries represented in the Gallup survey.

In this chapter, we examine two primary questions asked to respondents in the Gallup survey. The first question asked is whether Japanese respondents believe that their country is governed by the will of the people. Although Japan has achieved a high level of economic development in the postwar period, higher economic growth may not translate into greater belief that the country is governed democratically. In particular, we are interested to compare Japan's responses with other countries at similar and different stages of economic development. We also investigate the extent that differences in the preference of citizens exist at the individual level.

The second survey question that we use examines what sorts of things Japanese respondents feel are the most important in life. By comparing Japan's responses with those of other countries, it is possible to examine the case of Japan from a broader comparative perspective. Additionally, we want to investigate whether differences exist at the individual level in terms of age, education level, and gender. We might anticipate, for example, that differences exist between younger and older respondents in Japan for a variety of reasons that include the indirect effects of Japan's postwar economic growth on values.

Finally, we assess the preferences of the Japanese respondents for specific things in life such as family, religion, peace, and freedom. A higher level of economic development and democracy might be expected to translate into greater respect for democratic values such as freedom or more abstract values such as peace. At the same time, Japan may fall into the category of a 'disaffected democracy,' where a high level of cynicism toward the ideals of freedom and government by the will of the people are evident (Pharr and Putnam 2000). At the individual level, we also anticipate considerable heterogeneity across respondents given their varied experiences and positions in life. For example, a wide gap may be found between the preferences of men and women, which may be shaped by Japan's specific historical, socioeconomic, and political trajectory.

The outline of this chapter is as follows. First, we offer a brief discussion of Japan's status as a late developer as it pertains to current questions of democratic governance. We then analyze the questions from the Gallup survey discussed above. Both efforts are geared to facilitate comparisons between Japan and other countries represented in the Gallup survey.

The developmental state and governance in Japan

The concept of the developmental state can be understood if one examines the history of industrialization in Japan.[3] In the mid-nineteenth century, Japan was a latecomer on the world economic stage. With a large agricultural base and a small manufacturing sector, Japan faced unequal commercial treaties with the West, a situation which continued until 1911. Japan sought to overcome this latecomer status one step at a time. First, the government stressed the importance of learning from the West. Knowledge of western technology and practices was viewed as a means to overcome the unequal treaties. Second, the government promoted the slogan 'rich country, strong army.' The government borrowed western technologies and attempted to quickly adapt them for Japanese use. The generation of capital and technology from within was a motto for both the government and business firms (Samuels 1994).

Third, the government sought to increase exports in order to earn foreign reserves and to afford the import of energy and other natural resources. The export of products such as textiles, cars, and semi-conductors enabled firms to earn foreign reserves and helped spearhead Japanese industrialization. Initially, Japan was apprehensive at the prospect of becoming a western colony. Later it was concerned at being economically and culturally overwhelmed by the West. In response, Japan built an economy that contained fairly comprehensive sectors within its national territory, and experienced exponential growth. The theory and practice of national self-sufficiency were very important for Japan. Finally, Japanese technological know-how spread to neighbors that were also latecomers to the international economy. This was because Japan steadily increased its level of technological development, while at the same time shifting its production sites to the near-abroad and abroad, including East and Southeast Asia. This contributed to the formation of what is referred to as the 'flying geese' pattern of industrial development, led by Japan and followed by other countries in the region.

The developmental state as it evolved from the 1930s through the 1970s in Japan had distinctive features that influenced governance. First, the government was basically technocratic and authoritarian, as symbolized by the practice of administrative guidance (Banno 1996). Second, the government focused on the national goal of advancing economic development, and tended to play down other goals such as human rights and democracy, which could be pursued, it was argued, after material wealth had been achieved. Finally, the developmental state was able to make best use of both state-accumulated capital and the education of intermediate-level workers and engineers. The developmental state successfully promoted and brokered the large-scale production of manufactured goods at competitive prices.

After the 1970s, Japan joined the ranks of developed countries and not only enjoyed a relatively high per capita gross domestic product (GDP), but also considerable freedom in terms of political rights and civil liberties. Among the Asian countries surveyed in this volume, the case of Japan fares the highest in terms of both economic development and its rating by the Freedom House organization.[4] In Figure 2.1, we plot per capita GDP (logged value) and Freedom House scores for Japan along with the other Asian countries featured in this volume.[5] The political rights and civil liberties scores from the Freedom House have been summed together and reversed for the purposes of this analysis; higher scores indicate greater levels of freedom.

The countries fall into roughly four quadrants, which we label with the letters A–D. Along with Japan, South Korea and Taiwan fall into the highest quadrant (A) in terms of both indicators. Below this group is the second quadrant (B) of Malaysia and Singapore—which

Figure 2.1: Freedom House scores and per capita GDP

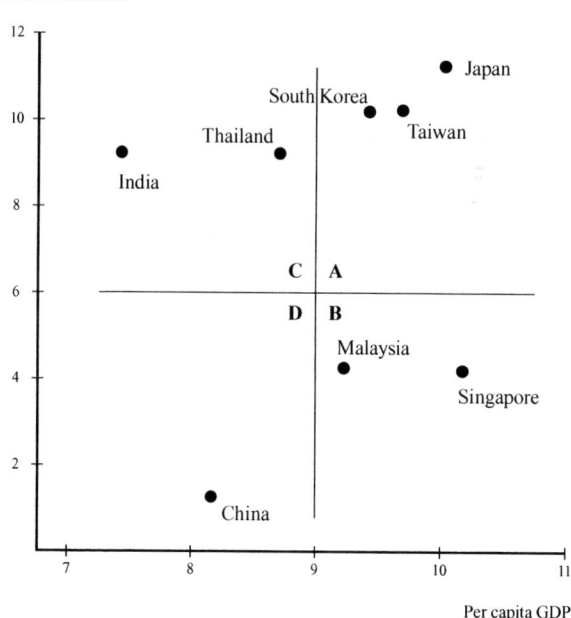

Source: Freedom House and CIA World Factbook available at *http://www.cia.gov/cia/publications/factbook/*.

Note: Political rights and civil liberties scores are summed and reversed on a scale of 0 to 12, where higher scores reflect greater freedom. The per capita GDP figures are logged.

fare higher on per capita GDP than the Freedom House evaluation. In the far left corner are Thailand and India, which fall into the third grouping (C) with their slightly lower scores. Finally, China falls into the last quadrant (D) with the lowest scores on both indicators.

These general groupings of countries are useful when we examine the results of the Gallup survey for Japan and the other Asian countries. In the case of Japan, the indicators for economic development and democracy rank the highest of the countries included in Figure 2.1. This achievement is likely related to the indirect achievements of its impressive economic record during the postwar period. Obviously, it is difficult for us to directly link Japan's historical and political context to explain the results of a survey that was conducted more recently. Ideally, we would like to use a longer time series of survey data available for Japan and other Asian countries.

Beyond the specific historical and political context, which is difficult to pin down, the survey results can also be analyzed at the individual level in terms of age, education level, and gender. At the individual level, age is important to consider because it is possible that the younger and older generations hold different perspectives on politics. The younger generation in Japan, for example, likely grew up after the country had already become a developed economy. Moreover, they may have had more opportunities to complete a college degree. In a similar vein, the youngest generations of female respondents may have experienced fewer difficulties and less discrimination in the labor market. This could be one possible factor among many that could contribute to possible gender differences in public opinion.

Comparing Japan's level of support for democracy

We begin by analyzing the responses to a question asked in the Gallup survey: 'Would you say that this country is governed by the will of the people?' The percentage of respondents who answered 'yes,' 'no,' and 'don't know' are presented in Table 2.1 for Japan and several of the other countries featured in this book, plus Singapore.

Despite Japan's impressive scores for per capita GDP and the level of democracy, only 22.3 percent of respondents in the poll believed that the country is governed by the will of the people. In fact, among the countries we examine, Japan's percentage of 'yes' answers is the second lowest after Korea. In Figure 2.1, Korea falls into the upper quadrant along with Japan and Taiwan, but for this particular question, along with Japan, Korea has the smallest percentage of

Table 2.1: Governance by the will of the people by country (%)

	Yes	No	Don't know
Japan	22.3	46.9	30.9
Korea	18.7	75.6	5.7
Thailand	51.2	47.6	1.2
Malaysia	77.3	17.7	5.0
Singapore	50.4	31.6	18.0
Taiwan	54.4	41.4	4.2

Source: Gallup survey, question 5.

respondents who believe that the country is governed by the will of the people.

In Taiwan, however, approximately 54.4 percent believe that the country is ruled by the will of the people, which is the second highest level of approval of the group and is roughly commensurate with its high scores for per capita GDP and state of democracy. Interestingly, the highest percentages of respondents with the exception of Taiwan are found in Malaysia and Singapore—countries with comparatively high levels of economic growth but lower evaluations of their political rights and civil liberties record.

The percentage of respondents who answered 'don't know' in Table 2.1 is also revealing. Approximately 30.9 percent of Japanese respondents do not know whether their country is governed by the will of the people. Singapore trails Japan at 18 percent, whereas the percentages of 'don't know' responses are below 6 percent in the remaining countries. The high response rate of 'don't know' answers for Japan is not uncommon and is noted in other literature. Susan Pharr and Robert Putnam (2000: 12), for example, note the extremely high proportions of Japanese responding 'don't know' to survey responses, which they link to the generation of leaders discredited by wartime defeat and to the new political institutions imposed by the American occupation authorities.

With the Gallup survey being conducted in 1999, the results presented in Table 2.1 reflect some of this characterization of Japan as having low confidence in democracy. As the above passage suggests, some of this may be related to the new and untested institutions of the Japanese state that the American occupation authorities set up in the wake of Japan's defeat in World War II. An additional factor mentioned in the same edited volume is the scandal-prone nature of government officials in Japan. Based on the analysis of survey data and newspaper coverage of scandal reports, Pharr (2000: 199) argues that reports of officials' misconduct are the best single predictor of confidence in government over the past two decades. She finds that as the number of stories about leaders' misconduct in office increases, the confidence of the Japanese public in government decreases.

The results of the Gallup question for Japan likely reflect cynicism toward government for some of the above reasons. As our chapter is confined to the analysis of only one survey done in 1999, we can only speculate about the complex causes that explain the Japanese case. We are, however, able to examine the results of this particular question in more detail through consideration of whether salient differences in opinions exist between younger and older respondents. As many younger respondents were born only after Japan joined the ranks of developed countries, their life experiences and education may diverge from older generations.

In terms of the likely effects of officials' misconduct on different generations, the Lockheed scandal of 1976 generated the greatest amount of coverage for the postwar period (Pharr 2000: 195). Although all respondents in Japan are likely to have been exposed to media coverage of scandals, those old enough to remember the Lockheed scandal might be expected to be more critical in their perceptions of whether the country is governed by the will of the people. An examination of the results of this question by age groups is useful to compare Japan against some of the other countries in this volume.

We have graphed the 'yes' and 'no' responses to the question about whether government is ruled by the will of people in Figure 2.2 for Japan and five other countries. We use five age groups constructed from the Gallup survey: 18–24; 25–34; 35–44; 45–54; and 55–64. Ideally, we would have wanted to construct age groups for individual decades, although respondents were only asked to specify their age bracket in the survey. The Gallup's age groups, however, suffice in considering the potential impact of age. In terms of relating the age categories to actual years, the youngest group of respondents was born roughly between 1975–1981, whereas the oldest group was born approximately between 1935–1944.

In the case of Japan, Figure 2.2 captures differences on the 'yes' and 'no' responses for each of the age groups. The percentage of 'yes' responses reached a high of 39.2 percent from the oldest age group (55–64), followed by 30.6 percent and 28 percent from the first and third age groups, respectively. In contrast, the percentage of 'no'

Figure 2.2: Governance by the will of the people by age group

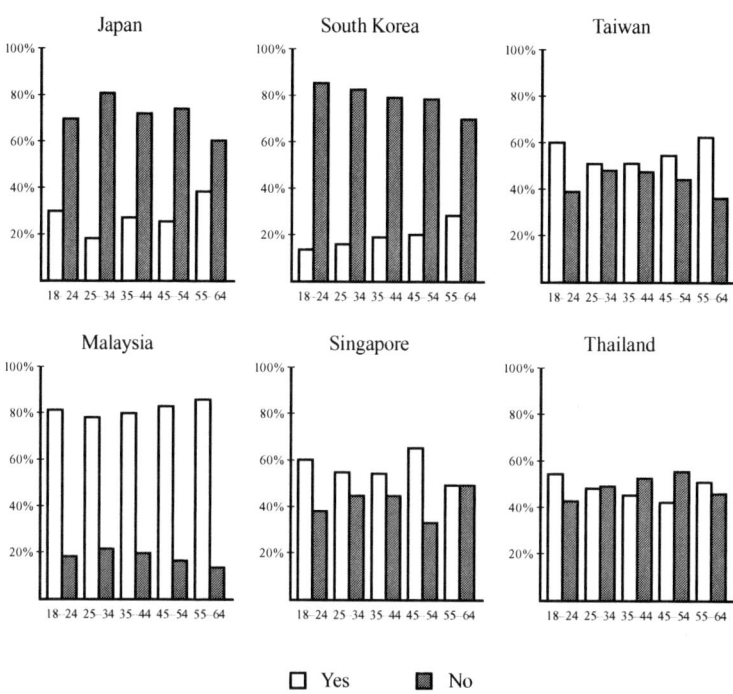

Source: Gallup survey, question 5.
Note: 'Don't know' responses are excluded.

responses was the highest for the second age group (25–34) at 81.2 percent, followed by the fourth (45–54) and third (35–44) age groups. The overall trend for this question suggests that the oldest respondents are the most likely to believe that the country is governed by the will of the people. Moreover, the youngest age group of respondents demonstrated the second highest positive response.

An explanation for this observation is more difficult to pinpoint. On the one hand, the significance of the Lockheed scandal cannot be easily surmised in the above figure. Most of the respondents from the first age group were not yet born in 1976, and the oldest respondents from the second age group were only eleven years old when the scandal erupted. The second age group averaged the highest 'no' response to the question of whether the country is governed by the will of the people. This might suggest that other events in post–Lockheed Japan are responsible for this strong response. At the same time, the percentage of 'no' responses can be still viewed as high for the remaining age groups. The respondents aged 45–54, for example, were in their twenties and thirties when the Lockheed scandal occurred. Nearly 74 percent of this group did not believe that the will of the people govern the country. This percentage, however, drops to 60.8 percent for the oldest age group—the respondents were in their thirties and early forties in 1976 and are likely to remember the Lockheed scandal.

The impact of the Lockheed scandal, of course, may be consequential for citizens' perceptions of governance in Japan. The survey responses suggest a relatively high level of cynicism for whether the country is governed by the will of the people. The most cynicism was uncovered for the second youngest age group (25–34), followed by the fourth oldest age group (45–54). The oldest age group (55–64) averaged the highest positive 'yes' response of 39.2 percent, although nearly 61 percent did not agree with the statement.

Yet it may be the case that older generations are more favorable toward viewing the country as being governed by the will of the people because of Japan's postwar economic success and the long period of stable rule under the Liberal Democratic Party. Despite the history of corruption scandals, older respondents may simply be more inclined than younger respondents to state a more favorable assessment on this issue. Moreover, the American occupation authorities soon after the war introduced the current constitution of Japan. To the extent that older respondents may compare Japan's postwar government structures with the prewar period, they may be more inclined to offer favorable assessments. However, as the nature of the Gallup survey is relatively limited for a more in-depth exploration of these results in the case of Japan, we are only able to speculate on possible explanations for the above patterns.

We are, however, able to compare the results for Japan by age with several of the countries presented in this book. To the degree that Japan's particular economic and political development are indirectly related to the patterns we have thus observed, we might also expect some discernible differences between Japan and the other countries. It is useful to first compare the responses from Japan with Korea and Taiwan given some of the similarities previously mentioned in terms of economic development and level of democracy. In the three countries, the oldest age group (55–64) expressed the highest percentage of 'yes' responses. The second highest percentage for Japan and Taiwan is the first age group (18–24), whereas the first age group in Korea has the lowest percentage of 'yes' answers. In terms of the absolute levels of 'yes' responses, Japan is closer to Korea based on the higher levels of satisfaction expressed in Taiwan.

Beyond Korea and Taiwan, we can compare Japan's patterns of responses to those of Malaysia and Singapore, countries that have high per capita GDP scores but lower political and civil rights scores among the surveyed countries. In contrast to Japan, these two countries have a higher percentage of 'yes' responses. That said, these two countries have little variation across the responses by age category. In Malaysia, for example, the lowest 'yes' average is 78.5 percent and the highest 86.7 percent. Singapore has slightly more fluctuation, which is driven primarily by the second oldest age group (45–54). Finally, the pattern for Thailand differs slightly from the countries mentioned above. The percentage of 'yes' responses gradually decreases from the first (18–24) to the fourth (45–54) age groups with the exception of the last age group (55–64) that has the second highest average.

Some caution is required when analyzing these broader patterns. First, the sample size across the age categories varies, and this could bias our results. Additional research that uses alternative surveys is necessary to identify whether these patterns hold for similar survey questions. Second, our analysis is based on only one survey question, which makes it difficult to generalize our results. From what has been shown thus far, one might make an argument that the survey responses for Japan do not differ considerably from the other Asian countries with the exception of perhaps South Korea. To the extent this may be true, the impact of Japan's postwar economic growth period on public opinion may not be so clear to discern. In the next section, we examine the responses for the same set of countries with attention to a question that asks respondents what matters most in life.

Turning from questions about governance and the rule of the people, we are interested to analyze the responses for Japan in terms of what respondents think are some of the most important things in life, based on a selection of items listed by the Gallup survey. By focusing on a question less directly related to government performance and the notion of democratic rule, we are able to consider how the pattern of responses is different or similar within Japan and across the countries sampled. Similar to preferences for governance issues, the choices for what things matter the most in life are likely to be indirectly shaped by a host of factors within the particular country in question.

It is useful to consider some of the broader indirect effects, such as the level of economic development, that might lead to specific changes, and that may shape the preferences and attitudes of individuals. As a country industrializes, for example, its economy is likely to undergo considerable transformations, such as an increased emphasis on manufacturing and production. Changes in the economy may further lead to other indirect effects, such as increased affluence for some of the population as well as increased migration to urban areas where centers of production are located. For countries, including Japan, this broader change should shape and affect the specific values of its citizens, including those of the youngest generations.

The process of economic development is also important as it shapes the socialization process through which people acquire shared norms and values. In countries that have not industrialized, for example, the traditional family unit or even the church may be the primary means through which the younger generations of society are educated and socialized. As more countries industrialize, we tend to expect that some of the importance accorded to the traditional family unit or church lessens, particularly as a country invests more resources into public education or a system of higher education. It is possible, however, that a considerable passage of time may be required before the effects of economic development can be observed.

What matters the most in life

In this section, we rely on the response to a second question from the Gallup survey that was broached in the following way: 'I would now like to ask you what you say matters the most in life.' Respondents were requested to select two values that matter the most in life out of the following choices: to have a job (*Job*); to get an education (*Education*); to be faithful to my religion (*Religion*); to have a good standard of living (*Standard of Living*); to live in a country where there is not war (*Peace*); to have a happy family life (*Family*); to live in freedom (*Freedom*); to live in a country without violence and corruption (*No Violence*); and finally, to have a good health (*Health*). The percentages of respondents that selected these values are listed in Table 2.2 for Japan and five other Asian countries.

Using the broader clustering of countries suggested in the previous section, we can make some general comparisons across the countries. First, respondents in Japan, Korea, and Taiwan selected *Health* and *Family* as two of the things that matters most in life. *Health* came in first and ranged from a high of 67.9 percent in Japan, 58.3 percent in Korea, and 48.1 percent in Taiwan. *Family* came in second with a

Table 2.2: What matters most in life (%)

	Japan	Korea	Thailand	Malaysia	Singapore	Taiwan
Job	27.8	18.9	29.3	12.2	9.4	14.0
Education	3.7	9.8	33.8	15.6	14.3	12.5
Religion	2.1	4.8	5.5	20.4	14.3	3.5
Standard of living	1.9	21.1	26.9	14.1	8.2	9.6
Peace	24.8	6.7	11.4	23.9	18.7	13.3
Family	48.0	58.0	42.2	48.6	44.0	41.5
Freedom	13.0	10.4	7.7	9.4	11.5	19.4
No violence	6.2	11.4	14.7	15.0	15.5	33.7
Health	67.9	58.3	27.7	27.5	41.8	48.1

Source: Gallup survey, question 22.
Note: Excludes 'don't know' and 'no' answer. Because respondents were asked to select two responses, the rows do not total 100 percent

high of 58 percent in Korea, 48 percent in Japan, and 41.5 percent in Taiwan. In contrast to what matters the most in life, the least popular selections in these three countries were *Standard of Living*, *Religion*, and *Peace*. *Standard of Living* was the least popular response in Japan (1.9%) and the second least popular in Taiwan (9.6%). In Korea, the smallest percentage of respondents selected *Religion*.

In terms of the remaining countries, *Family* and *Health* were selected as what matters the most in life in Malaysia and Singapore. The least popular response in Malaysia was *Freedom* (9.4%) and *Job* (12.2%). In Singapore, *Standard of Living* (8.2%) and *Job* (9.4%) were the two values least selected. Finally, in Thailand, *Family* (42.2%) and *Education* (33.8%) were the top two selections, whereas *Freedom* (7.7%) and *Religion* (5.5%) were the least selected.

Overall, the selections of *Health* and *Family* prevailed in the set of six countries. In five of the six countries, these two selections received either the first or second highest percentage of respondents. At the same time, *Religion* was the least popular in three of the six and *Standard of Living* in two of the six countries. What might explain these broader patterns? One explanation could be linked to the debate over 'Asian values.' Asian countries may share a set of similar values and cultural traditions that may explain some of the convergence in the response patterns. Confucianism, for example, is often viewed as a reason why the industrializing economies of East Asia have flourished (Davis 1987; Harrison 1992; Tai 1989).

The debate over 'Asian values' or the argument that these Asian countries share a similar set of values, however, cannot easily explain the considerable amount of heterogeneity in the response patterns. Moreover, this sort of explanation may underscore the importance of economic factors in shaping broader patterns of responses. For example, in Japan, Singapore, and Taiwan—which have the highest per capita GDP among the countries examined in this chapter—respondents gave little weight to the importance of having a good standard of living. Respondents in these three countries may be more inclined to focus on alternative selections since the standard of living is already fairly high in their countries.[6] In Korea, Thailand, and Malaysia, where the per capita GDP is smaller than the former set of countries, the selection of *Standard of living* did not rank at the bottom. In Korea alone this selection was the third highest.

Similar to *Standard of Living*, *Education* was one of the least selected responses in Japan. When Japan joined the ranks of developed countries in the 1970s, the importance of education was strongly stressed and parents made considerable efforts to send their children to the best schools. After 1952, the percentage of students continuing beyond compulsory education increased steadily in the years to reach a high of 85 percent in 1971.[7] Although the importance of education continues to this day, many of the Japanese respondents may be less inclined to select it as a valued item in life, because its importance was established several decades ago.[8] In contrast to Japan, *Education* was selected as a response more frequently in countries such as Thailand (33.8%), Malaysia (15.6%), and Singapore (14.3%). Perhaps as the level of economic development progresses in Thailand, the selection of *Education* as one of the most important things in life will fall to a level more comparable to Japan.

Another item that received relatively little selection across the Asian cases was *Freedom*. In the debates over 'Asian' values, a frequent criticism is that Asian governments focus too heavily on economic growth, at the expense of things such as individual freedom and human rights (Leary 1990). Indeed, the low response pattern for countries like Malaysia and Singapore would also appear consistent with the Freedom House's low rating for their political and civil rights record.[9] To the extent that the level of economic development might explain broader patterns that concern the selection of *Freedom*, we might expect considerable differences even within Asian countries, if we take a magnifying glass to examine the trends more carefully.

Although a broader discussion of economic development may help explain some of the patterns uncovered in the Gallup survey, obvious limitations exist in pushing this explanation too far. First, we lack adequate time series data that allow us to compare across countries during different time periods. This makes it difficult to study how public opinion and support for such things as *Education* and *Freedom* may change over time and in response to the indirect effects of economic development and the socialization process. Second, it is important to examine broader trends beyond the Asian region. If economic development, for example, can help explain Japan's selection of what matters in life, it should also help identify larger patterns across the entire Gallup survey. In the next section, we focus more specifically on the selection of *Freedom* using a broader set of countries and with attention to differences across age groups.

Support for freedom

The mention of freedom has become a favorite vocabulary word for U.S. President George W. Bush, particularly after the events of 9/11. In his September 2004 speech to the United Nations, Bush remarked that the desire for freedom resides in every human heart.[10] The U.S. president also used the term, freedom-loving people, in the context of the terrorist threats faced by the United States and other countries.[11] Given the recent connotations over what exactly the word freedom means in the public discourse, it is useful to discuss how respondents might have made sense of the word in the Gallup survey.

In the Gallup survey, which was conducted well before the events of 9/11, the meaning of freedom is likely to differ considerably for respondents, depending where they live. Obviously, the meaning of freedom to many is not a political question as implied by the U.S. president. In advanced economies where citizens do not face high levels of government repression, freedom may be desirable as a personal commodity. People may desire personal freedom to make their own choices, freedom from social pressures, freedom to decide where to go to school, and who to marry. In countries where citizens experience high levels of government repression, the meaning of freedom is likely to be considerably different: for example, the freedom from various forms of discrimination based on religion, gender, language, color, or political opinion. Given that the meaning of freedom can vary widely, it is useful to examine the broader pattern of responses for those who selected *Freedom* across all of the countries in the Gallup survey.

Figure 2.3 plots the percentage of the respondents in fifty-eight countries who selected *Freedom* as one of the two most important things in life by the level of economic development as measured by

Figure 2.3: Selection of freedom and per capita GDP

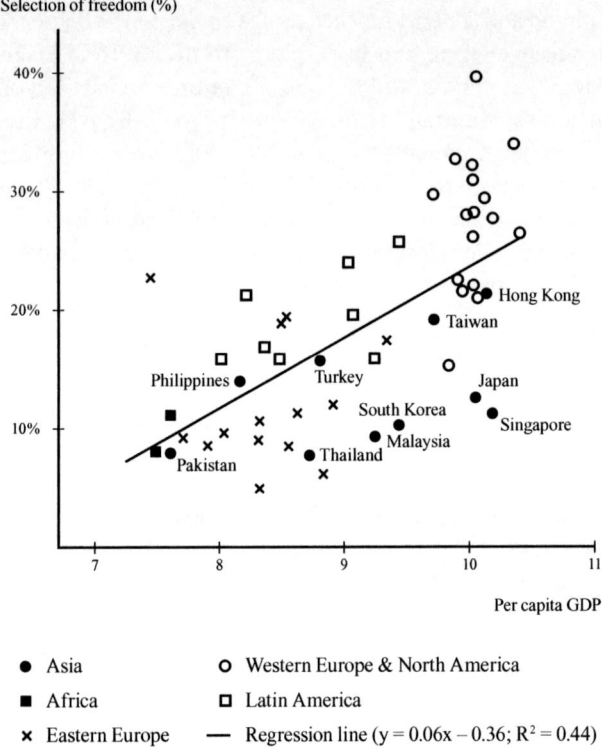

Source: Gallup survey, question 22, and CIA World Factbook.
Note: Per capita GDP is logged.

per capita GDP. The names of all of the Asian countries are specified along with their data point using the symbol of a filled-in triangle. We have also classified countries based on their geographical region. For example, all of the countries in Western Europe and North America are indicated with triangles that have not been filled in. By looking at the groupings of countries in terms of their selection of *Freedom* and per capita GDP, we can make several broad observations.

First, nearly all of the Western European and North American countries are grouped at the top right of the figure. Both the selection of *Freedom* and the per capita GDP levels for these countries are high. Under this clustering is Hong Kong, Singapore, and Japan. These countries have equally high levels of economic growth compared to Western European and North American countries, although the selection of *Freedom* is not as great. For the remaining Asian countries, considerable variation exists both in terms of per capita GDP and the percentage of respondents in the country that selected *Freedom*. Higher per capita GDP might be associated with the greater selection of *Freedom* in a country, although there are many cases of countries at similar stages of economic growth that demonstrate considerably divergent patterns. The cases of Thailand and Turkey, for example, are close in terms of per capita GDP scores, but Turkey ranks much higher on the selection of *Freedom* than Thailand.

Given the many political, economic, and social situations found across Asia, it is not easy to evaluate the sources of the survey differences without additional analyses. In light of George Bush's comments about the universality of freedom and the distinction of freedom-loving people, the results captured in Figure 2.3 may also not be entirely obvious. If support for *Freedom*, for example, depends partly on the level of economic development, then this possibility was not mentioned in the speeches. Moreover, it seems unlikely that the United States would criticize countries such as Japan for low levels of support for such abstract values as freedom or democracy. Of course, it is useful to examine the selection of *Freedom* in terms of age groups, as strong responses from particular age groups may drive the broader patterns captured in Figure 2.3. At the same time, perhaps the seemingly low support levels for *Freedom* in Asia may not be as problematic if, for example, certain age groups embraced the concept more than others.

In Figure 2.4, we have graphed the selection of *Freedom* for Japan and five other Asian countries according to the age groups of the respondents. What is clear is that for most of the countries, the selection of *Freedom* is most enthusiastically received by the youngest age group (18–24). This age group in Japan and South Korea are at the top of this selection of countries in support of *Freedom*, whereas this age group in Malaysia and Thailand are at the bottom. The selection of *Freedom*, however, does not always lessen as we move to older groups of respondents. In Taiwan and Singapore, for example, the second age group (25–34) demonstrated a higher average than the third age group (35–44).

It is useful to consider the patterns in Figure 2.4 with our analysis in the previous sections. When we analyzed the question of whether the country was governed by the will of the people, we noted that the oldest age group, followed by the youngest age group, averaged the highest amount of 'yes' responses—although the absolute values are

Figure 2.4: Selection of freedom by age

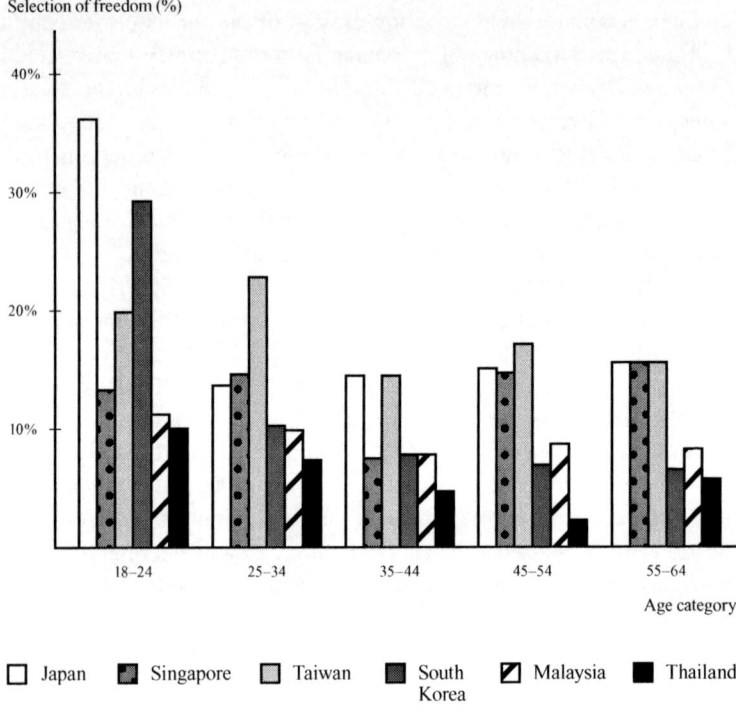

Source: Gallup survey, question 22.

both below 40 percent. In the case of *Freedom*, the youngest groups appear to be more favorable. Although the patterns are not exactly the same, the youngest age group appears to hold less cynical attitudes toward the first question and also to hold abstract values such as *Freedom* in high regard.

In the case of Japan, for example, economic development proceeded after the end of the World War II. Respondents aged 18–24 years were, therefore, born during a high period of economic growth. This age group likely benefited from not only higher income levels, but also from considerable changes in the education, legal, and political system initiated during the U.S. occupation of Japan. Thus, it is somewhat expected that this young group of respondents would be less cynical toward the government in the Gallup survey and that they would emphasize the selection of *Freedom* the most in comparison to those born prior to Japan's high period of economic growth.

Among the Asian countries, Japan and Korea also appear to exhibit some major similarities that set themselves apart from other countries in the Gallup survey. In terms of the overall percentage of respondents in Japan that selected *Freedom* as an important value, Japan ranks thirty-six, and Korea forty-third, out of fifty-eight countries. To the extent that Korea's economy has also taken off in the last few decades in a similar trajectory to Japan, perhaps the similarities are more than just coincidence.

A multivariate analysis of freedom

The analyses conducted thus far in this chapter have not yet examined the Gallup survey questions while controlling for multiple factors at the individual level. The effects of age, for example, may be stronger or weaker depending on whether we also control for such factors as education level and gender. Although many other factors could impact at the individual level, we opt here to focus only on these three. In particular, we are interested in how the selection of *Freedom* in Japan fares when individual-level factors are controlled for in the same model. Moreover, we seek to compare the results for Japan with the other Asian countries as well as with those in Western Europe and North America.

The dependent variable in our model is the percentage of respondents in each country that selected *Freedom* as one of the most important things in life. We include all of the countries classified by the Gallup organization as being part of the Asian region as well as from Western Europe and North America. The independent variables in our model are age, education, and gender. Exact expectations are difficult to specify for each of these variables as they are not likely to have uniform effects on each country, particularly as the historical, political, and socioeconomic contexts can differ considerably. However, it is possible to suggest a few expectations for Japan and for developed countries.

First, there is some reason to expect that the effect of age will be positive on the selection of *Freedom* for Japan and for other countries, although the exact causal mechanisms are not entirely clear. In Japan, it is possible that younger respondents may have benefited the most from the high growth economy or that they are somehow more enamored with abstract values like *Freedom* than their older, possibly more conservative, counterparts. In other countries, however, the expectation is harder to specify without discussing the specific circumstances faced by each country. Like age, the effects of education may prove to be mixed. On the one hand, education is believed to boost cognitive skills and practical knowledge, which helps people make sense of politics (Inglehart and Norris 2003: 103). Higher levels of education could lead to more critical attitudes about such values as freedom, or alternatively could foster greater appreciation for them. The empirical record of the effects of education on specific values is mixed (see, for example, Fuchs et al. 1995).

Finally, the model includes a control for gender. In the literature, attitudes between men and women are frequently attributed to cultural arguments or to theories of economic development, where structural changes can affect the socioeconomic position between women and men (Inglehart and Norris 2003: 89). To the extent that women may be more or less favorable to the selection of *Freedom* as one of the most important elements of life would seem to depend on the sorts of broader structural changes experienced in particular societies. To the extent that this variable may intersect with age and education in specific countries, however, it is important to include it as a control in the model.

The results of the multivariate model are reported in Table 2.3. The results for Japan are listed first. Here the variable for age is negatively associated and statistically significant. In other words, as age increases the tendency becomes greater to not select *Freedom* as one of the most important aspects of life. In contrast, greater levels of education are positively associated with *Freedom* selection. Similarly, more men than women tended to select *Freedom*. The multivariate results for age do not diverge from the analyses presented previously. The results of this model, however, further demonstrate that this relationship still holds when measures for education and gender are included.

We can also examine the results for Japan with the rest of Asia and the other regions. Among the Asian countries, Japan is the only case where all three independent variables are statistically significant. Korea, the Philippines, and Taiwan follow after Japan as cases in which two of the three variables are significant. Interestingly, all of the variables that are statistically significant for Asia have a similar impact: age is negatively associated with *Freedom*; education is positively correlated; and gender has a negative effect. Only Japan appears to differ because it is the only country where all three variables achieved statistical significance. This may somehow be related to its high growth period after the war that enabled it to quickly join the ranks of developed countries.

Table 2.3: Logistic regression for selection of freedom

Country	Region	Age β	Education β	Gender β	Constant β	Cox & Snell R^2	N
Japan	Asia	−0.20[a]	0.72[a]	0.37[b]	−3.55[a]	0.04	1272
Hong Kong	Asia	−0.11	−0.03	0.24	−0.88	0.01	502
Malaysia	Asia	−0.13	0.11	0.26	−2.27[a]	0.00	997
Pakistan	Asia	0.15	−0.21	−0.15	−2.22[a]	0.01	432
Philippines	Asia	−0.03	0.27[b]	0.46[b]	−2.83[a]	0.01	998
Singapore	Asia	−0.04	0.62[b]	0.25	−4.01[a]	0.01	495
South Korea	Asia	−0.47[a]	0.00	0.42[b]	−0.66	0.03	1505
Taiwan	Asia	−0.17[b]	−0.14	0.46[b]	−0.63	0.02	519
Thailand	Asia	−0.67[a]	−0.12	0.54	−0.54	0.04	297
Turkey	Asia	−0.05	0.05	0.31[b]	−1.70[a]	0.01	1941
Canada	N. America	−0.01	0.17	0.09	−1.51[a]	0.00	851
U.S.A.	N. America	0.13[a]	0.24	0.12	−2.13[a]	0.01	970
Austria	W. Europe	−0.04	0.33[b]	0.08	−1.93[a]	0.01	778
Belgium	W. Europe	−0.09[b]	0.38[a]	0.36[b]	−2.33[a]	0.02	991
Denmark	W. Europe	−0.01	0.47[a]	0.09	−1.82[a]	0.04	994
Finland	W. Europe	−0.03	0.35[a]	−0.13	−1.77[a]	0.01	1019
France	W. Europe	−0.09[b]	0.52[a]	0.64[a]	−2.36[a]	0.07	1003
Iceland	W. Europe	−0.05	0.31[b]	0.10	−1.61[a]	0.01	593
Ireland	W. Europe	−0.01	0.14	0.27	−2.19[a]	0.00	1363
Italy	W. Europe	−0.19[a]	0.24[b]	0.40[b]	−1.32[a]	0.03	981
Luxembourg	W. Europe	−0.11	0.19	0.39	−1.37[a]	0.02	490
Netherlands	W. Europe	−0.05	0.19[b]	−0.04	−1.29[a]	0.01	583
Norway	W. Europe	−0.16[a]	0.32[b]	−0.06	−1.16[b]	0.03	532
Spain	W. Europe	−0.09	0.40[a]	0.50[a]	−1.96[a]	0.06	590
Sweden	W. Europe	0.01	0.16	−0.09	−1.21[a]	0.00	986
Switzerland	W. Europe	0.01	−0.20	−0.03	−0.40	0.00	491
U.K.	W. Europe	−0.03	0.23	0.08	−1.67[a]	0.01	1007

Source: Gallup survey, question 22.
Notes: 'Don't know' responses are excluded. a: significance at the .01 level. b: significance at the .05 level.

We can also compare the results of the same model between Japan and Asia with North America and Western Europe. Of the two North American countries, only the United States reports any statistically significant independent variables. In contrast to Japan and many countries in Asia, age is positively associated with the selection of *Freedom*. The same trend does not appear for Western Europe, where the age variable fails to demonstrate any effects, with the exception of four countries where age is negatively correlated with the selection of *Freedom*.

For the rest of the Western European countries, the effects of education and gender all demonstrate similar patterns to those found in Japan and Asia. In ten of the fifteen European cases, for example, education positively correlates with *Freedom*, whereas gender negatively correlates in all but one country. In the 1970s, Japan joined the group of developed economies, and perhaps it is this that may explain some of the similarities between Japan and these countries.

Conclusion

We began this chapter by discussing the broader historical, political, and economic context of Japan from defeat in the war to becoming a developed country. Instead of emphasizing cultural explanations, we emphasized the importance of the historical and political context as well as the important indirect effects that economic development can have on peoples' perceptions and values. By using the Gallup survey, we examined and compared the case of Japan to other countries with a focus on two specific questions asked to respondents.

First, we examined responses to the question of whether respondents believed that the country is governed by the will of the people. Among the Asian countries we considered, we noted that Japan came in second to last after Korea. This result stood in contrast to Japan's high positive rating by the Freedom House organization and its high per capita GDP. We surmised that this result may be a consequence of having new and untested institutions or related to the misconduct of government officials. The results of our analysis based on age revealed that the highest percentage of 'yes' responses came from the oldest and youngest age groups. We were unable to confirm a clear relationship between the Gallup survey results and the Lockheed scandal of 1976.

Second, we examined a battery of answers to a question about what matters the most in life. Like most of the Asian cases we covered, respondents in Japan tended to select *Health* and *Family* most frequently, with *Religion* and *Standard of Living* being the least popular responses. To some extent the particular selections for each country may be related to the indirect effects of economic development. In the case of Japan, rapid economic growth in the postwar period may have weakened interest in the selection of such values as *Education*, *Standard of Living* or *No Violence*, particularly because these areas have already shown high levels of achievement.

Finally, we conducted an in-depth examination on the selection of *Freedom*. In light of the frequent criticism that Asian governments neglect human rights and of the popularity of the word freedom in U.S. foreign policy discourse, the results of this section suggest that considerable heterogeneity exists across the Asian countries in the selection of *Freedom*, and that its selection depends on the level of economic development. In the case of Japan, we further discovered that the youngest generation of respondents demonstrated the most enthusiastic response for the selection of *Freedom* in comparison to the older generations. This suggests that the period of recent rapid economic growth in Japan has likely had an important effect on the youngest generations.

The analysis of Japan and other countries presented in this chapter only focused on a few of the questions asked in the Gallup survey. Additional analysis is necessary to evaluate some of our tentative claims and to extend the discussion to other areas related to democratic governance in Japan. Moreover, we lack time series data that would allow us to consider whether our initial analyses might hold up for a longer time frame. Despite these challenges, however, we hope that future cross-country research on the case of Japan will better document more of the indirect effects of economic development on public opinion formulation.

Notes

1 The literature in this area is extensive. For some examples of this debate, see Johnson (1982), Wade (1992), Hane (1996), Pyle (1996), and Forsberg (2000).
2 Some examples of studies that focus on public opinion in Japan include Richardson (1974), Flanagan (1978), and Ladd and Bowman (1996).
3 We wish to thank Takashi Inoguchi for contributing to this section.
4 Unlike the volume at large, we include the case of Singapore in order to broaden our analysis.
5 The Freedom House rates political rights and civil liberties separately on a scale from 1 to 7, with 1 representing the highest level of freedom. We combine both scores and reverse the scale for the purposes of our analysis. For more discussion of the methodology employed by Freedom House, see their website, available online at *www.freedomhouse.org*.
6 During the late 1990s when the Gallup conducted this survey, it is worth noting that the Japanese economy was in a downturn. Although respondents in Japan did not select *Standard of Living* with great frequency, they did select *Job* as the third most important thing in life.
7 This statistic is from *Japan's Modern Educational System* published in 1980 by the Ministry of Education, Science and Culture previously available online at: *http://www.mext.go.jp/english/index.htm*.
8 Although the importance of education in Japan may be relatively low today, we would expect the opposite to be true during Japan's high period

of economic growth. We note, for example, that the numbers of students attending college and high school in Japan peaked just after the OPEC oil embargo in 1973, which occurred just after a period of high economic growth. If time series data was available, we might expect to see a stronger level of support for education sometime after the attendance peak of 1973.

9 For further debate about Asian values and economic development, and the cases of Singapore and Malaysia in particular, see Sen (1997).

10 'President Speaks to the United Nations General Assembly', Office of the Press Secretary, September 21, 2004. Document available online at: *http://www.whitehouse.gov/news/*

11 'Remarks by the President to Employees at the Pentagon', Office of the Press Secretary, September 17, 2001. Document available online at: *http://www.whitehouse.gov/news/*

Bibliography

Banno, Junji (1995), *Establishment of the Japanese System*, London and New York: Routledge.

Davis, Winston (1987), 'Religion and development: Weber and the East Asian experience', in Myron Weiner and Samuel Huntington (eds.), *Understanding Political Development*, Boston: Little, Brown.

Flanagan, Scott, Shinsaku Kohei, Ichiro Miyake, and Bradley Richardson (1991), *The Japanese Voter*, New Haven: Yale University Press.

Forsberg, Aaron (2000), *America and the Japanese Miracle*, Chapel Hill: University of North Carolina Press.

Fuchs, Dieter, Giovanna Guidorossi, and Palle Svensson (1995), 'Support for the democratic system', in Hans-Dieter Klingemann and Dieter Fuchs (eds.), *Citizens and the State*, Oxford: Oxford University Press.

Hane, Mikiso (1996), *Eastern Phoenix: Japan since 1945*, Boulder: Westview Press.

Harrison, Lawrence (1992), *Who Prospers? How Cultural Values Shape Economic and Political Success*, New York: Basic Books.

Inglehart, Ronald and Pippa Norris (2003), *Rising Tide: Gender Equality and Cultural Change around the World*, Cambridge: Cambridge University Press.

Inglehart, Ronald and Wayne Baker (2000), 'Modernization, cultural change and the persistence of traditional values', *American Sociological Review*, 65 (1), pp. 19–51.

Jackman, Robert, and Ross Miller (1996), 'The poverty of political culture', *American Journal of Political Science*, 40 (3), pp. 697–716.

Johnson, Chalmers (1982), *MITI and the Japanese Economic Miracle*, Stanford: Stanford University Press.

Ladd, Everett Carll and Karlyn H. Bowman (1996), *Public Opinion in America and Japan: How We See Each Other and Ourselves*, Washington, D.C.: American Enterprise Institute Press.

Leary, Virginia (1990), 'The Asian region and the international human rights movement', in Claude Welch and Virginia Leary (eds.), *Asian Perspectives on Human Rights*, Boulder: Westview Press, pp. 13–27.

Pharr, Susan and Robert Putnam (eds.) (2000), *Disaffected Democracies: What's Troubling the Trilateral Countries?* New Jersey: Princeton University Press.

Pharr, Susan (2000), 'Officials' misconduct and public distrust: Japan and the trilateral democracies', in Susan Pharr and Robert Putnam (eds.), *Disaffected Democracies: What's Troubling the Trilateral Countries?* New Jersey: Princeton University Press.

Pyle, Kenneth (1996), *The Making of Modern Japan*, 2nd ed., Lexington: D.C.: Heath and Company.

Samuels, Richard (1994), *Rich Country, Strong Army: National Security and Technological Transformation of Japan*, Ithaca: Cornell University Press.

Sen, Amartya (1997), 'Human rights and Asian values: what Lee Kuan Yew and Le Peng don't understand about Asia', *The New Republic*, 14 July, pp. 33–41.

Tai, Hong-chao (ed.) (1989), *Confucianism and Economic Development: An Oriental Alternative?* Washington, D.C.: The Washington Institute Press.

Wade, Robert (1992), 'East Asia's economic success: conflicting perspectives, partial insights, shaky evidence', *World Politics*, 44 (2), pp. 270–320.

Chapter Three
Trust and Confidence in the Government of South Korea

Chung-Si Ahn and Won-Taek Kang

Introduction

Democracy has emerged as the leading political system of the post-Cold War world. Although liberal democracy has no real rival, political distrust and the growth of 'critical,' 'disaffected' citizenry is the troubling reality of contemporary democracy everywhere. Studies show that over the past decades, a loss of confidence in government and public institutions is almost universal. Citizens in most democracies have become less satisfied with their political institutions than they were decades ago (Nye, Zelikow, and King 1997; Norris 1999; Pharr and Putnam 2000). Confidence in government has declined in many of the old, established democracies, as well as in the new, nascent democracies. Trust, confidence, and public satisfaction in politics are widely believed to be intimately connected with the effectiveness of government and the durability of democratic institutions (Putnam 1993; Fukuyama 1995; Warren 1999).

Contemporary South Korea is well known for its citizens' lack of political trust and low confidence levels in government. The country had a relatively soft transition to democracy in 1987 and has since made remarkable progress in democratic change (Ahn and Jaung 1999). In 1998, South Korea also became the first among Asia's new democracies to peacefully transfer power to an opposition party. In spite of this, its political process is torn by discontent with gridlock and bickering, and the performance of democratic institutions lag far behind the expectations of their citizens. Mass dissatisfaction with government, feelings of alienation from politics, perceptions of a widening gap between the elite and the masses, and a low regard for public agencies are familiar words in the politics of democratizing

South Korea (Shin 1999). A declining confidence in government is feared to have disengaged people from activities of 'positive social capital,' and instead caused them to revert primarily to 'personal trust' based on kinship, regional identity, and informal networks of patron-client relationships (Ahn 2000a: 467). Therefore, the need to address the problems of political distrust and a declining level of confidence in the South Korean government is paramount.

Does it matter when people do not have trust and confidence in government? If we follow the classical liberal vision of society, democracy is better when government is smaller. The core belief of traditional liberalism is that government '...will have incentives not to act in the citizens' interest,' and that '...citizens should distrust and be wary of government' (Hardin 1999: 23). Accordingly, a low level of confidence and mistrust in government (at least to a modest degree) are considered healthy for democracy. If the subjective political feelings of citizens reflect 'wariness rather than cynicism,' then a lack of trust about politics and public institutions may be sensible and necessary for democracy to continue.[1]

Indeed, citizens' trust and confidence in politics is highly significant for democratic systems and their sustained performance. Distrust, dissatisfaction, and a low level of confidence in government are said to affect the sustainability of democracy and the strength of democratic institutions in many ways. Moreover, political trust, satisfaction, and confidence in government are strongly associated with one another. Trust builds effective institutions, which helps government perform more effectively. And this in turn encourages confidence in public institutions, and helps to build a vibrant civil society.

Conversely, a continuously declining level of confidence in government might cause 'a cumulative downward spiral' (Nye et al. 1997: 4). Or, 'poor government performance as manifested, for example, in rampant political corruption may create a cycle that contributes to widespread social distrust' (Pharr and Putnam 2000: 72–73). Representative democracy requires public support to sustain its durability and effectiveness. Loss of public trust may also breed low support and unstable government, which negatively affects the ability of government to provide public goods. It also follows that inefficient, unstable government may foster cynicism about politics and elected officers, which in turn may reduce citizens' participation and support for democracy in principle and in practice.

The reasons for a low level of trust in government can be many— inefficiency, corruption, high costs, inappropriate policies and programs, authoritarian leaders, and so on. Attempts, both theoretical and empirical, to explain the causes and problems of low public trust abound in literature. Among them, three explanations stand out. The first looks to economic performance as the main cause for low public trust. It posits that economic prosperity leads to public satisfaction, while economic downturns erode public confidence in government. The second explanation is based on social and cultural hypotheses. The cultural model attributes a decline of political trust to a long-term secular trend that argues that disrespect of authority is part of a post-modern society as it moves from survival to quality-of-life values (Inglehart 1997). The civil society model is another popular explanation and is synonymous with social capital theory. According to this theory, confidence in government diminishes when social capital runs low, and flourishes when civil society is endowed with a good supply of social capital (Putnam 1993). The third explanation attributes the decline in confidence primarily to political and institutional factors. This approach emphasizes unaccountable, unresponsive political leaders and institutions (e.g., parties, legislature, and bureaucracy), constitutional arrangements, dishonest leaders, and political corruption as the main causes of dissatisfaction and low levels of confidence in government (Norris 1999; Pharr, Putnam, and Dalton 2000: 3–27; Pharr 2000; Newton and Norris 2000).

In this chapter, we explore where South Korea stands in the evolution of democratic governance. We compare how well the citizens of South Korea and those of other neighboring Asian countries believe that their respective governments perform various functions. The term political trust is synonymous with words such as 'civic-mindedness and participation,' 'citizenship,' 'political interest and involvement,' 'concern with public interest/public good,' 'political tolerance,' 'ability to compromise,' and 'confidence in political institutions' (Newton 2001: 205). For the sake of analytical simplicity and extended applicability for empirical indicators across countries, we define political trust broadly in this study as interchangeable with confidence and satisfaction in politics. Trust, confidence, and satisfaction in politics refer here to the aggregate property of politics seen from citizens' evaluation of the political world. They are expressed in citizens' perception that a political system and its institutions perform their functions satisfactorily.

This study uses the Gallup International Millennium Survey (henceforth, Gallup survey) conducted in 1999 for the pragmatic reason that: the data is available for public use and provides a good basis for cross-national comparison of political trust and confidence. The survey, one of the largest on global opinion at the turn of the new millennium, included nearly sixty countries, including many in Asia. (See the Appendix for details). In our analysis we do not limit our cases to only those countries included in this book. Rather we make use of the following Asian countries in addition to Korea: Japan, Hong Kong, Malaysia, the Philippines, Singapore, Taiwan, and Thailand.

The following sections first provide comparative statistics to show how South Korea stands among our selected countries in terms of several survey questions that tap citizens' confidence in politics. We then look into plausible causes of South Korea's low levels of trust and confidence in politics. Our purpose in this exposition is not to provide complete answers, or to provide solutions for the problem of public disaffection in politics. By examining a series of political, economic, and social-cultural hypotheses about the causes and correlates of political disaffection, we want to clear the ground for an in-depth examination of the institutions, governance, and performance of South Korea's new democracy.

Perceptions of governance: a comparative assessment

Democratic representation and democratic responsiveness

Democratic government should represent the will of the people. Democracy may also expect that governments respond to the will of its people. How citizens perceive their government and the role of democracy is the focus of our first analysis using the Gallup survey. To examine this issue, we make use of two questions that the survey posed to respondents. The first question asked respondents whether their country is 'governed by the will of the people.' The second question asked them to select from several choices which words describe their perception of government. Here, we are specifically interested in whether respondents mention that their government 'responds to the will of the people.'

We use the first question as a measure that taps democratic representation and the second question to tap the issue of responsible governance. Using the responses to these questions, we plot the percentages of respondents that thought government is governed by the will of the people on the 'x' or horizontal axis. We also indicate the percentage of respondents who described their government by mentioning that it 'responds to the will of the people' on the 'y' or

Figure 3.1: Democratic representation and government responsiveness (%)

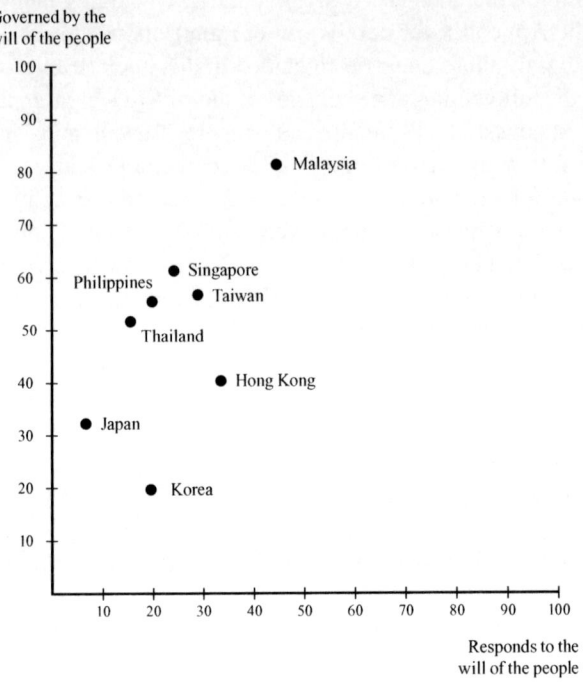

Source: Gallup survey, questions 5 and 7.
Note: Question 5 is measured as the percentage of respondents who answered 'yes' to whether their country is governed by the will of the people. Question 7 is the percentage of respondents who described their perception of the government as one that 'responds to the will of the people.' See the Appendix for specifics of Gallup's questionnaire.

vertical axis. Figure 3.1 captures this effort for Korea and the other seven Asian countries. We exclude missing and 'don't know' responses for this figure and all other calculations.

Despite Korea's hard-won democratization, its position in Figure 3.1 is intriguing and reveals that Korean respondents are the most dissatisfied among the selected countries for the question tapping 'democratic representation.' Only 20 percent of South Koreans responded positively when asked if their country is governed by the will of the people. This is considerably below the average of 50 percent for the eight Asian countries and comes in more than 12 percentage points behind Japan, which came in as the second most dissatisfied among the surveyed countries.

Korean respondents as a whole also appear discontent on the question that taps responsible governance. Only 19 percent of the respondents described their perception of the Korean government as one that 'responds to the will of the people.' Although this percentage is higher than that of Japan and Thailand, it remains nearly 5 percentage points below the average for the entire group. Korea's position on both questions suggests that the feelings of political efficacy, including feelings of trust and confidence, are rather low among its citizens. The case of Japan appears to come closest to Korea in this regard.

Government efficacy and performance

Next, we examine perceptions of governance in South Korea and Asia by focusing on the issues of government efficacy and performance. We do this by analyzing the results of the previously mentioned question that asked respondents to describe their perception of the government. Instead of focusing on the responses to whether the country is viewed as responding to the will of the people, we focus on the words that tap issues of government efficacy and performance. Specifically, we are interested in the extent to which citizens view their government as efficient and just or bureaucratic and corrupt. These are four of five possible words (as well as 'responds to the will of the people') that respondents could chose in the Gallup survey to indicate perceptions of government in their country.

First, we plot the percentage of respondents who mention 'efficient' and 'just' in Figure 3.2. Higher percentages indicate greater mention of these words from the available choices. For the first dimension, it is clear that only 8 percent of South Korean respondents agree that their government is efficient. South Korea comes in second lowest out of the selected countries and just behind Japan's low 3 percent. Singapore and Malaysia, in contrast, capture the most favorable views for efficient government.

For the second dimension, it is evident that very few South Koreans view their government as 'just.' Only 4 percent offer a positive evaluation, which is the second smallest percentage after Japan. Respondents in Malaysia and Singapore perceive their government as the most efficient, while the Philippines and Hong Kong fall between the three East Asian democracies (Japan, Korea, and Taiwan) and the two Southeast Asian semi-authoritarian governments (Singapore and Malaysia).

Second, we plot the percentage of respondents who mention 'bureaucratic' and 'corrupt' in Figure 3.3. We can take higher scores to

Figure 3.2: Perceptions of government as efficient and just (%)

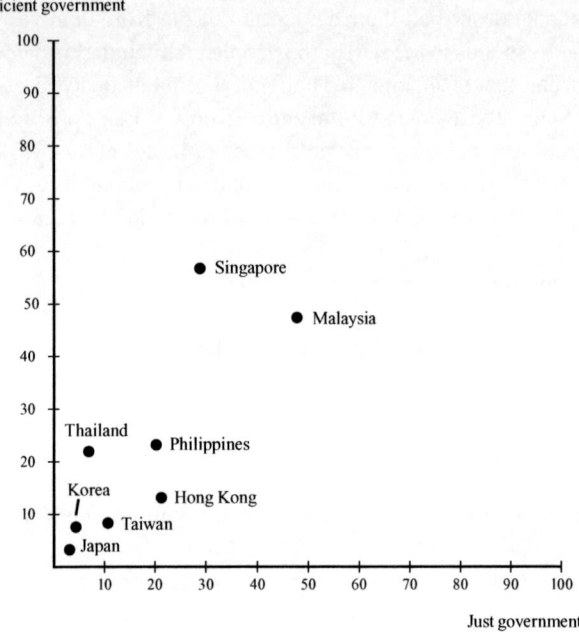

Source: Gallup survey, question 7.
Note: Question 7 is the percentage of respondents who mentioned either 'just' or 'efficient' when asked to describe their perception of the government in their country.

indicate more 'critical' evaluations of the government in their country. We can see that more than one-half of South Korean respondents indicate that their government is bureaucratic. This is the third highest position after Taiwan and Japan. In contrast, the countries of respondents with the least mention of bureaucratic government are Singapore, the Philippines, and Malaysia; Hong Kong and Thailand fall in the middle of the group.

In terms of perceptions concerning corruption, nearly three-quarters of South Korean respondents view their government as corrupt. This is considerably higher than the average 40 percent for this group of Asian countries. In fact, South Korea ranks first followed by Thailand at 71 percent and the Philippines at 50 percent. At the other end of this spectrum is Singapore, where only 2 percent view the government as corrupt.

In short, a majority of South Koreans perceive their government to be highly bureaucratic, mostly corrupt, of extremely low efficiency,

Figure 3.3: Perceptions of government as bureaucratic and corrupt (%)

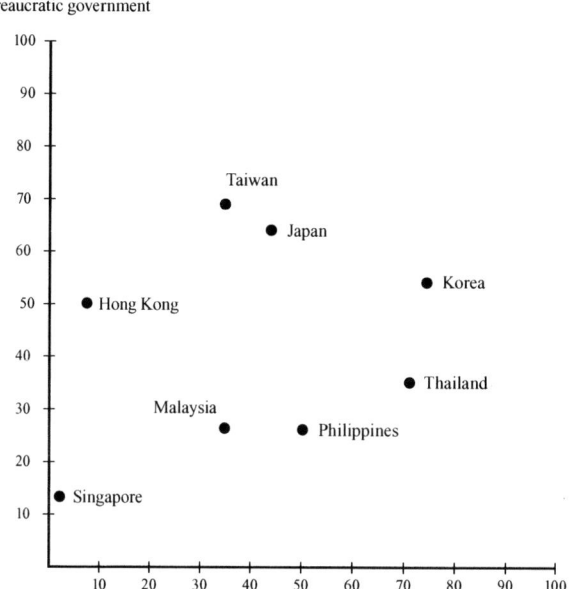

Source: Gallup survey, question 7.
Note: Question 7 is the percentage of respondents who mentioned either 'bureaucratic' or 'corrupt' when asked to describe their perception of the government in their country.

and unjust. The data clearly imply that democracy in South Korea lacks the support and trust of its citizens. Another interesting point is the seeming contrast between East Asian and Southeast Asian countries in the way citizens evaluate government. People in South Korea, Japan, and Taiwan tend to be more critical than those in Southeast Asia. In the questions examined thus far, South Korea, Japan, and Taiwan have a similar response pattern.

Human rights and equality

Human rights and equality are two core values of democracy. To analyze perceptions on these issues, we make use of several questions from the Gallup survey. On the issue of human rights, respondents are asked whether they think that human rights are being fully respected, partially respected, or not being respected at all in their country. Respondents are also asked about specific human rights mentioned in the United Nations' Universal Declaration of Human Rights such as the right to freedom of speech. We also draw upon a question that asks whether women have equal rights with men and whether discrimination on the basis of gender occurs in respondents' countries.

In Figure 3.4 we graph the percentage of respondents who answer that human rights are 'fully respected' in their country. In the case of South Korea, only a tiny 4 percent seem to agree, which ties with Japan for the lowest percentage of the eight countries. The vast majority of South Koreans believe that human rights are not respected. Given the decade-long period of uninterrupted democratic development in South Korea, such low levels of confidence in the protection of human rights might seem surprising. Intriguingly enough, Japanese respondents also express a huge level of discontentment with human right practices in their country.

Beyond the general question of human rights, the Gallup survey also polled citizens about specific rights mentioned in the Universal Declaration, including the right to freedom of speech, equality before the law, and equal pay for equal work. In Figure 3.5, we plot the percentage of respondents who believe that freedom of speech is fully protected in their country. It appears that not only are South Koreans

Figure 3.4: Human rights are fully respected (%)

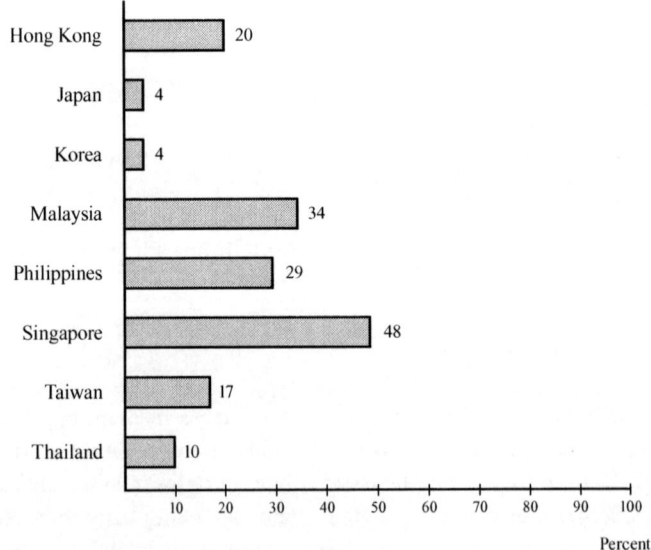

Source: Gallup survey, question 7.

Figure 3.5: Right to freedom of speech respected (%)

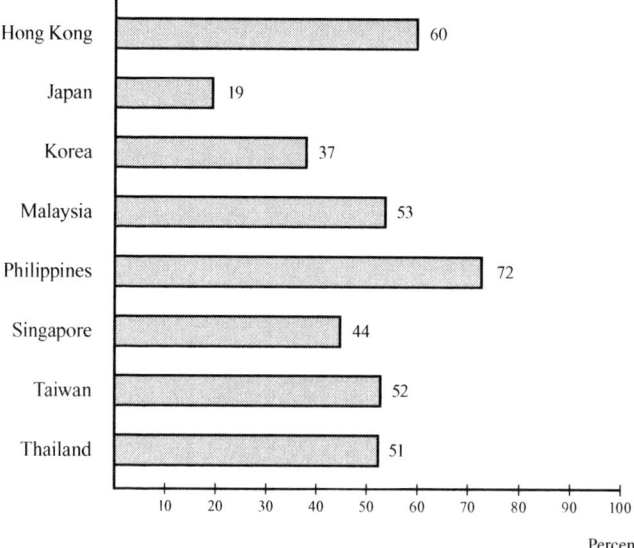

Source: Gallup survey, question 26.

discontent about human rights in general, but also to the specific political right of freedom of speech. Only 37 percent agree that this right is fully protected, which is nearly half the approval rating of Filipinos. Korea is closest to Singapore, where 44 percent are fully content.

Koreans appear discontent with human rights in general and with the right to freedom of speech. Are Korean citizens also disillusioned with the norm of equality in their society? We make use of several Gallup questions to analyze equality from a variety of economic, political, and social dimensions. First, we make use of the aforementioned question pertaining to specific rights mentioned in the Universal Declaration. Specifically, we utilize the responses to two of the items asked in this question: whether the rights pertaining to 'equality before the law' and the 'right to equal pay for equal work' are fully respected in the respondents' country.

In Figure 3.6, we plot the responses to the question pertaining to 'equality before the law' against the 'right to equal pay for equal work.' Twenty-three percent of South Koreans agree that 'equality before the law' is respected in their country, whereas 35 percent said that the 'right to equal pay for equal work' is guaranteed. Koreans' approval

Figure 3.6: Equality before the law and equal pay for equal work

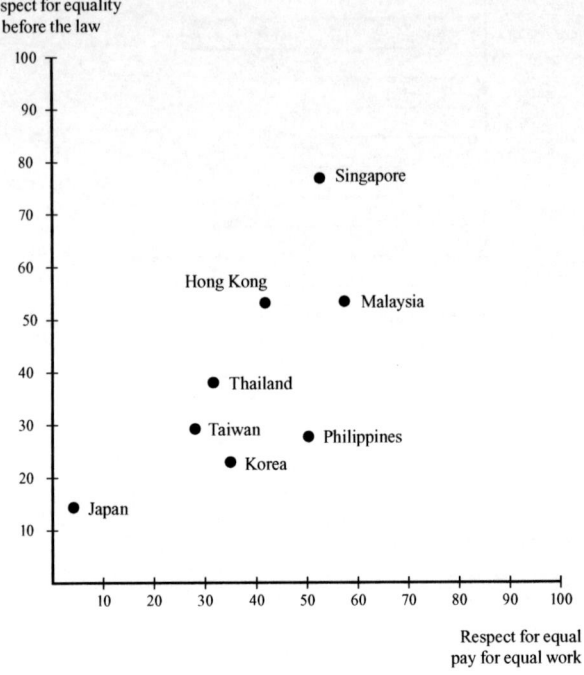

Source: Gallup survey, question 26.

rates for 'equality of law' are the second lowest after Japan; they place fourth after Japan, Taiwan, and Thailand for 'right to equal pay for equal work.' Korea's percentage is considerably below the average 39 percent for the first right, but much closer to the median of 38 percent for the second right. Nonetheless, that almost eight out of ten South Koreans think that they are not fairly treated by the law implies a very high level of distrust in the justice system.

The final dimension of equality that we analyze pertains to the issue of gender equality. Here we are interested in two particular questions asked in the Gallup survey. The first question asked respondents whether women have the same rights as men in their country. The second question asks whether gender discrimination occurs frequently. Both questions tap perceptions pertinent for considering equality as it pertains to women's rights.

The plotting of the responses for both questions in Figure 3.7 clearly attests that South Korean society is highly male-dominant. On the

Figure 3.7: Perceptions of equality between women and men

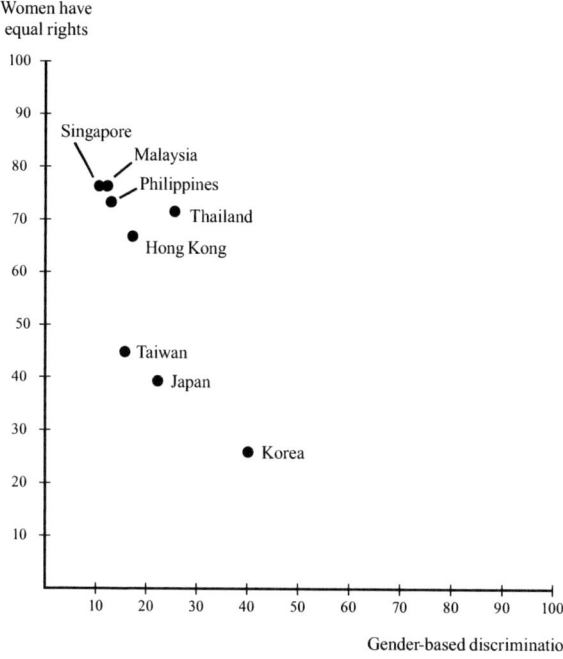

Source: Gallup survey, questions 14 and 28.

question of equal rights between men and women, South Korea ranks the lowest among the surveyed Asian countries with 26 percent of South Koreans agreeing that equality between the sexes exists—close to half the average for all of the countries and about one-third that of Malaysia. The response rate is also highest among South Koreans on whether gender discrimination occurs, with 40 percent saying that discrimination on the basis of sex 'frequently' takes place.

Explanations for Korea's disaffected citizenry

The foregoing analysis reveals striking features of the 'Korean syndrome' in political values. First, for the group of Korean respondents, low levels of trust prevail in almost all of the survey questions pertaining to democratic governance. This is unique to South Korea, although it may be true of Japan as well, and is in sharp contrast to the aggregate properties of other Asian survey samples. In considering the many democratic achievements of the last ten years, that South Korean citizens hold their government in such low esteem seems hardly justifiable. For example, in 2000, the Freedom House rated South Korea with a score of a '2' for both political rights and civil liberties—relatively high compared with other Asian countries. Yet only 37 percent of South Korean respondents to the Gallup survey indicated that 'everyone has the right to freedom of speech.' This is well below the average (49%) of the eight countries under comparison, followed only by Japan (19%). In short, South Koreans tend to be unusually critical and disaffected with their democratizing government.

Why are South Korean people so dissatisfied with their newly won democracy? What makes up the seemingly unique culture of political disaffection in South Korea? How can we explain the extremely low confidence and erosion of trust in democratic governance? Interpreting the 'Korean syndrome' and explaining the context and dynamics of political distrust in South Korea is a paramount task.

South Korean economy, society, and politics underwent a radical transformation over the past several decades. In this regard, it is natural to assume that those changes affected attitudes, values, social norms, and networks, and have caused shifts in how South Korean people feel about, and evaluate government and public institutions. We look at the 'Korean syndrome' by starting first with hypotheses drawn from an economic perspective.

Economic factors

South Koreans in recent years have experienced both the exhilaration of political liberalization and the frustration of economic downturn. The country had decades of prosperity under authoritarian rule before undergoing the transition to democracy in 1987. From 1988 to 1996, the country made slow but relatively steady progress from a soft transition to democratic consolidation. Political involvement by the military was completely eliminated during the presidency of Kim Young Sam. In 1996, South Korea was admitted to the Organization of Economic Cooperation and Development (OECD). The financial crisis of 1997, however, shattered the reputation of South Korea as a nation capable of achieving both an 'economic miracle' and a 'democratic breakthrough.' The crisis forced the Kim Young Sam government to seek a bailout from the International Monetary Fund (IMF). In a hard fought political campaign, Kim Dae Jung won the presidency at the end of 1997, largely because he effectively capitalized on the 'critical mood' of voters against the ruling party for making a fiasco of the country's economy.

The Gallup survey was taken while South Koreans were in the midst of a financial crisis. Presumably, timing and the specific social context biased the results of South Korean data, but it is equally plausible that, in the wake of an economic crisis, more people would be dissatisfied with the way the national economy was governed. However, the economic explanation must not be taken simplistically for several reasons. First, other countries such as Thailand and Malaysia underwent similar economic crises, but the statistics of these countries do not match those of South Korea. Second, the sheer intensity and consistency of responses from the South Korean sample attest that more than timing and a financial crisis were at play.

Another hypothesis based on economic reasoning is that people become angry and tend to hold a low regard for politics when a good economic record is sharply reversed. Generally speaking, management of the South Korean economy under democratic regimes is far from impressive. Economic performance in post-transition South Korea was not as good as that under the authoritarian government. Annual growth rates continued to decline from a high of 10.5 percent under Park Chung Hee and 9.5 percent under Chun Doo Hwan to 6.9 percent and 4.9 percent during Kim Young Sam and Kim Dae Jung's presidencies. The current account surplus turned to a net deficit in 1990 and remained that way throughout the entire period of the Kim Young Sam government. In 1996, the annual deficit was especially high at U.S. $2.3 billion.

Moreover, the lingering memory of 'miraculous' economic development under past authoritarian regimes may well explain part of the declining confidence in the democratically-elected government of the day. Until the late 1980s, when the downturn started, the South Korean economy looked good. The government of Chun Doo Hwan stabilized consumer prices. Both the regimes of Park and Chun effectively maintained full employment and rapid growth. In contrast to those glittering economies, economic performance under democratic governments was meager. At the same time, new groups formerly oppressed under authoritarianism began to claim the right to participate in the wake of democratization. Labor is a case in point. Authoritarian regimes forced workers to remain underpaid, and effectively keep them from any volatile level of participation in the labor movement. However, with democratization, radical demands for high wages and better working conditions fervently burst out. In fact, the eruption of sectional interests was not limited to trade unionism, but dispersed to other parts of society. A newly democratized government tends to be vulnerable to collective action problems, which may result in inconsistency and lack of coordination in economic policymaking.

The combination of low growth and reduced effectiveness in managing the national economy, followed by good economic times after the financial downturn in the late 1990s, might have aroused a sense of exclusion, deprivation, dissatisfaction, public distrust and disaffection in the newly democratizing regime. This explanation is convincing to those who take the economy seriously as a tool to understand the dynamics of citizen support for government. However, we find it difficult to establish that a reduction in public confidence in government was primarily due to an economic downturn or economic crisis. Widespread discontent and perceptions of government ineffectiveness were on a growth trend even before the 1997 economic crisis erupted. As Table 3.1 suggests, low and declining levels of confidence in government actually preceded the outbreak of the economic crisis. As Doh Chull Shin (1999: 35) reports, the proportion of citizens who felt that the democratic Sixth Republic did a better job than the previous authoritarian government in running 'the government by and for the people' had declined significantly between 1994 and 1996.

We do not prematurely rule out that, in the South Korean context, an economic downturn combined with the ensuing economic crisis in 1997 significantly disaffected citizens from government. We are inclined, however, to limit the generalization only to specific circumstances (that is, hard times such as the economic crisis) in

Table 3.1: *Changes in political efficacy and system responsiveness in South Korea, 1994–1996*

	Political efficacy		**System responsiveness**	
	1994	**1996**	**1994**	**1996**
Increased	56.1%	40.8%	53.7%	44.9%
Stayed about the same	34.5%	51.6%	34.7%	47.8%
Decreased	9.4%	7.6%	11.6%	7.3%
Number of respondents	1,475	1,000	1,475	1,000

Source: Shin (1999: 34), Table 1.6.
Note: The original table with five categories is collapsed into three.

conjunction with certain socio-political contexts or settings (that is, in semi-democracies or transition economies). It may be that people become disenchanted with a certain socio-political context during economic hard times.

Socio-cultural dynamics

Is something unique about the South Korean culture that makes its citizens reluctant to acknowledge what the government does? Are South Koreans culturally inclined to be 'critical,' 'rebellious,' and 'cynical' toward government? Are they intrinsically less trustful of politics than, for example, Malaysians or Singaporeans? Indeed, we find some indications that the measures of confidence and trust in government for the three Confucian states of South Korea, Japan, and Taiwan tend to cluster together somewhat. However, the data at hand do not warrant any systematic evidence to show that Confucian East Asians are more disrespectful of authority than other Asians. Another hypothesis that pertains to cultural exposition is the gap theory. The theory posits that the actual or perceived gaps between the ideal and reality, between expectation and achievement, between socioeconomic and political development, produce dissatisfaction, mistrust, and low levels of confidence in government. Critical attitudes may also reflect lagging social, political, and economic development or the lingering effects of an authoritarian era.

A related, but analytically differentiated, mode of placing the 'Korean syndrome' onto a socio-cultural plane of analysis is found in the debates on 'Asian values' toward democracy and its performance. Singapore's senior minister Lee Kuan Yew has long argued that Western-style democracy has deleterious effects on Asian society (Zakaria 1994; Emmerson 1995). A 'soft' form of authoritarianism, according to Lee, is more appropriate to East Asia's Confucian tradition than Western-style liberal democracy. On the basis of this (illiberal) logic, he justifies the suppression of freedom of speech and political dissent. According to this view, (liberal) democracy represents not universal values, but is uniquely rooted in Western culture, and is, therefore, not always appropriate for 'Asian culture.'

In contrast, Kim Dae Jung, while still an opposition leader, challenged Lee's view on democracy and Asian values, refuting it with the point that democracy represents the same human principles regardless of whether the states are in the East or the West. Kim also argued that economic development could not take the place of democratic values. He said that democracy and economic prosperity should be pursued simultaneously. In his presidential inaugural address in 1998, Kim declared that his government would pursue the 'parallel development of democracy and free market economy.' Kim's view parallels the development of democracy and market economy and can be contrasted to Lee Kuan Yew's notion that Asian values are less conducive to 'Western-style' democracy.

South Korean society widely debated these two opposing views. By and large—perhaps somewhat dissimilar to Singapore or Malaysia—a majority of South Koreans have been socialized to oppose the view that democracy is alien to South Korea or to Asian culture(s). Few South Koreans, whether supporters of Kim's government or not, challenged his view that democracy and a market economy could develop in parallel. The South Korean people tend to understand that democracy represents universal values that cannot be confined to the Western world. This notion implies that democratic values and culture, its institutions, and practices in Western countries are not ethnocentric; achievements made in the West such as political freedom, human rights, fair and free elections, and rule by law are models and standards for every country to emulate. The standards formulated in 'advanced' democracies are 'normal' and 'desirable' and can serve as 'universal' categories to judge and compare any government and its performance.

Culturally and psychologically, South Korean views of democracy may lead to an unduly high level of expectation, which in reality may be difficult to achieve. Such difficult-to-achieve expectations are likely to cause the public to hold their government in low esteem, and may increase the number of 'critical citizens.' Even if some improvements are made in democratization and its consolidation, people will want 'more democracy' and 'better governance' with reference to ever rising comparative grounds for 'asking for more and better' governance.

Although we do not have sufficient data to test the validity of this hypothesis, we do not rule out such a possibility in the South Korean context. Formal education in South Korea has long instilled modern, democratic values of liberal individualism into its youth. Progressive ideology, drawn from the leftist literature of the West, has deeply affected student activism and working class movements. With economic globalization, leaders and policymakers emphasize the need for South Koreans to restructure the society and economy to global standards. South Korea's early entry, and to some critics, premature one, into the OECD was welcomed by many as a means of providing the country with a good opportunity to reach and meet global standards. One editorial highlighted the positive consequences of joining the OECD:

> It is very important that by joining the OECD the principles of pluralist democracy, market economy and human rights will be obviously applied to the Korean society in general. Domestic policies, from human rights, labor, and environment to finance, education, and health, should be revised to meet 'international standards.' With the entry we will actively participate in the international economic order led by the advanced economies (*Dong-A Ilbo*, November 18, 1996).

President Kim Young Sam also said in 1996 that the South Korean government would reform and liberalize its domestic systems to match 'the standards of advanced countries' (*Chosun Ilbo*, December 12, 1996).

One ramification of the above discussion is that the South Koreans' low approval of government performance in the Gallup survey does not necessarily mean that citizens see no improvement in the democratization of South Korea. Although South Koreans are critical of their democratic institutions and elected leaders, studies widely support the conclusion that people would not allow a return to the authoritarian past, and are more satisfied with the quality of life under democracy than under authoritarian regimes (Shin 1999; Ahn 2000b). It may be that those who aspire for a high level of democratic achievement tend to become more critical toward government, and that the South Korean people as a whole do not see that the changes made so far in democratization have brought sufficient progress to meet their aspirations. Poor grades from the public may reflect, on the other hand, that people are becoming exasperated with the sluggish pace of reforms. Testing these hypotheses requires further work with improved theory and data that go beyond the scope of this study.

Constitutional arrangements and institutional flaws

Constitutional arrangements adopted at the time of the democratic transition in South Korea have the built-in defects of producing divided government and dual legitimacy. That may have caused ineffective governance, in turn, resulting in disenchantment with government. High public disaffection with government can also be attributed to the poor performance of political leaders, representative institutions, political parties, and policy implementing agencies. South Korea's party alignment is primarily based on regional rivalry and poses additional problems. The hypothesis that underlies these arguments is that it is primarily the performance of political leaders, public institutions/agencies, and policies that produce (or reproduce) citizen trust and confidence in politics.

In all elections held after the 1987 transition, the country's voting turnout was divided into four politically distinctive regions, on which three or four parties heavily relied for backing. Voters are strongly aligned with 'their' region-based parties. The ramifications of regional voting are in the emergence of divided governments. Since 1988, no governing party has succeeded in securing a majority of seats in the National Assembly in all four elections. In fact, every election in post-transition South Korea produced a divided government. Unlike American politics, presidents with divided governments in South Korea have to deal with a hostile and united opposition in the legislature. According to Giovanni Sartori (1994: 89), three factors help the U.S. presidential system to function effectively: lack of ideological principles; weak and undisciplined parties; and locally centered politics. The United States has weak political parties in which electoral politics are run on the basis of 'individualistic' campaigning. Campaign resources are made available mainly to individual candidates rather than through political parties (Ware 1996: 295). Such a weak grip by the political parties allows the lawmakers to defy the party line, if any, when voting in Congress.

Despite an apparent similarity in terms of a lack of ideology, South Korean parties operate under a different logic. National issues dominate party politics and all parties are under the tight control of top leaders who monopolize political resources. Individual lawmakers cannot effectively challenge the official party policy without running the risk of being disciplined or even expelled. Such strong party discipline prevents individual legislators of opposition parties from freely cooperating with the government party or the president in the Blue House, even when they are sympathetic with government policy positions. Accordingly, problems arise when the government party fails to win the majority in the National Assembly. As parties are solidly united, political disagreement with an opposition party (or parties) can lead to conflict between the president and the legislature and result in a stalemate.

Dual legitimacy is not unique to South Korea. It can be found in any presidential system of government. The problem in the South Korean case is that its constitutional system lacks institutionalized solutions to settle conflicts, at the time they arise, between the president and the opposition-dominated legislature. In the United States, presidential leadership and power to persuade opposition lawmakers plays an important role in settling disagreements with Congress (Neustadt 1980: 10). The French way is much subtler. Even though the architects of the Fifth Republic intended the presidency to be strong, the president is able to wield strong power only when his party (or coalition of parties) wins a majority in the National Assembly. Otherwise, administrative power goes to the opposition that controls the National Assembly, which is often dubbed 'cohabitation.'

Unlike the United States or France, the South Korean presidential system has yet to invent an institutional mechanism that can settle a deadlock of dual legitimacy. In the absence of such a mechanism, political disagreements often develop into serious showdowns between president and legislature, resulting in protracted stalemates. The deadlock inevitably lessens the effectiveness of policymaking and policy implementation. In this situation, a president who wants to reform the system can easily be blocked in the National Assembly. Many bills can be delayed or even canceled. When urgent reform bills in wake of Korea's economic downturn in 1997 were delayed by legislative entanglement, huge public outcry and criticism arose. The widespread political negativism of the South Korean respondents as expressed in the Gallup survey can be interpreted in this context.

Another facet of institutional flaws in the South Korean political system is the timing of executive and legislative elections. The Latin American experience shows that non-concurrent elections (executive and legislative elections on separate dates) are likely to result in a multiparty structure (Jones 1995: 103–118). The effects of non-concurrent elections in Korea are twofold. First, they are more likely to produce a divided government. Elections in the middle of the executive's term (especially after the 'honeymoon period') are interpreted as polls on the popularity of the incumbent president. When the governing party (or a coalition) does not fare well, a divided government can result. Second, mid-term elections often cause the momentum of reforms to run out of steam. During election campaigns, every party tries to woo as many voters as possible. Reforms inherently entail changes in the status quo, which is likely to turn some voters against the ruling party. To avoid the loss, the president compromises or softens reform programs. Consequently, the political momentum slows down. This partially explains why successive presidential attempts to reform the bureaucracy have been aborted.

Political distrust may also reflect the unpopularity of the incumbent president, the political parties, and the politicians, as well discontent with the conduct of these political actors. Less than three years into their respective tenures, all presidents of the Sixth Republic of Korea lose much of their credibility as leaders, becoming lame ducks. Many people perceive that not only the president but also all legislators are to be collectively blamed for inefficiency, dishonesty, and excessive partisan interest. Frequent occurrences of political deadlock and partisan bickering turn people off from politicians as a whole, regardless of party or position. The level of public support for main parties is low. According to a survey reported by *Joong-Ang* daily in September 2000, 40 percent of the respondents said that they were not close to any party, 25.5 percent favored the main opposition (Grand National Party), and 22.7 percent supported the ruling New Millennium Democratic Party. Civic movement groups and nongovernmental organizations (NGOs) were rated much more favorably than political parties. Independent candidates were no less favored than party affiliated candidates in legislative elections (Hwang and Kang 1998).

The widened scope of press freedom and freedom of speech brings an unceasing flow of disclosure of corruption at high levels and official misconduct in electoral democracy that provides further grounds for mounting public distrust in government and cynicism toward politicians. Electoral democracy enhances political transparency and mechanisms for institutional checks on the governing processes. Democratization expands the scope of civic participation in decision making and subjects officials to closer public scrutiny and greater accountability. The National Assembly has been substantially empowered to oversee executive misconduct. Local councils have been established to check local government. Mass media, freed from government control and intervention, finds it more 'profitable' to scrutinize or criticize government activities. In addition, many voluntary civic watchdog groups sprang up during and after the democratic transition. NGOs regularly monitor government policies, covering various issues such as environment, women's issues, political financing, and elections. The activities of NGOs have also been expanded to subnational levels in order to watch over local policymaking processes. Trade unions (particularly white-collar trade unions) play an important role in enhancing transparency within large firms and conglomerates.

All in all, when compared with the authoritarian period, democracy has made South Korean society much more open, transparent and contentious at all levels. Growing civil society and monitoring institutions pressure those in political power and public institutions to enhance responsiveness and accountability. Given the level of openness and transparency, it is no small surprise that a large majority of South Korean people regard their government as inefficient, corrupt, bureaucratic, and unjust.

Interestingly, almost three-quarters of the South Korean sample in the Gallup survey said that 'government is corrupt.' That is the highest number among the eight Asian countries, with Thailand coming second. How can this seeming paradox be explained? It makes little sense to assume that democratization lead to greater levels of corruption from those experienced in Korea's authoritarian past. According to Transparency International, a non-governmental organization, the level of perceived corruption placed South Korea roughly in the middle of the ninety countries in its annual expert-based survey called the *Corruption Perceptions Index*.[2] If we compare this ranking with previous surveys, South Korea's rating has improved steadily as democratization proceeded, which suggests that corruption is becoming less rampant, albeit still continuing

One possible way to solve the puzzle is to look at changes in public attitude toward corruption from a regime perspective, that is, even though corruption is less rampant (than before under authoritarianism), it causes more serious disaffection in a democratic regime. People might have taken corruption for granted in the past, either because they had no alternative, or because they had no institutional channels in which to express their frustrations. However, in a democratic environment with an expanded scope of monitoring institutions and public participation, citizens are probably more willing to openly deplore and defy them. In consequence, practices that were 'ordinary' under authoritarian regimes are no longer tolerated.

On many occasions, presidents and their cabinets have embarked on anti-corruption campaigns. Moreover, corruption scandals in which powerful politicians are implicated are more frequent under democracy than before. Without exception, democratically elected presidents or close aids and relatives have been involved in corruption. Two former presidents, Chun Doo Hwan and Roh Tae Woo, were jailed for illegally accumulating huge amounts in slush funds. A son of

President Kim Young Sam was charged with bribery and tax evasion. Kim Dae Jung's presidency was no exception to this cycle. Naturally, these scandals provoked furious reactions from the public. Unlike the period of authoritarian rule, people nowadays do not condone corrupt behavior and official misconduct. Citizens and social groups are more inclined to publicize their dissatisfaction than with an authoritarian regime. Statistics from the Gallup survey data may reflect this public discontent and political disaffection.

Also, public scrutiny and institutional monitoring allowed many otherwise, concealed cases of corruption to be disclosed to the public. As press freedom expanded, the mass media would disclose malpractice, bad conduct, and corruption cases much more frequently than before. Such frequent disclosures of corruption, in turn, make many people believe that the 'government is corrupt.' Moreover, frequent revelations of corruption can create an image of weak control or a lack of discipline within government. The impression, however, that corruption greatly increases as democratization proceeds cannot be justified objectively. Authoritarian regimes would have swept many of these corruption cases under the carpet by preventing the press to publicize them. If we take this into consideration, it would be inappropriate to say that democratization has brought about more corruption. Thus, we conclude that the extreme negativism expressed in the political orientation of the South Korean people as seen in the facts and figures in this chapter is overstated to some extent., Instead, such critical attitudes show that although South Korea is slowly proceeding toward democratic consolidation, its people are not content. In fact, they are still far from being proud of how they are governed in an electoral democracy.

Conclusion

Public opinion and mass political culture have received marginal attention in past studies of Asian politics, reflecting a view in part that ordinary people matter little under military regimes or authoritarian government. Instead, greater scholarly attention has been given to studies of dominance by elites, characteristics of the regime, political and economic dynamics, and international linkage. Yet, as democracy spreads widely, public opinion and citizen values are taken increasingly as important subjects of inquiry. Accordingly, studies on mass culture and citizen orientation have emerged as vital areas of research in comparative democratization. We based the approach of this chapter on the assumption that studying subjective evaluations of citizens toward their government is one of the most effective methods to understand and explain the dynamics of democratic change in Asia. Analysis undertaken here is a modest attempt to fill the academic gaps in this emerging research.

The findings in the study lead to the conclusion that South Korean politics today, a decade since the transition to democracy began in 1987, is still far from stable and mature. The quality and performance of South Korea's new democracy has a long way to go. The general public sentiment is that the electoral democracy that the South Koreans won a decade ago has not progressed much in delivering on its promises of accountability, responsiveness, effectiveness, and respect for the rule of law. The record in human rights, freedom, and equality is still far from what is expected. Only a few are satisfied with the current state of democracy. Public support for the regime and the representative institutions remains remarkably low, even when compared with the illiberal, authoritarian governments of Southeast Asia. On the whole, we find little evidence of a declining public commitment to the principles of democratic governance among Korean citizens. We do not see the democratic regime in South Korea at risk of being supplanted by 'a return to authoritarianism.' Both in perception and reality, the authoritarian past has been effectively relinquished in favor of electoral democracy. However, evidence shows a decline in political confidence among South Koreans. A majority of South Korean citizens are disillusioned with politicians, political parties, and political institutions. Growing segments of the people are publicly disaffected with government and the institutions of representation.

Growing negativism in politics and government may reflect a postmodern trend, that is, general anti-authority attitudes that grow with broad socioeconomic transformation. But, our analysis appears to confirm that, in shaping public confidence in politics, what happens in politics matters much more than what happens in the economy and society. The problem could in part be that popular expectations of a hard-won democratic government after long authoritarian rule have been too high. It may be that the performance of South Korea's electoral democracy is poor, or that South Korean political culture tends to incite overly high expectations. Either way, low levels of confidence and high amounts of distrust in politics tell us that something is deficient in South Korean democracy. The heart of the problem may be in the inability of government to fill the gap between expectations and actual performance (Norris 1999: 2–3, 21–25).

Does the high level of political distrust in South Korea reflect a 'crisis of democracy?' Or does the tension between the expectations and reality bode well for the future of democratic governance in Korea? The growth of a more critical citizenry in the 1980s increased the pressure on the democratic transition of South Korea in the 1990s (Ahn 2001). Will the same be true of the consolidation process? The answer lies in how we make our elected government more accountable to the public before citizens become highly skeptical of democratic principles. To achieve this outcome, the challenge is first to reform existing institutions and structures so that we can quickly correct the flaws and improve the quality of democratic government. To sustain and strengthen a democracy requires public trust and popular support. Hence, the next critical problem that faces South Korea's democracy is to foster responsible leadership and democratic governance under which trust and confidence can be generated and upheld.

Notes

1 In the words of James Madison: 'The aim of every political constitution is, or ought to be, first to obtain for rulers men who possess most wisdom to discern, and most virtue to pursue, the common good of society; and in the next place to take the most effectual precautions for keeping them virtuous whilst they continue to hold their public trust.' Federalist Paper No. 57.
2 For more information about this organization and the methodology of its annual surveys is available at: *http://www.transparency.org/*.

Bibliography

Ahn, Chung-Si (2000a), 'Korean democracy under Kim Dae Jung: a stalled progression?' *Journal of Korean Politics*, 10, pp. 457–447.
Ahn, Chung-Si (2000b), 'Fifty years of Korean politics: political culture and political values', *Journal of Korean Politics*, 10, pp. 131–161 (in Korean).
Ahn, Chung-Si (2001), 'South Korea's "critical citizens" in the 1980s: culture and socialization of post-Korean War generations', unpublished paper.
Ahn, Chung-Si and Hoon Jaung (1999), 'South Korea', in Ian Marsh, Jean Blondel, and Takashi Inoguchi (eds.), *Democracy, Governance, and Economic Performance: East and Southeast Asia*, Tokyo, New York, Paris: United Nations University Press, pp. 137–166.
Emmerson, Donald (1995), 'Singapore and the 'Asian values' debate', *Journal of Democracy*, 6 (4), pp. 95–105.
Fukuyama, Francis (1995), *Trust: The Social Virtues and the Creation of Prosperity*, New York: Free Press.
Hardin, Russell (1999), 'Do We Want Trust in Government?' in Mark E. Warren (ed.), *Democracy and Trust*, Cambridge: Cambridge University Press, pp. 22–41.

Hwang, Su-Ik and Won-Taek Kang (1998), 'Independent candidates in South Korean legislative elections', *Korean Journal of Legislative Studies*, 4 (2), pp. 138–161.

Inglehart, Ronald (1997), *Modernization and Post-modernization: Cultural, Economic, and Political Change in 43 Societies*, Princeton: Princeton University Press.

Inoguchi, Takashi (2000), 'Can Asian values be the basis of democratic governance in the Asia-Pacific region?' Paper presented at the conference on 'Changing Values and Challenges of Democratic Governance in Asia,' Seoul National University, Seoul, Korea, November 17–18.

Jones, Mark (1995), *Electoral Laws and the Survival of Presidential Democracies*, Notre Dame: University of Notre Dame Press.

Kim, Sunhyuk (2000), 'The politics of reform in South Korea: the first year Kim Dae Jung government, 1998–1999', *Asian Perspective*, 24 (1), pp. 163–186.

Neustadt, Richard (1980), *Presidential Power*, New York: John Wiley.

Newton, Kenneth (2001), 'Trust, Social Capital, Civil Society, and Democracy', *International Political Science Review*, 22 (2), pp. 201–214.

Newton, Kenneth and Pippa Norris (2000), 'Confidence in Public Institutions: Faith, Culture, or Performance', in Susan Pharr and Robert Putnam (eds.), *Disaffected Democracies: What's Troubling the Trilateral Countries?* pp. 52–73.

Norris, Pippa (ed.) (1999), *Critical Citizens: Global Support for Democratic Government*, Oxford: Oxford University Press.

Norris, Pippa (1999), 'Institutional explanations for political support', in Pippa Norris (ed.), *Critical Citizens: Global Support for Democratic Government*, pp. 217–235.

Nye, Joseph S., Jr., Philip D. Zelikow, and David C. King (1997), *Why People Don't Trust Government*, Cambridge, Massachusetts: Harvard University Press

Pharr, Susan J. and Robert D. Putnam (eds.) (2000), *Disaffected Democracies: What's Troubling the Trilateral Countries?* Princeton: Princeton University Press.

Pharr, Susan (2000), 'Officials' misconduct and public distrust: Japan and the trilateral democracies', in Susan Pharr and Robert Putnam (eds.), *Disaffected Democracies: What's Troubling the Trilateral Countries?* pp. 173–201.

Putnam, Robert (1993), *Making Democracy Work: Civic Traditions in Modern Italy*, Princeton: Princeton University Press.

Pye, Lucian (1985), *Asian Power and Politics: The Cultural Dimensions of Authority*, Cambridge, Massachusetts: Harvard University Press.

Sartori, Giovanni (1994), *Comparative Constitutional Engineering: An Inquiry into Structures, Incentives and Outcomes.* London: Macmillan.

Shin, Doh C. (1999), *Mass Politics and Culture in Democratizing Korea*, Cambridge: Cambridge University Press.

Ware, Alan (1996), *Political Parties and Party Systems*, Cambridge: Cambridge University Press

Warren, Mark E. (ed.) (1999), *Democracy and Trust*, Cambridge: Cambridge University Press.

Zakaria, Fareed (1994), 'Culture is destiny: a conversation with Lee Kuan Yew', *Foreign Affairs*, 73 (2), pp. 109–126.

Chapter Four
The Social Foundation of Taiwan's New Democracy: Public Perceptions of Democratic Governance
Hsin-Huang Michael Hsiao

Introduction

Taiwan's new democracy has come a long way. Since the 1980s, Taiwan has gone through several phases of major political transformation: liberalization (December 1980 – June 1987), democratic opening and uncertainty (July 1987 – July 1988), democratic transition (July 1988 – December 1994), and democratic consolidation (January 1995 – March 1996) (Hsiao and Koo 1997). The March 1996 presidential election was the first direct election of a president in the history of Taiwan, and marked a clear break with the authoritarian past. The electoral win of the presidential office by the opposition party, Democratic Progressive Party (DPP), in March 2000 and the success of the DPP to win control of the Legislative Yuan in 2001 marked the most significant political changes ever for Taiwan's democratic consolidation. Indeed, the long transition to democracy took the final two decades of the twentieth century to complete. The arrival of the twenty-first century has finally witnessed great achievements for the democratic struggles on the island state of Taiwan.

Thus far, the new democracy established in Taiwan has gone beyond the shallow and merely procedural systems for which many third-wave democracies are criticized. Democracy should be more than the procedural matter of having free, secret-ballot elections to choose political representatives under a multiparty setting (Inoguchi, Newman, and Keane 1998). Without a doubt, political leaders who advocate democracy should have a substantive and normative commitment to institutionalizing a social foundation to safeguard the notion of 'democratic governance,' in which state–society relations are governed by 'accountability' (measures to ensure the availability of checks and balances and the rule of law) and 'social liberalism' (mechanisms to protect citizenship and participation, human rights, equality, and social capital). In other words, the rise and growth of the so-called third-wave democracies, as defined by Samuel Huntington's (1991) 'minimal-procedural indicators,' need to be reassessed against the above mentioned 'reasonable-substantive indicators' of democracy—'accountability' and 'social liberalism.'

Since 1972, Freedom House has published an annual report, entitled *Freedom in the World*, that has advanced two composite indexes of substantive democratic governance, which consist of political rights (measured by ten items) and civil liberties (fifteen items). Each year, an expert team is asked to evaluate the performance of sixty countries using twenty-five indicators of freedom status. The 1999 Freedom House report ranked Taiwan twenty-eighth out of the sixty countries evaluated; in the 2000 report, it was upgraded to thirteenth—most likely because of the successful and peaceful democratic transition of power in 2000. On the basis of the Freedom House's assessment, Taiwan's new democracy has been recognized and praised, and given the same rank as Japan, an established democracy in Asia.

In this chapter, I reassess the social foundation of Taiwan's new democratic governance, as subjectively evaluated by the Taiwanese public. The public opinion data on which this chapter is partially based are drawn from the Gallup International Millennium Survey (henceforth, Gallup survey). The Taiwanese sample covers 526 individuals, with an equal distribution of males and females, about half concentrated in the age group from 25–44 years old, and a tendency toward high education, as more than 90 percent had education above middle school. It is important to note that the survey was conducted in 1999 prior to the 2000 presidential election.

Trust and democracy

At the beginning of 2000, although the opposition DPP had not yet won the presidential election, more than half of the respondents (54.4%) in the survey said that Taiwan is already being governed by the will of the people, and that the country is indeed a democratic one. However, 41.4 percent of the public did not agree. Furthermore, with regard to the minimal procedural definition of democracy as measured by free and fair elections, approximately 40 percent of the respondents agreed that Taiwan has reached such standards, while more than 56 percent remain weary. Significantly, only a very small percentage of the respondents selected the 'don't know' category to the above two questions (4.2% and 3.8%, respectively). This can be seen as another indicator of the free and open nature that characterizes Taiwan's society today.

Since the 1980s, organized civil society protests and social movements have mobilized the public, which has learned to be critical of the government, especially after the first popular direct presidential election in 1996. Citizens have become more and more demanding toward, and even suspicious of the government's conduct and performance. Although 54.4 percent of the Taiwanese respondents in the Gallup survey consider Taiwan to be a country already governed by the will of the people (a democratic state in nature), only 27.4 percent said that the government responds to the will of the people (democratic governance in practice). This confidence gap, as expressed between the two public attitudes, is an important socio-political phenomenon, related to the public evaluation of the actual government's efficacy under democracy. In fact, when assessing the government's efficacy, using positive adjectives such as efficient and just, and negative ones such as bureaucratic and corrupt, the public confidence gap or the lack of trust is even more evident in Taiwan's new democracy.

The public perception of the government as reflected in Table 4.1 cannot be described as rosy. Only 8.2 percent of Taiwanese respondents consider the government to be 'efficient,' and just 9.7 percent view it as 'just.' In other words, less than 10 percent of the public agreed that the government is 'efficient and just.' On the other hand, about two-thirds (66.5%) criticized the government for being 'bureaucratic,' and about one-third (33.7%) also condemned it as 'corrupt.'

Table 4.1: Democracy and trust in Taiwan (%)

	Yes	No
1. Taiwan is governed by the will of the people	54.4	41.4
2. Elections are free and fair	39.7	56.5
3. The government responds to the will of the people	27.4	72.6
4. The government is efficient	8.2	91.8
5. The government is just	9.7	90.3
6. The government is bureaucratic	66.5	33.5
7. The government is corrupt	33.7	66.3

Source: Gallup survey, questions 5–7.

Note: For items 3–7, the 'yes' responses indicate the percentage of respondents that described their perceptions of government out of the choices given in question 7.

In looking at other new democracies in the Asia-Pacific region, we found that all third-wave democracies suffer from relatively low degrees of public trust and confidence. Among these countries, Taiwan's democratic government enjoys a higher level of public confidence than its counterpart in South Korea. The public in the new Asian democracies, along with the established democracy of Japan, tend to be much more critical of the government than those in other less democratic states such as Malaysia, Singapore, Thailand, and Hong Kong. It is intriguing to discover from the Gallup survey that a sizeable portion of the public in Malaysia, for example, view their country as already being governed by the will of the people, and see their government as responsive to the will of the people. More Malaysians consider their government to be 'efficient' and 'just' than 'bureaucratic' and 'corrupt.' Judging by many objective indicators of democracy and freedom, Taiwan, South Korea, and the Philippines definitely outperformed Malaysia in 1999, but the public's subjective evaluations revealed opposite results.

This contrast between positive attitudes and a higher level of trust toward an authoritarian government and the negative perception and lower levels of confidence given to democratic governments can only be explained through the irony that it is the democratization that has, in fact, stirred and increased the distrust and mistrust of the citizens toward their government. Distrust and a low level of confidence toward the government are even considered by some theorists to be necessary and healthy to create a democracy (Hardin 1999; Warren 1999). The tricky part, however, of this idea of 'necessary and inevitable distrust and low confidence,' as argued in the democratization literature and individualization theory (Ester, Halman, and de Moor 1993) is the dilemma of how to determine a reasonable and tolerable level of distrust toward the government, as well as how to prevent this low level of confidence from turning into widespread cynicism and feelings of powerlessness.

A previous study found that in the early 1990s the Taiwanese public was already skeptical of their democratic future, and worried about the chaos that would accompany political transformation. During the period of political democratic transition, the social esteem enjoyed by politicians and business leaders was already lower than that of social elites. Moreover, the Taiwanese people were already cautious about the excessive power and influence of big business, but showed more trust in the top government leaders (e.g., the President) and the executive organ (the Executive Yuan) than the legislative body (the Legislative

Yuan). This certainly reflected the very nature of political democratization that was occurring at that time (Hsiao and Wan 1998).

In other words, since democratization, the public attitude toward the government and big business has been one of open questioning, and this has actually served as a collective sentiment that pushes the democratizing government toward further political reforms and democratic institutionalization. This was the positive side of the rising consciousness of distrust toward the government. Despite the low level of confidence, the public valued the political reforms that had taken place since the 1980s and continued to aspire for a more democratic government in Taiwan. The negative side, however, was the inevitable emergence of public cynicism, meaning that people became skeptical about attaining a satisfactory democratic system (Hsiao and Wan 1998).

Serious consideration should be given to the emerging cynicism in Taiwanese public sentiment since the 1990s under democratization. After all, public confidence and trust are essential to enhance sociopolitical integration and to sustain democracy. Ubiquitous public cynicism was once identified as the single greatest challenge facing America's well-established democracy, and it is undoubtedly even more deleterious to a nascent democracy like Taiwan (Goldfarb 1991).

In a recent survey conducted in late 2000 by Academia Sinica, after the significant 2000 presidential election, the above trust pattern was discovered to still hold true, and the mistrust level to have even increased in the ten-year period that encompasses the two phases of democratic transition and consolidation. Public distrust of the presidential office increased from 2.6 percent in 1992 to 40 percent in 2000, distrust of the Executive Yuan grew from 10 percent in 1992 to 44.2 percent in 2000, while the non-confidence rate toward the Legislative Yuan deteriorated to 62 percent from 46 percent (Institute of Sociology, Academia Sinica 2002). It may be disturbing and ironic to detect that the successful decade of democratic development has also produced a substantial number of critical and distrustful citizens who, in turn, have low levels of confidence for a democratic government that they have helped to create.

Yet the Taiwanese public has not lost faith in democracy as a desirable political system. In the above 2001 survey, more than 48 percent of the respondents said that they believe that even ordinary citizens could influence government policies, and 49 percent indicated that people such as themselves, as long as they constantly pose requests and articulate their opinions, have the ability to influence developments in society. This reflects a general faith in democratic governance and a trust in the actual existence of a democratic government in Taiwan.

Furthermore, in another recent survey carried out in January 2002, right after the December 2001 Legislative Yuan election, more than 36.3 percent of people went as far as praising the improvement of the quality of democracy in Taiwan over the past year, 37.3 percent said that it remained the same, and only 19.4 percent argued that the quality of Taiwan's democracy had declined between 2000 and 2001 under the new DPP government (Commonwealth 2002).

Protection of civil liberties

Democracy is said to have the moral obligation and societal capacity to protect the human rights of citizens and to enhance overall social equality. The Gallup survey included a series of questions that can be used to gauge perceptions of civil liberties in Taiwan. The most general measure is the extent to which people believe that human rights are being respected. In Table 4.2, 16.5 percent regard Taiwan's human rights as being fully respected and protected, and 80 percent that they are being partially respected. Altogether, 96.5 percent positively evaluated the human rights situation in present-day Taiwan, and only 2.1 percent responded that human rights are not respected.

Table 4.2: Human rights in Taiwan (%)

	Fully respected	Partially respected	Not respected	Don't know
1. Human rights in general	16.5	80.0	2.1	1.3
2. No one shall be subject to torture	28.3	50.0	13.3	8.4
3. All are equal before the law	28.3	53.2	16.3	2.1
4. Marriage shall be entered into only with the free and full consent of the partners	64.8	30.4	2.7	2.1
5. Everyone has the right to freedom of religion	74.5	21.5	2.3	1.7
6. Everyone has the right to freedom of speech	51.1	41.6	5.3	1.9
7. Everyone has the right to equal pay for equal work	27.6	54.8	15.0	2.7

Source: Gallup survey, questions 26–27.

As for the level of protection of the six specific domains of human rights mentioned in the Universal Declaration of Human Rights, the public ranked the six domains according to the degree that they are being fully respected, as follows: (1) freedom of religion (74.5%); (2) free and full consent of the partners for marriage (64.8%); (3) freedom of speech (51.1%); (4) freedom from being subjected to torture (28.3%); (5) all equal before the law (28.3%); and (6) equal pay for equal work (27.6%). The difference or discrepancy among the six human rights areas is evident: the freedoms of religion, marriage, and speech receive a much more positive evaluation, whereas the freedoms of equal treatment before the law and equal pay for equal work, as well as freedom from torture, still show room for improvement.

The composite approval rating, or the total percentage that responded in the fully and partially respected categories across the six human rights domains, ranges from 78.3 percent for freedom from torture, to 81.5 percent for equal treatment before the law, 82.4 percent for equal pay for equal work, 92.7 percent for freedom of speech, 95.2 percent for freedom of marriage, and finally to a high of 96 percent for freedom of religion. One can conclude that under the democratic government, the public is generally satisfied with the progress in improving the quality of human rights in Taiwan. It is also important to note, however, that more than 10 percent of the respondents are still dissatisfied with right to be free from torture (13.3%), the right of equal pay for equal work (15%), and the right that all are equal before the law (16.3%).

The Gallup survey also includes questions on five areas of discrimination—on the bases of sex, color, language, religion, and political opinion—which are prohibited under the proclamations of the Universal Declaration of Human Rights. Based on the results of this survey, it is evident that Taiwan's new democracy still suffers, to various degrees, from different forms of discrimination in the public mind. As presented in Table 4.3, discrimination on the basis of public opinion was the most serious in the public's perception, with 37.8 percent saying that it takes place frequently, and another 35 percent complaining of occasional occurrence. In other words, 72.8 percent of the respondents feel that discrimination, on the basis of political opinion, still exists in Taiwan's new democracy. The next most common form of perceived discrimination was gender discrimination (with 55.5% of respondents contending it frequently or sometimes occurs), followed by language discrimination (40.1%), religious discrimination (33.3%), and discrimination on the basis of color (31.2%).

Table 4.3: Discrimination in Taiwan (%)

	Frequently	Sometimes	Rarely	Never	Don't know
1. Discrimination on the basis of sex	15.0	40.5	26.6	16.0	1.9
2. Discrimination on the basis of color	8.0	23.2	38.0	28.5	2.3
3. Discrimination on the basis of language	9.1	31.0	38.8	19.0	2.1
4. Discrimination on the basis of religion	7.4	25.9	38.6	24.7	3.4
5. Discrimination on the basis of political opinion	37.8	35.0	15.8	8.9	2.5

Source: Gallup survey, question 28.

As pointed out earlier, 13.3 percent of the public expressed dissatisfaction with the freedom from torture, with as many as 28.3 percent openly agreeing that the use of torture has been documented in Taiwan. In considering that greater than 92 percent and 78 percent, respectively, of the public believe that the freedom of speech and the freedom from torture are fully or partially respected in Taiwan, the above mentioned negative subjective evaluations of political discrimination should be seen as qualifications of the overall condition of Taiwan's political freedom.

Nevertheless, the public is fairly concerned about what is being done to reduce or eliminate the use of torture. Of the public, 86.7 percent believe that greater public awareness of incidents of torture is crucial to reducing it, and 81.2 percent that stricter control over police/law enforcement officers would be an effective means. In addition, 77.8 percent advocate stricter international laws against the use of torture, 74.9 percent are in favor of increased prosecution of those suspected of torture, and finally, 70.5 percent support grassroots campaigns to ban torture (Gallup survey, question 28). These pro-political human rights attitudes in the public perception can be effective for mobilization against any further abuse of political freedoms.

The survey further reveals that gender inequality is at the top of the list for types of discrimination in Taiwan. More than half of the respondents (54.8%) recognize that women do not have equal rights with men (Gallup, question 14). To change the current undesirable situation would certainly require proper policy remedies and strong public support. It is interesting to discover that among the perceptions held by the Taiwan public, the value of equal rights for women is already well recognized. For example, 79.7 percent disagree that education is much more important for boys than for girls; 89.2

percent maintain that both husbands and wives should contribute to the household income; 84 percent agree that women in advanced countries must work for the rights of women in the developing world; 52.5 percent reject the view that men make better political leaders than women; and finally, 53.2 percent object to the idea that when jobs are scarce, men should be given more job opportunities than women (Gallup survey, question 15). The existence of such progressive values toward gender equality should serve as a useful social foundation to help upgrade and enhance women's rights in the future.

Taiwan's new democracy did bring about better institutional protection of human rights in general in the last decade, and the public has seen and recognized this. The public, however, also appears to believe that progress of two specific areas of human rights—politics and gender—has not been satisfactory.

Environment and public safety

Democracy does not necessarily guarantee a better quality of society, but it can provide a rational socio-political framework for the government and civil society to deal with existing and emerging social problems. Under a democratic political system, the public may be in a better position to express concerns about various social issues, and even to make demands that the government be responsive and responsible.

The Gallup survey includes four questions on the public's view of the environment and six questions on concerns regarding public safety and crime. As Table 4.4 shows, it is no surprise that the public in democratic Taiwan openly expressed grave concerns over the worsening conditions of the environment and crime, as has been well documented in previous surveys since the 1980s. The data on the environment and public safety from the Gallup survey further reinforce these findings.

In the Gallup survey, just 2.1 percent of respondents are very satisfied with the overall state of Taiwan's environment, and 56.3 percent consider the environment to be mainly satisfactory. Hence, less than 60 percent of the public hold positive views of current environmental conditions, with the remaining 40 percent holding rather negative attitudes. Although more people are satisfied than dissatisfied with the current environmental quality, approximately 74 percent of the respondents still condemn the government for not having done enough to address environmental issues. Following the

Table 4.4: Attitudes toward environmental problems in Taiwan (%)

	Very satisfactory	Mainly satisfactory	Mainly unsatisfactory	Very unsatisfactory	Don't know
1. How satisfactory do you find the overall state of the environment in Taiwan?	2.1	56.3	33.1	6.8	1.7

	Too little	Too much	The right amount	Don't know
2. In your opinion, has the government done too little, too much or the right amount to address the environmental issues in Taiwan?	74.0	2.5	19.8	3.8

3. Which of the follow statements do you tend to agree with more?

1) It is more important to protect the environment than to ensure economic growth	65.8
2) It is more important to ensure economic growth than to protect the environment	25.9
3) Don't know	1.4

	1st mention	2nd mention
4. The biggest threat to future generations not only in Taiwan but in the whole world as well:		
1) Industrial pollution	25.5	14.4
2) Holes in the ozone layer	16.7	15.2
3) Accidents with nuclear energy	12.2	12.7
4) Traffic pollution	12.2	11.6
5) Pollution of drinking water	12.0	13.1
6) Loss of rainforests, species and wildlife	9.3	10.3
7) Global warming	7.2	10.8
8) Pollution from farming	2.1	2.1

Source: Gallup survey, questions 2–4.

results of the survey, the two most critical environmental problems that threaten Taiwan's future generations are industrial pollution and holes in the ozone layer. The following environmental problems are also seen by the Taiwanese public as threatening to the well-being of future generations of the country and abroad: accidents with nuclear energy, pollution of drinking water, traffic pollution, and the loss of rainforests, species, and wildlife.

Since the 1980s, the normative conflict between economic growth and environmental quality has been a salient issue in Taiwan society. Three environmental movement streams—the anti-pollution protests, nature conservation movement, and the anti-nuclear power movement—have been promoting greater public concern over the controversy of growth versus environment, by means of collective actions in civil society (Hsiao 1998). It is evident that public concern over worsening environmental problems has been consistently high since the 1980s, as manifested in various surveys in the 1980s and 1990s. The percentage of the public who subjectively rated environmental problems as very serious or as serious social problems in Taiwan in different years came to 70 percent (1983), 88 percent (1986), 77 percent (1990), 81 percent (1991), 82 percent (1992), 86 percent (1999) and 75 percent (2001) (Hsiao 1998; Hsiao, Stone and Chi 2001; Institute of Sociology, Academia Sinica 2002).

As a result of the growing concern over the environment since the 1980s, a majority of Taiwanese have come to consider environmental protection to be more important than ensuring economic growth. In a 1983 survey, 53 percent held this view; the figure rose to 55 percent in 1986, and again to 57 percent in 1999 (Hsiao, Stone, and Chi 2001). In the Gallup survey, the percentage increased to 65.8 percent, the highest record to date. However, in a more recent survey, in July 2001, public perception may have changed on the growth versus environment controversy. For the first time since the 1980s, pro-environment values lost to pro-growth ones, with a ratio of 40.8 percent versus 46.9 percent (Institute of Sociology, Academia Sinica 2002). It is intriguing to see the gap between the continuously increasing concerns over the environment followed by a sudden decrease in 2001. This inconsistency in public perception can be explained, to a great extent, by the public's preoccupation over Taiwan's worsening economic conditions and increasing joblessness from 2000–2001. It is likely that support for pro-environment values, however, will survive, persist, and continue to grow in the years to come.

Beyond the environment, the public expressed great concern over public safety and crime in Taiwan as captured in Table 4.5. Approximately 46.6 percent of respondents indicated a great deal of concern over crime and another 47.9 percent a fair amount of concern. In total, 94.5 percent expressed worries about the crime situation. Furthermore, as much as 47.5 percent of respondents admitted that in the past five years their concern has increased a lot, with an additional 25.5 percent saying their concern has increased a little. This means that 73 percent said that they have become more concerned about crime problems in recent years.

In another survey conducted in 2001, as many as 85.3 percent and 82.2 percent of the respondents, respectively, agreed that juvenile

Table 4.5: Attitudes toward public safety and crime in Taiwan (%)

	A great deal	A fair amount	Not very much	Not at all	Don't know
1. How concerned are you about the level of crime?	46.6	47.9	4.9	0.4	0.2

	Increased a lot	Increased a little	Stayed the same	Decreased a little	Decreased a lot	Don't know
2. To what extent has your concern about crime increased or decreased in the past five years?	47.5	25.5	21.1	3.8	1.1	1.0

	Very well	Fairly well	Not very well	Not at all well	Don't know
3. How well do you think the government is handling the issue of crime?	0.8	30.8	50.2	16.9	1.3

	Too much	Too little	About right	Don't know
4. What do you think about the control of guns?	6.3	49.8	42.4	1.5

5. What should be the main aim of imprisonment?	
1) To make those who have done wrong pay for it	30.6
2) To act as a deterrent to others	26.8
3) To protect other citizens	22.8
4) To re-educate the prisoner	16.9
5) Don't know	2.9

6. Are you in favor or against the use of the death penalty?	
1) In favor	83.3
2) Against	13.5
3) Don't know	3.2

Source: Gallup survey, questions 16–21.

delinquency and public safety problems are very serious or serious social problems in Taiwan. In fact, among the fifteen social problems listed for respondents to choose from, the two above mentioned crime-related social issues ranked as the number two and three problems facing Taiwan (Institute of Sociology 2002). Furthermore, in the 2002 Commonwealth survey, 53.5 percent of respondents said that they do not feel safe under the present public safety conditions (Commonwealth 2002).

Given the high level of anxiety about crime problems, it is only natural that the public in Taiwan is also concerned about the government's handling of public safety issues. As predicted, respondents to public opinion polls do not express any satisfaction at all with what the government has done so far on crime problems. In the Gallup survey, more than half (50.2%) of the respondents feel that the government has not done the job well, and another 16.9 percent criticize it for having failed in its tasks. Only 31.6 percent indicate that the government has handled crime very or fairly well. It appears that the public in Taiwan is preoccupied with the problem of public safety, and even feels victimized. Thus, it is no surprise to discover that public satisfaction with the government's measures to control crime is relatively low.

It is also important to point out that Taiwanese people, because of their great concern about the issue of public safety and their sense of being victimized by the crime problem, tend to take conservative and tough stands on policy issues such as gun control and the death penalty. Roughly half (49.8%) contend that there is too little control of guns, with 42.4 percent agreeing that gun control is about right, and only 6.3 percent saying that control is too much. A very high percentage (83.3%) of Taiwan's public is in favor of the death penalty—a sign of a mass reaction to the worsening crime problems and resulting conservatism. Moreover, 30.6 percent of the respondents take a punitive rather than rehabilitative view toward the imprisonment of criminals, saying that they should pay for their crimes, with another 26.8 percent arguing that imprisonment is a deterrent to others, 22.8 percent that it is a way to protect the innocent, and a low 16.9 percent perceiving it as a means to reeducate prisoners. All of the above mentioned indicators of conservative and tough stances toward punishment and the death penalty well reflect the public's worries and fear about the increasing victimization of innocent citizens.

In sum, using the two examples pertaining to the environment and public safety to assess the performance of Taiwan's democratic government to produce social betterment for all, the regrettable finding is that democracy does not necessarily guarantee a better quality of society. Democracy, however, does guarantee the civil rights and freedom of citizens to make demands toward the government to take necessary and effective policies and measures to improve society. The analysis of public opinion in Taiwan offers support for this general claim.

Conclusion

The above discussion of Taiwanese public perceptions and attitudes toward the new democracy, using data from the Gallup survey, helps characterize the social foundation of democratic governance in Taiwan. It is argued that Taiwan's new democracy has already gone beyond a mere procedural change. It has transformed, to various degrees, government conduct and new responsibilities of government—societal relations, the quality of social liberties and human rights, and the prospects for governmental response to emerging social issues. Surveys suggest that the public has found that the government has changed its conduct and become more responsive and accountable. Civil society appears to exert much more power in influencing the direction and content of government policies. When the government does not respond in the way the public expects, people become frustrated and resentful. Therefore, the public is becoming more and more critical and demanding, and may have even developed a sense of cynicism and distrust toward the government and other public institutions.

However, people have not lost faith in the idea of democracy and the practice of democratic governance. Under Taiwan's relatively new democratic political system, the public is generally satisfied with progress in the protection of human rights. Civil liberties have been respected and safeguarded. However, many people believe that discrimination on the basis of political opinion still persists in today's Taiwan. People are also concerned about the persistence of gender inequality, although pro-women rights values have risen over the last two decades, facilitated by the democratic transformation.

Taiwan's new democracy also has not produced, at least in the short run, a better society for all. Worsening environmental problems and public safety issues have been a constant public worry over the years, and the government has failed to adequately handle these problems. The frustration and mistrust of the public originates in the inadequacy of governmental policies and actions to solve problems involving the environment and crime. Yet it is clear in the mind of the public that their rights and freedom to make further demands toward the government can only be properly protected under the newly established democracy.

Democracy has created and raised expectations among the Taiwanese public for a more accountable government that can respect civil liberties and human rights, and also build a better society with improved environmental quality and more safety for citizens. The Taiwanese public may be discontent, they may be suspicious, and they may even be cynical, but they are not apathetic. The notion of democracy as a way of public life that involves rights and duties needs to be educated and internalized among the public in Taiwan. Only when that notion is fully appreciated by both the citizens and the government, can the social foundation of Taiwan's new democratic governance be firmly established. The story of democracy in Taiwan is still in its first few chapters, and the rest remains to be written together by all parties concerned.

Bibliography

Ahn, Chung-Si and Woo-Taek Kang (2002), 'Trust and confidence in government in transitional democracies: South Korea in comparative perspective', paper presented at the International Workshop on Changing Values and Challenges of Democratic Governance in Asia, Seoul National University, Seoul, Korea.

Commonwealth Magazine (2002), '*2002 national situational survey*', January, pp. 72–85.

Ester, Peter, Loek Halman, and Ruud de Moor (eds.) (1993), *The Individualizing Society: Value Change in Europe and North America*, Tilburg: Tilburg University Press.

Goldfarb, Jeffrey C. (1991), *The Cynical Society: the Culture of Politics and the Politics of Culture in American Life*, Chicago: University of Chicago Press.

Hardin, Russell (1999), 'Do we want trust in government?' in Mark E. Warren (ed.), *Democracy and Trust*, Cambridge: Cambridge University Press, pp. 22–41.

Hsiao, Hsin-Huang Michael and Hagan Koo (1997), 'The middle classes and democratization', in Larry Diamond and Marc Platter (eds.), *Consolidating the Third Wave Democracies*, Baltimore: Johns Hopkins Univ. Press, pp. 312–333.

Hsiao, Hsin Huang Michael and Po-San Wan (1998), 'Confidence gap in Taiwan and Hong Kong', in *Ritsumeikan Journal of Asia–Pacific Studies*, no.1, pp. 45–68.

Hsiao, Hsin-Huang Michael, Russell Stone and Chum-Chieh Chi (2002), 'Taiwan environmental consciousness: indicators of collective mind toward sustainable development', paper presented at the Workshop on Sustainable Development Indicators, Chung-Li, Taiwan: National Central University.

Huntington, Samuel P. (1991), *The Third Wave: Democratization in the Late Twentieth Century*, Norman: University of Oklahoma Press.

Inoguchi, Takashi, Edward Newman and John Keane (1998), *The Changing Nature of Democracy*, Tokyo: United Nations University Press.

Inoguchi, Takashi (2000), 'Can the Asian Values Be the Basis of Democratic Governance in the Asia–Pacific Region?' paper presented at the International Conference on Changing Values and Challenges of Democratic Governance, Seoul National University, Seoul, Korea, November 17–18.

Institute of Sociology, Academia Sinica (2002), *Social Change Survey in Taiwan 2000*, Ying-Hua Chang and Yang-Chi Fu (eds.), Taipei: Institute of Sociology, Academia Sinica.

Warren, Mark E. (ed.), (1999), *Democracy and Trust*, Cambridge: Cambridge University Press.

Chapter Five

A New Era of Politics in Malaysia: Ferment and Fragmentation

Francis Loh Kok Wah

Despite a history of continuous parliamentary rule and regular elections since independence from British rule in 1957, Malaysian politics has experienced an increasing concentration of governmental powers in the executive at the expense of the judicial and legislative branches, the mass media, and, in general, civil society. The Malaysian political system is described variously as a 'quasi democracy' (Zakaria 1989), a 'semi democracy' (Case 1993), a 'repressive-responsive regime' (Crouch 1996), or even a 'syncretic state' (Jesudason 1996). For other critics, the present-day Malaysian political system is better described as a system of *rule by law*, no longer one of *rule of law* (Rais 1995). In this chapter, my focus is not on the coercive laws and institutional constraints that restrict the scope of political participation in Malaysia (Saravanamuttu 1992; Loh 2000) but on the discourses and practices, or the political culture(s), defined loosely, that permeate Malaysian society. Specifically, I want to understand why Malaysians seem to acquiesce to this authoritarian *rule by law*.

I begin this chapter by providing a brief background to Malaysia, followed by a discussion of the democratic ferment—the so-called *reformasi* movement and the formation of an opposition coalition—that occurred in 1998–1999 after Malaysia's 'dual crises:' the regional financial crisis and the dismissal and incarceration of Anwar Ibrahim, the then deputy prime minister. Despite anticipation that a change of government was in the offing, the Barisan Nasional (BN or National Front) ruling coalition was returned to power in the November 1999 general election. Many Malaysians were disappointed because they had believed that the Barisan Alternatif (BA) would displace the BN.

Next, drawing from the Gallup International Millennium Survey (Gallup survey), I discuss some aspects of Malaysian political culture.

Contrary to those who argue that a set of 'Asian values' prevail among Malaysians, and other Asians, I suggest that the current political values, attitudes, and orientations of Malaysians derive from the rise of 'developmentalism,' the cultural corollary to the *dirigiste* developmental state that characterized the Malaysian (and many other East and Southeast Asian) regimes during the 1980s and early 1990s. Accordingly, I discuss how this new culture of developmentalism became embedded among Malaysians. It is this developmentalism, therefore, that explains the values, attitudes, and orientations of the Malaysians, which in turn imposes limits on democratization. However, the fact that democratic ferment did occur, especially evident during the dual crises period of the late 1990s, suggests that this developmentalism is being contested.

From independence to the New Economic Policy

Approximately 23.3 million people inhabited Malaysia in 2000. Officially the people are categorized into *bumiputera* (indigenous) people and non-*bumiputera* (non-indigenous) people. Malays and the aboriginal groups in peninsular Malaysia and the 'natives' of Sabah and Sarawak states (both in northern Borneo) total some 60 percent of the population, and constitute the *bumiputera*. Chinese (about 28 % of the total) and Indians (about 8% of the total), who began immigrating to Malaysia during British colonial rule in the nineteenth and early twentieth centuries, comprise the non-*bumiputera*. Apart from linguistic and cultural differences, religion further distinguishes the ethnic groups from one another. The Malays are invariably Muslim, the Chinese predominantly Buddhist and Taoist, and the Indians mostly Hindu with smaller numbers of Muslims and Sikhs. Finally, about 9 percent of Malaysians (from all ethnic groups, with the exception if Malays) are Christian.

From independence in 1957 to 1969, the Federation of Malaysia was ruled by the Alliance Party, a multi-ethnic coalition government that comprised of the United Malays National Organization (UMNO), the dominant partner, the Malaysian Chinese Association (MCA), and the Malaysian Indian Congress (MIC). Nominally, it practiced a Westminister system of government and held federal and state elections regularly. For some observers, Malaysia was an example of consociationalism wherein political elites of various ethnic groups reached consensual power sharing arrangements (Lijphart 1977).

In reality, and in spite of regular elections and parliamentary rule, a strong state dominated by the executive had been in place since independence. However, its control of civil society was achieved not through the use of brute force or the suspension of the constitution or elections, but through coercive legislation passed by parliament. The most important consideration in this regard was how the British expanded and consolidated the Malaysian (then colonial) state quickly as a result of the communist uprising, euphemistically termed the Emergency (1948–1960). It was only with the advent of independence that a set of participatory governmental institutions was introduced by the British. The state's coercive powers granted under the Emergency Regulations were then amended and incorporated into the Independence Constitution and other laws for the state's use in ordinary times in post-independence Malaysia. Ironically, the Malaysian nationalists worked hand in glove with the British to expand and consolidate the national state, ensuring the defeat of the communist insurrection.

The post-independence executive used these strong foundations to further reform the state to serve its own political ends. Through promulgation of new laws and amendments to these new laws and constitution, the executive ensured uninterrupted control and domination of the Malaysian state. Consequently, very few independent organizations have developed that are capable of advocating the rights and interests of civil society in a sustained fashion. Hence, the Alliance Party, (and its successor the Barisan Nasional) has maintained an ironclad grip on power since 1957.

The absence of consensus outside the Alliance leadership and an economic slowdown in the late 1960s contributed to worsening ethnic relations that culminated in the worst-ever incident of communal riots in May 1969. The riots led to the suspension of parliamentary rule. The National Operations Council—largely drawn from the ruling Malay elites in UMNO and the upper echelons of the administrative and security forces also dominated by Malays—ruled for almost twenty-one months. Several important changes to the original consociational arrangements, geared toward the promotion of Malay interests, were introduced before parliamentary rule was restored in early 1971.

First, the political elite expanded the Alliance multi-ethnic ruling coalition to include the erstwhile opposition parties and renamed it the Barisan Nasional (BN, National Front). At the same time, a shift occurred from participative to executive institutions. Following amendments to the constitution and to the Sedition Act, certain 'sensitive issues' were declared beyond the bounds of public discourse. These issues included the special rights of Malays, the position of traditional rulers as heads of state, Malay as the national language, and Islam as the official religion on the one hand, and the citizenship rights of non-Malays on the other.

Second, the government undertook various moves to promote a common national identity. These included the introduction of a National Cultural Policy (which emphasized Islam and the cultural attributes of the majority and indigenous Malays as the essential bases of the Cultural Policy); the belated implementation of the National Language (Malay) and National Educational policies (including the progressive use of Malay as the sole medium of instruction in secondary schools and universities beginning from 1971), which had been passed in the 1960s; and the pronouncement of the *Rukunegara*, the national ideology based on a set of five universal principles.

Third, the government formulated and launched the New Economic Policy (NEP, 1971–1990) as its principal policy response to the May 1969 communal riots. The objectives of the NEP was to deal with Malay poverty and resentment of inter-ethnic income and wealth inequalities, and with the ethnic division of labor that favored the more urbanized non-*bumiputeras* and discriminated against the rural *bumiputeras*. Under the auspices of the NEP, the 'Outline Perspective Plan (OPP) for 1971–1990,' proposed poverty eradication regardless of ethnic group (the poverty rate was especially high among rural *bumiputeras*) and the increased share of corporate equity for the *bumiputera* from 2.5 percent in 1970 to 30 percent by 1990. Hence began a massive affirmative action program favoring *bumiputeras*. To ensure that the overall financial well-being of the non-*bumiputera* were not adversely affected, the NEP was set within the context of achieving rapid economic growth during the duration of the OPP. Foreign domination of the economy, which in 1970 accounted for 60.7 percent ownership of equity in the corporate sector, was also to be reduced drastically.

Malaysians, according to their ethnicity, differed in their opinions about the NEP. The *bumiputera* welcomed the restructuring as necessary to foster national unity, whereas the non-*bumiputera* tended to resent it as racial discrimination, arguing that it worsened inter-ethnic relations. Non-Malay leaders of the BN ruling coalition who claimed to support the NEP, nonetheless, were apt to complain about its overzealous implementation by Malay bureaucrats. Non-Malays and opposition Malay parties criticized it on the grounds that a political patronage system had been spawn as a result of the NEP (Gomez 1996). At the root of the problem was the availability of business licenses, government projects, and soft loans that, in accordance with NEP quota requirements, targeted *bumiputeras*. The proliferation of public enterprises and the establishment of companies by these enterprises further resulted in the creation of numerous directorships, managerial and executive positions as well as ordinary job opportunities.

The most lucrative business opportunities and top positions often went to UMNO leaders, who either acted as trustees on behalf of UMNO or in their own private capacities. In turn, these UMNO leaders made available the less lucrative opportunities and positions to their own supporters. Ultimately, UMNO ended up in business. This involvement of UMNO in business and subsequently other BN political parties has led to the so-called phenomenon of 'money politics' in Malaysia. Indeed, public debates over the NEP were sometimes acrimonious. Yet, in the end, Malays and non-Malays forged a general acceptance of the NEP and of some form of state intervention in the economy on behalf of Malay interests.

Such consensus was facilitated by the steady economic growth of the 1970s and early 1980s (Jomo 1990). Fortuitously, the first decade of the NEP coincided with Malaysia's discovery of offshore petroleum and an international commodities boom that resulted in favorable export earnings that enabled the government to implement the NEP. But the growth was also spurred on by increased foreign direct investments (FDIs) in Malaysia's export-oriented industrialization programs, which began in the 1970s. Free trade zones were created and various incentives offered to foreign companies. With industrialization and rapid growth generally, employment opportunities expanded. Unemployment rates fell while per capita income rose (Jomo 1990). By any standards, growth was impressive, even more so when the need for inter-ethnic restructuring of the economy is considered. In 1985–1986, however, Malaysia experienced a severe recession due to falling commodity prices including that of petroleum. Local and foreign investments also fell. Many mismanaged and unprofitable public enterprises were closed. It was under such circumstances that the NEP was held in abeyance.

To resuscitate the economy, the Malaysian government liberalized guidelines for foreign equity ownership in manufacturing. Malaysia also adopted other economic deregulation policies and privatization projects, in line with neoliberal global trends, (Loh 2000: 71–72). Because of these critical changes in development policy, favorable growth rates resumed in the late 1980s and continued into the 1990s. By that time, however, the NEP had officially come to a close

Meanwhile, the BN coalition consolidated its rule. Political ferment that had occurred during the mid-1980s recession was halted through the mass arrests of activists belonging to nongovernmental organizations (NGOs), opposition leaders, unionists, and educationists in an operation code named *Operasi Lalang* in October 1987. Following the tightening of various laws, the government initiated an assault on the conservative, but independent judiciary in 1988. The upshot was the removal of the head of the Supreme Court and suspension of five other judges.

Although the opposition gained ground in the 1990 general election, the BN recovered its support base in the the 1995 general election. On that occasion, the BN coalition polled 66 percent of the votes and won four-fifths of all seats in parliament. A year earlier in the 1994 Sabah state election, the BN had also performed well replacing the *Parti Bersatu Sabah* (PBS, or United Sabah Party), which had been in power since 1985. In Sarawak, the *Parti Bansa Dayak Sarawak* (Sarawak Dayak People's Party), which had quit the Sarawak BN coalition in 1983, rejoined the BN in 1994. Finally, the Malay opposition party, *Semangat 46* (Spirit of '46)—created after the split of UMNO in 1987/1988—voted to dissolve itself in October 1996 after eights years in opposition. Its leaders and their followers returned to the UMNO fold. Prior to the dissolution of *Semangat 46*, the Islamic movement Darul Arqam, which had been banned in 1994, was successfully disbanded too. All told, it appeared that the BN had consolidated itself by the mid-1990s, after a political hiccup in the mid-1980s (Loh 2002: 38–40).

Reformasi and the democratic ferment

It was, therefore, an unexpected twist of fate that a *reformasi* movement emerged in 1998–1999. No doubt, this *volte face* had everything to do with the so-called Anwar saga.

The 1997 financial crisis brought differences between Prime Minister Mahathir Mohamad and his deputy prime minister, Anwar Ibrahim, to a head, particularly over how the crisis should be managed. Anwar, who was then finance minister, severely cut government expenditure and allowed interest rates to float upwards. Privatized 'mega projects,' such as the Bakun hydroelectric power project in

Sarawak and a mass rapid transit system that linked the capital city to the new international airport (the KLIA) in Sepang, were shelved. Calls to bail out Malaysian companies that faced bankruptcies were rejected. But Dr Mahathir considered these decisions and related measures taken by Anwar to miss the point. They were no different from the International Monetary Fund's response to the crisis and, in his mind, failed to recognize that the crisis was not a result of domestic shortcomings. Rather, it was caused by international currency speculators and the hedge fund managers. In refusing to assist the Malaysian, specifically the *bumiputera* corporations, Anwar was allowing the gains secured under the NEP to promote *bumiputera* commercial and industrial interests to become unstuck.

Consequently, a different set of policies that focused attention on how to deal with foreign manipulation of the Malaysian economy, on the one hand, and on bailing out Malaysian corporations via restructuring, debt relief, and access to new credit, on the other hand, were proposed by the National Economic Action Council (NEAC), headed by former finance minister and Mahathir's confidante, Daim Zainuddin. In June 1998, when an Anwar associate launched an attack on cronyism and nepotism, a veiled attack on Mahathir, the latter hit back openly. By September 1998, Anwar was ousted.

Anwar's sacking from government, expulsion from UMNO, subsequent arrest, prosecution, and six-year prison sentence galvanized his supporters in and outside UMNO into a mass movement, and led to public rallies and street demonstrations in support of Anwar. His treatment and the regime's abuse of power generally were widely criticized in publications, video-cassette tapes, and on numerous websites. But the demands of the movement quickly moved beyond concern for Anwar's well-being to reformist issues such as 'rule of law,' 'participatory democracy,' and 'justice for all.' It also called for the repeal of coercive laws, like the Internal Security Act (ISA—which allows for detention without trial), and for 'accountability' and 'transparency' in decisionmaking in order to end 'corruption, cronyism and nepotism,' and to initiate Dr. Mahathir's ouster. Ultimately, Anwar's supporters launched *Parti Keadilan Nasional* (National Justice Party), led by Dr. Wan Azizah Ismail, Anwar's wife. In anticipation of the general elections scheduled for mid-2000, *Parti Keadilan Nasional* and three opposition parties—the Malay-based *Parti Islam SeMalaysia* (PAS, Islamic Party of Malaysia), the Chinese-based *Democratic Action Party* (DAP, *Parti Tindakan Demokratik*) and the small multiethnic socialist-inclined *Parti Rakyat Malaysia* (PRM, Malaysian People's

Party)—subsequently formed a new opposition coalition, the *Barisan Alternatif* (BA, Alternative Front) in mid-1999. Put simply, the discourse of participatory democracy, previously the purview of small groups of middle-class, (western) educated Malaysians, especially those involved in NGOs, now developed into a significant counter-discourse that involved the opposition parties, too.

Just as a leopard cannot change its spots, neither did the opposition parties change theirs. Many in PAS continue to maintain a literalist fundamentalist notion of Islam and to understand the party's goals in terms of furthering Islamic laws, with the ultimate goal of an Islamic state. Moreover, some members of PAS reject democracy as a western imperialist legacy and as an extension of secularism. These particular leaders and supporters of PAS also have a narrow ethnic outlook, which stands in contrast to Islamic preachings of universalism. Yet PAS also has members who believe that Islam is not incompatible with democracy (Syed Ahmad 2002). This latter group became more publicly articulate and was responsible for steering PAS toward supporting Anwar's plight, *reformasi*, and formation of the BA. The issues of justice and democracy that the BA highlighted, and which PAS supported in the run-up to the 1999 polls, indicate that PAS, while maintaining its Islamic credentials, nonetheless, supported the democratic momentum.

The DAP, while advocating the deepening of democracy, apparently conducted its internal party affairs in a high-handed fashion. In 1998–1999, several party stalwarts and their supporters, who accused Lim Kit Siang and the other DAP national leaders of authoritarianism and nepotism, were suspended or expelled. In fact, many within the party also harbored strong anti-Islamic sentiments and disagreed with the leadership's decision to cooperate with PAS in the elections. At the same time, UMNO leaders and supporters, who had joined *Parti Keadilan Nasional*, not surprisingly displayed signs of UMNO-styled exclusivist ethnic politics, too. Some leaders of BA, reportedly, disagreed with the proposals of the new opposition coalition toward greater cultural liberalization. Yet the formation of the BA was not merely a 'marriage of convenience' among incompatibles. Many leaders and members of the four parties that formed this coalition subscribed to the democratic discourse. And through extended debate and give and take, the BA reached agreement on the distribution of electoral seats, the contents of a joint manifesto 'For a Just Malaysia' (which contained many social democratic features), and even on a 'people friendly' alternative budget, which sought to jump-start the economy by increasing public spending for social programs.

A related development was the proliferation of NGOs and other independent groups, which also made their voices heard in the run-up to the elections. Although these nascent organizations and groups appeared to be critical of the BN and its policies, they were also expressing their concerns to the BA and, indeed, to whomsoever wished to rule the country. Their concerns included:

- the 'Women's Agenda for Change,' which demanded that the laws be enforced to protect women's rights and that these rights be furthered through new legislations;
- the 'Citizens Health Initiative,' which mobilized Malaysians from all walks of life to oppose the corporatization (a variant of privatization) of the public hospitals and other health services;
- the 'People are the Boss' campaign that involved Chinese youths who championed the original meaning of democracy;
- the 17-Point 'Election Appeals'(*Suqiu*), which focused on issues of justice and democracy rather than specific Chinese interests, and was endorsed by more than 2000 Chinese associations;
- the Election Watch (*Pemantau*) organized by 'Budi,' a new NGO, which rallied 40-odd NGOs to jointly monitor the electoral campaign and prepare a report of its findings;
- a petition with about 50,000 signatories demanding a monthly wage scheme and better working conditions for plantation workers—several busloads of whom converged on the doorstep of parliament to deliver their petition;
- a coalition of NGOs, principally Indian-based, which called for an inquiry into two separate incidents in which the police killed eighteen Indians suspected of being criminals;
- an unprecedented march through the streets of Kuala Lumpur in December 1998, by some 300 lawyers in support of a colleague who had been found guilty of 'contempt of court' for remarks uttered while defending Anwar Ibrahim;
- environmentalists who protested the continued resettlement of Sarawak natives, despite the shelving of the Bakun hydro-electricity project and the proposed construction of the Selangor Dam, which threatened to destroy pristine forests and required the eviction of indigenous peoples living in the area.
- a mass campaign led by the consumer organizations to encourage parliamentarians to pass the Consumer Protection Act;
- artists who parodied the unfolding events and protested against injustices through their compositions and songs, artworks

and installations, performances and skits, verses, and (in one instance) an entire novel; and
- many groups of ordinary Malaysians whose investments in housing development projects were now stalled on account of the economic crisis, and who now protested collectively against the developers and pressured the government to look into their plight.

Most of these groups and initiatives were not associated with the opposition coalition or directly concerned with the outcome of the election. But their emergence alongside the *reformasi* movement and the formation of the BA indicated that Malaysia was in political ferment. The impulses toward democracy demonstrated by them paralleled the burgeoning popular movement in the mid-1980s, which also occurred during a period of economic recession and similarly called for 'rule of law,' 'participatory democracy,' 'accountability,' etc. Mass arrests conducted during *Operasi Lalang* in October 1987, halted the latter movement. Indeed, some of these demands for justice and democracy were foreshadowed in the struggles of the radical wing of the independence movement in the 1940s and 1950s, and of the leftist opposition in the 1960s.

Yet the late-1990s movement was significantly different from earlier democratic movements. For the first time, a movement had the support of a significant proportion of the Malay middle class. Previously, this class had supported the BN-UMNO government, but in the late 1990s it considered the BN government cruel (*zalim*) and unjust (*tak adil*), and openly expressed its anger against the government. This change in attitude and orientation had everything to do with Anwar's unjust treatment, which for many Malay dissidents was considered to have breached 'traditional' norms and practices (Khoo 1999). Since these dissidents had contact with the grassroots through organizations like *Angkatan Belia Islam Malaysia* (ABIM, the Malaysian Islamic Youth Movement) *and Jama'ah Islah Malaysia* (JIM, the Malaysian Islamic Reform Movement), they drew in lower-class Malay support, too. Consequently, polls at that time showed high expectations for a change of government.

That change, however, did not occur. The BN, the 14-party ruling coalition led by UMNO, won 148 out of 193 parliamentary seats in the November 1999 general election, maintaining its two-third majority of parliament. In the face of the political ferment, how does one explain the BN's triumph? Before offering an explanation, I will consider the findings of the Gallup survey on the political values, attitudes and orientations of Malaysians.

The Gallup International Millennium Survey findings

In a study that compared democratic governance among nine Asian countries, Takashi Inoguchi (2000) highlighted an important discrepancy between the ranking of these countries based on objective indicators of democratic governance derived from Freedom House data on political rights and civil liberties, and that based on subjective indicators derived from the Gallup data.

Thus, whereas Japan, South Korea and Taiwan are clearly ranked as more democratic than Malaysia (and Singapore) in the Freedom House schema, they are ranked considerably lower according to data from the Gallup survey. Inoguchi (2000: 4–5) notes:

> It is those quasi-democratic and semi-authoritarian countries that are accorded highest scores for subjective democratic governance along with such seemingly highly democratic countries such as Switzerland, Netherlands, Denmark, Sweden and UK. It is those highly democratic countries such as Japan and South Korea that are given low scores of democratic governance along with Cameroon and Colombia [in the Gallup schema]. It looks as if how [they] respond to the questions on corruption, people's will, justice and governing efficacy made significant differences. Those quasi-democratic and semi-authoritarian countries are given bonuses to their democratic scores despite some illiberal practices.

A comparison of the Gallup data that pertains to Malaysia, Singapore, and Thailand supports Inoguchi's point. Table 5.1 indicates that Malaysians (even more so Singaporeans) perceive their government to be relatively efficient, just, and responsive to the people's will. Accordingly, the Malaysian government is not too bureaucratic or corrupt. By contrast, the Thais perceive their government to be less efficient, less just, and not particularly responsive to the people's will. Accordingly, the Thai government is regarded as more bureaucratic and clearly more corrupt.

The Gallup survey also registered similar high rates of confidence in, and trust of the government when Malaysians were asked whether they are 'governed by the will of the people,' and whether 'free and fair elections' occur. (See Table 5.2.) However, as Inoguchi (2000: 5)

Table 5.1: Perception of the government (%)

	Malaysia	Singapore	Thailand
Efficient	47.8	56.8	22.4
Bureaucratic	26.7	13.3	35.7
Corrupt	34.9	1.5	71.2
Just	47.5	28.4	6.3
Respond to the will of the people	44.1	23.9	15.1

Source: Gallup survey, question 7. The figures indicate the percentage of respondents that selected the word to describe their perception of the government in their country.
Note: 'Don't know' responses are excluded.

notes, such trust and confidence are often based on a procedural notion of democracy that emphasizes the existence of multi-party systems and free, secret ballot elections rather than the prevalence of the rule of law, the formation of independent associations, and joint action on the part of groups and associations for the betterment of civil society—in other words, a more participatory democracy.

I have investigated the Malaysian responses further by disaggregating the Gallup data according to the gender, educational level, and religion of the respondents. The disaggregated data according to gender does not readily reveal any major difference between the opinions of male and female respondents. When disaggregated according to the level of education obtained, it appears that those who possess a university degree are more critical than those with a secondary school education, and the latter, in turn, are more

Table 5.2: Attitudes toward procedural democracy (%)

	Malaysia	Singapore	Thailand
Governed by the will of the people?			
Yes	77.3	50.4	51.2
No	17.7	31.6	47.6
Don't know	5.0	18.0	1.2
Free and fair elections?			
Yes	71.3	75.3	31.0
No	18.3	11.7	66.3
Don't know	10.4	13.0	2.7

Source: Gallup survey, questions 5–6.

Table 5.3: Attitudes toward democracy by education level (%)

	Primary	Secondary	University
Governed by the will of the people?			
Yes	86.4	77.5	68.6
No	10.2	16.9	26.8
Don't know	3.4	5.6	4.6
Free and fair elections?			
Yes	71.0	73.6	64.4
No	13.1	17.8	24.7
Don't know	15.9	8.6	10.8
Perception of government			
Efficient	39.8	48.1	38.7
Bureaucratic	16.5	23.9	35.6
Corrupt	33.5	32.0	35.6
Just	46.0	46.6	35.6
Responds to will of people	32.4	44.8	36.6
None	4.6	2.0	3.6
Don't know	10.8	6.7	3.6
In general are human rights being respected?			
Fully respected	35.2	34.8	24.7
Partially respected	56.3	59.2	67.5
Not respected	1.1	3.6	7.2
Don't know	7.4	2.3	0.5

Source: Gallup survey, questions 5–7 and 27.

discerning than those who only received a primary school education (see Table 5.3). For instance, approximately 86.4 percent of those with primary education agreed that they are governed by the will of the people, whereas 77.5 percent of those with secondary school education agreed, and only 68.6 percent of those with university education concurred. Similar kinds of differences between these three categories pertain vis-à-vis the respondents' perceptions of whether the government is bureaucratic, corrupt, or just. Likewise, the better the respondent was educated, the less s/he thought that the government fully respected human rights.

The differences in attitudes toward procedural democracy and perceptions toward government are most evident when the data is disaggregated according to religion. Here, religion is used as a proxy for ethnic group since all Malays are Muslim, most Indians are

Hindu, and a large majority of Chinese is Buddhist. The data reveals that the Hindus are least critical of the government, the Buddhists most critical, and the Muslims in between the first two groups. For instance, 86 percent of Hindus believed that elections are free and fair, compared to 68 percent of Muslims, and only 71 percent of Buddhists. Hindus also consider the government to be more efficient, just, and responsive to the will of the people; Muslims are more critical and Buddhists are the most critical of all in these particular assessments. On the question of whether human rights are fully respected, 47 percent of Hindus answered in the affirmative, whereas 36 percent of Muslims and only 25 percent of Buddhists agreed.

Hence, Malaysians have differences in opinion. Such differences help to explain the emergence of the *reformasi* movement and the critical NGOs that we discussed earlier. The data suggest that these more critical Malaysians are Buddhists/Chinese as well as Malaysians in general who possess a higher level of education. That said, it should be recognized, nonetheless, that Malaysians, relatively speaking, are more positive in their evaluation of their government when compared to the other Asian countries (with the exception of Singapore). An explanation for this is surely because of the relative success of the Malaysian government in handling the 1997 financial crisis. Whereas in 1998 Indonesia saw an economic decline of more than 13 percent, and Thailand and the Philippines, 10 to 11 percent, Malaysia registered a 7 percent decline. (Singapore registered next to no growth that year). More importantly, the Malaysian economy began to turn around by mid-1999, emboldening the BN government to call for general elections in November 1999 (Saravanamuttu 2002).

Moreover, whereas the financial crisis led to ethnic conflict and political instability in the neighboring countries, especially in Indonesia, political stability ensued in Malaysia, the challenges of the *reformasi* movement notwithstanding. The Malaysian government was not oblivious of its relatively favorable circumstances and made much of this in the mass media by comparing itself to its less fortunate neighbors. No doubt, this was part of the BN's electoral strategy. Indeed, the BN electoral propaganda depicted the challenges of the *reformasi* movement and the NGOs as a threat to the prevailing political stability and the capacity of the BN government to further resuscitate the economy. Significantly, the Gallup survey was conducted in Malaysia in September 1999 amid such discursive contestations. But the attitudes and opinions of most Malaysians had already been shaped much earlier in favor of the quasi-democratic and semi-authoritarian status-quo, due to what I have termed 'developmentalism,' and which I next discuss.

Developmentalism and the limits to democratization

Some analysts have explained the victory of the BN in the November 1999 election by referring to the usual politics of ethnicism. No doubt, ethnic sentiments were intentionally stimulated, and ethnic separateness emphasized by the ethnic-based component parties of the BN. The electoral campaign of the BN shows clear evidence of this strategy—in the speeches made, the posters distributed, and the propaganda in the mass media, which the BN controlled (Mustafa 2000). As ethnic tensions re-emerged, the BN projected itself as the only proven and credible coalition capable of attending to the disparate needs and interests of Malaysia's multiethnic, multi-religious society. As a contrast, the new opposition coalition, also largely composed of ethnic-based component parties, was depicted as a 'marriage of convenience,' its partners as 'strange bedfellows,' and ultimately, incapable of ruling a multiethnic Malaysia. Yet I maintain that this politics of ethnicism was only one of several factors, perhaps even a minor factor, that contributed to the BN's electoral success. I argue that the appeal of BN can be principally attributed to 'developmentalism.'

With the end of the NEP in 1990, and global trends toward privatization and economic deregulation, the private sector replaced the public sector as the engine of growth under the auspices of 'Malaysia Inc.,' that is, a collaboration between the private and public sectors. These policies of economic liberalization, the double-digit economic growth rates, and the resultant 'trickle down' provided new jobs, opportunities, and improved living standards for most Malaysians (until the mid-1997 financial crisis set in). The new discourse of 'developmentalism' came into its own amid this economic growth and new opportunities, especially during the early 1990s. It further coincided with the consolidation of a multiethnic Malaysian middle class.

The new political culture valorizes rapid growth, the resultant consumerist habits, and the political stability offered by BN rule, even when the government resorts to authoritarian means. Since no other party has ever ruled Malaysia, many ordinary Malaysians, including the middle class, cannot imagine political stability being maintained in a multiethnic Malaysia without BN rule. Developmentalism, therefore, is the cultural consequence of the *dirigiste* developmental state, which occurs when citizens begin to enjoy improved living conditions as a result of the economic growth brought about by the state. In the 1990s, developmentalism increasingly displaced the former ethnic political discourse and practice. It is primarily this discourse of developmentalism, and not that of ethnicism, which now sets limits to the discourse of democracy. Developmentalism has two significant off-shoots—cultural liberalization and the consolidation of a politics of public works and services.

Cultural liberalization and utilitarian goals in the 1990s

The BN government endeared itself to a substantial proportion of the middle class by introducing a series of policies that lead toward 'cultural liberalization' in the early 1990s, especially when viewed from the perspective of non-Malays. Specifically, UMNO leaders appeared to have de-emphasized or re-defined the political significance of the most important emblems of Malay identity—the Malay rulers, Malay language and culture, and Islam—hitherto considered central attributes in the defining of the Malaysian nation.

UMNO's challenges to the Malay rulers in 1983–1984 and again in 1994 curtailed the symbolic and actual powers of the rulers. Indeed, this challenge of the rulers received widespread support, especially among middle-class Malays. Although reaffirming the status of Malay as the national language, Dr. Mahathir and other UMNO leaders also promoted the use of the English language on utilitarian grounds, especially with the onslaught of globalization. This included the use of English as the medium of instruction for certain technical subjects in local universities, a move that partially reversed the policy of using Malay as the sole medium introduced in 1971.

Additionally, the new Education Act of 1996 formally empowered the education minister to exempt the use of Malay as the medium of instruction for certain purposes deemed necessary, even in secondary schools. Through the introduction of other legislative acts and the amendment of existing ones that pertain to higher education, the government further facilitated the corporatization of public universities[1] and the setting up of private universities and branch campuses of foreign universities in Malaysia. Together with the expansion of public universities, opportunities were made available to many more Malaysians to pursue tertiary-level education, thereby ameliorating the previously intense competition among the various ethnic groups for limited places in local universities. The changes also have allowed students to enroll in 'twinning colleges' (attached to foreign universities) to complete their entire university education locally, which has decreased the cost of a post-secondary education. Since these private colleges and universities were encouraged to recruit foreign lecturers and students, English has become the medium of instruction. Other notable aspects of cultural liberalization were the promotion of non-Malay cultures by the Ministry of Culture, Arts and Tourism as a means to attract the tourist dollar, and the increasing use of English in the mass media, particularly by privatized radio and television stations. With the introduction of cable and satellite television, the pluralization of the mass media also occurred, which resulted in an increased range of choices for Malaysian audiences.

In response to the resurgence of Islam, the BN government introduced its own Islamization policies beginning in the early 1980s. But it has distinguished itself by advocating a more liberal interpretation of Islam that emphasized the promotion of Islamic values in administration and society *writ large*, rather than the realization of an Islamic state as PAS and other Muslim radicals advocated. Taken as a whole, the new policies appeared to stress a more inclusive rather than an exclusive notion of Malaysian nationhood. It also offered choices in the cultural realm as a result of increasing pluralism. Middle-class Malaysians, especially non-Malays, welcomed this cultural liberalization for utilitarian goals.

That said, political liberalization did not follow. Although citizens were offered some measure of choice and even the private space to pursue their ambitions and to express their identities, these individual pursuits did not extend themselves into a common effort toward enhancing liberal democracy. Put another way, individuals fought for, and gained the necessary private spaces to express themselves as individuals. But the end result was the 'privatization' of freedom, not the creation of a strong civil society and an autonomous public sphere.

Delivering public works and services

A re-definition of the role of political parties, and even of the meaning of politics itself, further accompanied this developmentalism. During this period of economic progress, the BN component parties not only avoided debate over policies, especially when they involved 'sensitive issues' (i.e. inter-ethnic), but also de-emphasized political education and mobilization. A politics of 'developmentalism'—that emphasizes the delivery of public works and services, sustained by economic development, and guaranteed by political stability, which the BN parties argued only they could provide—was promoted instead.

Put simply, the BN parties transformed themselves into extensions and instruments of the state, not merely to assist in the maintenance of the status quo, but to assist in the delivery of public works and services. Additionally, the Chinese-based BN parties, like the Malaysian Chinese Association (MCA), even established its own college, the Kolej Tunku Abdul Rahman (KTAR). Through its four campuses, KTAR now provides tertiary-level education to some 23,000 students annually. Its Langkawi Project further caters to the educational needs of primary school children (by organizing tutoring classes and providing books and other resources), especially in the Chinese 'New Villages.' Fund raising was also conducted on behalf of the independent Chinese secondary schools during the 1990s. Additionally, Kojadi, the MCA's savings co-operative, provides low-interest loans for the children of co-op members to attend universities and colleges.

The BN political parties also established so-called service centers and complaint bureaus throughout the country. These are partially financed by the constituency development funds, allocated by the government only to elected politicians belonging to the BN. Lower-class Malaysians, in particular, have resorted to these centers and bureaus, instead of the relevant government agencies, to resolve their everyday problems and needs, whether of a personal nature or for the local community. The problems range from applying for official documents, getting their children into a school of their choice, to acquiring business licenses, to repairing roads and drains, to equipping the local community with more amenities and facilities. Yet there are structural limits to the kinds of problems that the service centers and complaint bureaus can help to resolve. For instance, they could not help to prevent the repeal of the Rent Control Act in 2000, which led to escalating housing and shop rentals rates throughout cities in Malaysia, and which in turn, caused thousands of household occupants who were unable to pay the new rental rates to move out, under threat of eviction. Nor have these centers and bureaus been able to prevent the privatization of public utilities—such as water works, electricity and telecommunication services, and sewerage treatment—or the granting of concessions to build and maintain tolled highways to private corporations.

Finally, the BN parties themselves have ventured into business activities and forged close ties with other captains of industry and commerce. Together with them and their associations, such as the Chamber of Commerce and Industry, and other industry-specific bodies, such as the Federation of Malaysian Manufacturers, the BN parties have initiated various projects in support of the BN government's post-NEP economic policies, which have been friendlier to the private sector, in general, and beneficial to Chinese business interests, in particular. In sum, the BN political parties have assumed very different roles. Ironically, they seem to be encouraging their members to withdraw from popular political participation.

It is developmentalism, therefore, and the related offshoots of cultural liberalization and the supplementary delivery of services and goods by the BN parties down to the local level—in the process redefining the meaning of politics—that account for the continued support of the BN in the 1999 polls. It is in the context of this new discourse and practice of developmentalism that the Gallup survey findings should be understood.

Conclusion

It must be emphasized that ethnicity remains a very salient aspect of Malaysian politics. However, whereas ethnicity previously dominated the discourse and practice of Malaysian politics, and imposed limits on democracy ever since independence, but especially during the NEP years, it no longer does so, or at least not to the same predictable extent. Recent developments, especially in 1998–1999, suggest that a new discourse and practice of participatory democracy, not merely electoral and procedural democracy, has gained ground among some Malaysians of all ethnic groups. I refer specifically to the *reformasi* movement, the formation of an opposition coalition that made the 1999 general elections uncharacteristically meaningful by offering a real choice to the voters, and a cacophony of new voices that demanded justice, accountability, popular participation, and an autonomous public sphere.

Despite the ferment, however, the democratic impulse has not yet prevailed in Malaysia. Some observers have continued to resort to ethnic explanations to clarify this lag between Malaysia and other Southeast and East Asian countries where regime changes have occurred. Yet I argue that the politics of ethnicism, in and of itself, cannot explain this lag. Instead, it is 'developmentalism,' the cultural consequence of the *dirigiste* developmental state, which is principally responsible for setting the major limits on democratization since the 1990s. The findings of the Gallup survey indicate that Malaysians do seem to acquiesce with the illiberal political system in which they find themselves. However, rather than attribute this attitude to some essentialist 'Asian values,' I have argued that these attitudes are a result of developmentalism, a recent discursive construct. It is therefore, developmentalism, rather than Asian values that now limits democratization.

That democratic ferment is occurring and that politicians still resort to the politics of ethnicism, which still resonates in some quarters of Malaysian society, suggest that increasing contestations exist between the discourses and practices of ethnicism, participatory democracy, *and* developmentalism. In this study, the distinctions between the different discourses are used as heuristic devices. For in the real situation, they overlap with one another and are not mutually exclusive. This contestation between different discourses signals the internal divisions not only among non-Malays but also Malays. Such divisions in the non-Malay and Malay communities cannot be easily reversed. In all probability, further fragmentation will occur in the short to medium term. Hence, although regime change has not occurred, I believe that Malaysia has entered a new era of politics characterized by ferment and fragmentation. It augurs well for Malaysia's democratization.

Notes

1 Under corporatization, understood as a variant of privatization, the public universities became responsible for raising the necessary operating expenditures progressively. University assets, however, remain the property of government.

Bibliography

Anuar Mustafa K. (2002), 'The role of Malaysia's mainstream press in the 1999 general election', in Francis Loh Kok Wah and Johan Saravanamuttu (eds.), *New Politics in Malaysia*, Singapore: Institute of Southeast Asian Studies.
Case, William (1993), 'Semi-Democracy in Malaysia: withstanding the pressures for regime change', *Pacific Affairs*, 66 (2), pp. 183–205.
Crouch, Harold (1996), *Government and Society in Malaysia*, St Leonard's, New South Wales: Allen and Unwin.
Gomez, Edmund (1996) 'Changing ownership patterns, patronage and the

NEP', in Muhammad Ikmal Said and Zahid Emby (eds.), *Malaysian Critical Perspectives: Essays in Honour of Syed Husin Ali*, Kuala Lumpur: Malaysian Social Science Association, pp. 132–154.

Inoguchi, Takashi (2000), 'Can Asian values be the basis of democratic governance in the Asia–Pacific region?' paper presented at the conference on 'Changing Values and Challenges of Democratic Governance in Asia', Seoul National University, 17–18 November.

Jesudason, James (1996), 'The syncretic state and the structuring of opposition politics in Malaysia', in G. Rodan (ed.), *Political Oppositions in Industrializing Asia*, London: Routledge, pp. 128–160.

Jomo, K S (1990), *Growth and Structural Change in the Malaysian Economy*, London: Macmillan.

Khoo, Philip (1999), 'Thinking the unthinkable', *Aliran Monthly*, 19 (5), pp 2–8.

Lijphart, Arend (1977), *Democracy in Plural Societies: A Comparative Explanation*, New Haven, CT: Yale University Press.

Loh Kok Wah, Francis (2000), 'State–societal relations in a rapidly growing economy: the case of Malaysia 1970–97', in R.B. Kleinberg and J.A. Clark (eds.), *Economic Liberalization, Democratization and Civil Society in the Developing World*, Basingstoke, Hampshire: Macmillan Press, pp. 65–87.

Loh Kok Wah, Francis (2001), 'Where has ethnic politics gone? The case of the BN Non-Malay politicians and political parties', in Robert Hefner (ed.), *The Politics of Multiculturalism: Pluralism and Citizenship in Malaysia, Singapore and Indonesia*, Honolulu: University of Hawaii Press, pp. 183–203.

Loh Kok Wah, Francis (2002), 'Developmentalism and the limits of democratic discourse', in Francis Loh Kok Wah and Khoo Boo Teik (eds.), *Democracy in Malaysia: Discourses and Practices*, Richmond, Surrey: Curzon Press, pp 19–50.

Loh Kok Wah, Francis (2005), 'The March 2004 general elections in Malaysia: looking beyond the 'Pak Lah' factor', *Kasarinlan*, 20 (1), pp. 3–24.

Rais, Yatim (1995), *Freedom under Executive Power in Malaysia*, Kuala Lumpur: Endowment.

Saravanamuttu, Johan (1992), 'The state, ethnicity and the middle class factor: democratic change in Malaysia', in K. Rupesinghe (ed.), *Internal Conflict and Governance*, New York: St Martin's Press, pp. 44–64.

Saravanamuttu, Johan (2002), 'The eve of the 1999 general election', in Francis Loh Kok Wah and Johan Saravanamuttu (eds.), *New Politics in Malaysia*, Singapore: Institute of Southeast Asian Studies.

Syed Ahmad Hussein (2002), 'Muslim Politics and the Discourse on Democracy', in Francis Loh Kok Wah and Khoo Boo Teik (eds.), *Democracy in Malaysia: Discourses and Practices*, Richmond, Surrey: Curzon Press, pp. 74–107.

Welsh, Bridget (1996), 'Attitudes towards democracy in Malaysia', *Asian Survey*, 31 (9), pp. 882–903.

Zakaria, Ahmad (1989), 'Malaysia: quasi democracy in a divided society', in L. Diamond, J. Linz and Seymour Lipset (eds.), *Democracy in Developing Countries: Asia, vol 3*. Boulder: Lynne Rienner, pp. 347–381.

Chapter Six
Political Participation and Governance in Thailand
Chaiwat Khamchoo

Introduction

It is clear that stable, consolidated democracy has long evaded Thailand. The first attempt was made in June 1932 when a group of junior military officers and public servants overthrew the absolute monarchy and proclaimed the first democratic regime in the country. Although this democracy was more symbolic than factual, leading to a long period of paternalistic and authoritarian military dictatorships, it at least created new ways of thinking about political democracy and participation. In the period since 1932, there have been nine successful coups, and seven failed ones. These frequent transitions and the lack of political continuity have thwarted the development of a stable multi-party system. Typically, political parties in Thailand 'lack a mass base, a well-articulated organization, and, indeed, any identifiable ideology' (King and LoGerfo 1996: 103). Instead, as discussed later, the usual political practice is for parties to be oriented around personal ties and a well structured though fluid system based on patron–client relations.

A major watershed for democratization that followed the establishment of the 1978 Constitution came in 1991. At this time, the military, playing on urban middle-class discontent toward the money politics and vote buying of the previous government of Prime Minister Chatichai Choonhaven (1988–1991), launched a successful coup (LoGerfo 2000). This was Thailand's ninth successful coup since 1932; it was led by the National Peacekeeping Council (NPC), headed by strongman General Suchinda Krapayoon. A number of political parties took a stand against the NPC's dictatorship in a campaign leading up to the March 1992 elections. The coalition government that formed after these elections invited Suchinda to take the leadership. This led to massive protests around the country over the following two months and resulted in a deadly three-day crackdown in Bangkok, which claimed at least fifty-two lives and a number of missing persons (LoGerfo 2000). Finally, on May 20, King Bhumibol summoned the contesting leaders, pro-democracy activist Major-General Chamlong Srimuang and General Suchinda, together to resolve the conflict.

After the subsequent collapse of the Suchinda government, Anand Panyarachun was asked to form an interim government. He dissolved parliament and scheduled elections for September 1992. The parties were divided into two camps: those who were allied with Suchinda's NPC (which the print media called the 'devil parties'), and the more democratic parties (the 'angel parties') led by Chuan Leekpai's Democrats, the oldest political party in Thailand. Chuan took over as Thailand's twentieth prime minister and the first premier in some twenty years without a military background (King and LoGerfo 1996). He returned to form a second government in 1997, after the start of the Asian economic crisis, but lost the elections in January 2001 to the Thai Rak Thai ('Thai Love Thai') Party, led by entrepreneur and communications tycoon Thaksin Shinawatra.

The root causes of Thailand's political problems can be found in the connections between money politics (vote buying and the enduring patronage system), personal struggles for wealth, power and prestige (and endemic corruption), and weaknesses in the party system (factional conflicts). These factors lead to inherently unstable governing coalitions (Bunbongkarn 1999).

The period leading up to the last elections in January 2001 saw Thailand make a serious effort at political reform. There was an increasing shift from old-style politics, as described in the previous paragraph, to improved democratic governance. The reform process is embodied in the progressive 1997 Constitution (see below) and a corresponding 'growing awareness' in civil society of the need for change (Rathananongkolmas 2001).

Changes have occurred in a number of areas—such as civil and political rights, participation in the free selection of leaders and policies, and contestation in terms of positions of government power and elected offices—that indicate Thailand is headed in the direction of democratization (LoGerfo 1996). The transition from old-style money politics to a democratic political system is still in process and not enough time has elapsed since the 1997 Constitution and the implementation of new government reforms to make any firm conclusions. Yet using existing scholarly work on Thailand, supplemented by the results of the Gallup International Millennium

Survey (Gallup survey), it is possible to make some provisional judgments of how Thai politics have changed over time and what the future holds for democratization.

Thailand and calls for good governance

Kim Dae Jung and James Wolfensohn (1999) note that in addition to correct policies and social investments, development requires good governance, which implies transparent and accountable institutions able to carry out these tasks. They argue that governments must continue to reform alongside business. The market will ensure that the private sector reforms, while the people will ensure that governments will continue the fundamental tasks of institutional reform (it is hoped without ignoring the need for social safety nets). 'Financial crises are really human crisis. Politicians can no longer ignore the manifest urgency of building economic development in parallel with an environment of social and human justice' (Kim and Wolfensohn 1999: 6). Meanwhile, Amartya Sen (1999) emphasizes that development needs to be fused with the real freedoms that people enjoy, inherent in basic human rights. Although growth is one way to expand freedoms, it is only a part of the total picture. Freedoms depend on other factors, not least social, economic, political, and civic rights.

Thus, the growing interest in 'good governance' in the public sector is hardly limited to Thailand. Jon Pierre and Guy Peters (2000) identify various factors—including an ideological shift toward a belief in markets, and disappointment among people about what the government is supposed to do and what it has actually accomplished—that have spurred international interest in governance. These factors have contributed to the growth in calls for improved governance in Thailand, particularly since the late 1980s, when its economy grew at one of the world's fastest rates. Thus in 1999, the Office of the Prime Minister in Thailand identified six elements of good governance.

- The rule of law: To enact laws, regulations, rules, and directives that are fair, up to date, and are accepted and followed by citizens.
- The rule of integrity: To encourage ethical and exemplary behavior by government officials and to inculcate the values of integrity, fairness, hard work, and discipline among the people as national characteristics.
- The rule of transparency: To create a climate of mutual trust through changes in all sectors to ensure transparency and enable

public scrutiny, to guarantee access to accurate information throughout the system, and to provide information in a straightforward manner in language that is clear and easy to understand.
- The rule of participation: To welcome input from the general public and to encourage their participation in significant decisions of the country through public hearings, referenda, and public investigations.
- The rule of accountability: To raise public awareness of the rights of individuals, as well as the duties and responsibilities of citizens toward society, and to encourage the general public to be mindful of social problems and difficulties and to be active in seeking solutions. At the same time other opinions should be respected and there should be a willingness to accept the consequences of actions.
- The rule of value for money: To encourage all sectors to utilize and manage limited resources efficiently and effectively; to conserve natural resources; to promote thrift and economy to maximize the benefits from limited resources for the national good; and to support the production of quality products and services so as to be competitive in the global marketplace.

These, as expected, coincide with the aims of multilateral agencies, such as the Asian Development Bank's elements of good governance: accountability, participation, predictability, and transparency. The Office of the Prime Minister noted that in general, awareness has been growing, especially in the wake of the 1997 Asian economic crisis, among Thai leaders and the general public that good governance is essential to the creation of a peaceful, stable, and well-ordered society. This applies to both public and private organizations, and to individuals and communities. A system of good governance in Thailand needs to be based on transparency, fairness, and public participation in accordance with democratic principles and a constitutional monarchy. This should be a system of governance that adheres to human dignity and Thai cultural norms and values, and that is both local and global in vision.

Most scholarly observers and Thai citizens view Thailand's public sector as lacking many of the elements of good governance. The information in the Gallup survey reflects these beliefs, based on responses to the question: 'Which of the following words describes your perception of the government of this country?' The high percentage of people who perceive the government to be corrupt and the low percentage who believe it to be just particularly stand out.

Table 6.1: Perceptions of the Thai government

	Positive Mention (%)
Efficient	22.4
Bureaucratic	35.7
Corrupt	71.2
Just	6.3
Responds to the will of the people	15.1

Source: Gallup survey, question 7.
Note: Total sample size is 510.

Moreover, a recent poll on corruption in Asia noted that, although Thailand was not ranked in the highest category, corruption is growing and still seen as a normal way of life; additionally, the new government leadership seems rather complacent about resolving this problem (*Bangkok Post*, March 24, 2001). This is despite the fact that, in a nationwide survey conducted in late 2000, voters said that they believed corruption (and vote buying) to be the most serious, persisting problem in the political arena (*The Nation*, December 9, 2001).

Much of the blame for the lack of good governance can be pinned on the government itself, because of the following problems: endemic corruption in government contracts, a legislature that seems to represent a very limited set of business and political interests, a party system focused on personalized political goals instead of broad national policy objectives, and a judiciary subject to political influence and bribes. Yet good governance requires contributions from members of society as well, and Thais need to be made aware of their rights and become more active in assuming social responsibilities. The present emphasis (or rhetoric), encouraged by the new 1997 Constitution, is on increasing civic participation at all levels. As discussed below, judging from a number of mass public protests over issues of accountability, transparency, poverty, and participation, many of the ideas in the constitution are taking hold.

Thailand's 1997 Constitution

The current constitution, promulgated in 1997, is Thailand's sixteenth since the overthrow of the absolute monarchy in 1932. Sometimes referred to as the 'people's constitution,' it has broken some new ground from past practices and 'promised to transform Thai politics by spurring the introduction of new democratic principles, better politicians, and political stability' (Bowornwathana 2000: 93). The drafters incorporated many of the six elements of good governance outlined above.[1]

First, it is the first constitution where the drafting process involved wide-ranging and significant public participation. Much of the debate about the provisions of the constitution took place in the popularly elected Constitutional Drafting Assembly, a body with representatives from many sectors of Thai society and all of the country's seventy-six provinces. Second, the constitution explicitly provided for the decentralization of power from the central government to local government bodies in the provinces. Third, it created a set of independent organizations to monitor and sanction the government (e.g., the Election Commission and the National Counter Corruption Commission). The aim of these organizations is largely to remove some of the major constraints to democracy: money politics and political corruption. Popular perceptions of Thai politics have been, and continue to be, that politicians are of low quality and are mainly concerned with enriching themselves and supporters, and that money politics remains at the root of these problems (Laird 2000).

Fourth, the constitution significantly reformed the electoral system and composition of the National Assembly (Thailand's parliament). Elections for the House of Representatives (the lower house) moved from a multi-member district system to a combination of single-member districts and proportional representation based on national party lists. The Senate (upper house), which had been previously appointed, is now fully elected by popular vote. Lastly, the constitution changed the structure of the judiciary, particularly by creating an entirely new Constitutional Court to review the constitutionality of laws and government regulations.

In addition, the new constitution states that the people have the right to receive basic social services that the government should provide. This also reflects rising expectations that such services are a state responsibility. As more people become aware of their rights, the pressure on the government to provide an effective 'social safety net' (see below) will increase. Since the constitution encourages decentralization and increased participation from other civic organizations, the role of the government as provider of basic social services is also expected to change accordingly. Under Chapter 3 of the 1997 Constitution, which states the rights and liberties of the Thai people, three basic social services are considered to be rights: education, quality of health services, and support to achieve a reasonable livelihood.

In general, the new constitutional arrangements are supposed to strengthen the power of parliament over the bureaucracy. Section 182 states that: 'The House of Representatives and the Senate are, by virtue of this Constitution, vested with the power to control the administration of State affairs.' Although relations between the legislative and executive branches of government have taken various forms since the 1932 overthrow of the absolute monarchy, the legislature has typically held relatively less power over the policymaking and budget processes. Furthermore, Thai government ministries have not exemplified any of the six elements of good governance noted above.

Good governance and the new electoral system

Clearly, the constitution was supposed to ensure different roles for members of the House of Representatives and the Senate. House members elected directly from constituencies would be responsible for bringing the voice of the people into policy formulation and to monitor the implementation of government policies. The House would also provide thirty-five (formerly 45) members selected from the party lists to work in the executive branch as ministers in the cabinet.[2] To strengthen the fractious party system, various constitutional provisions and laws limit the extent to which House members can change party membership. This brought about some confusion in the run-up to the last elections, when many former MPs were 'pulled' into various parties, especially the present ruling Thai Rak Thai Party (Rathanamongkolmas 2000: 2).

The new constitution also introduced a popularly-elected Senate under a multi-member provincial constituency system. Senators are not allowed to be members of political parties. The constitutional drafters conceived the Senate as a watchdog over the highly political House, and as a body whose members would bring more representatives of civil society groups into the legislature.

The first Senate elections were held in May 2000 with a high voter turnout (about 72%, which was higher than in any previous election) (Bureekul 2001). The first House elections under the new rules were held in January 2001. The Election Commission conducted several electoral rounds, as many constituencies reported fraud. In many cases, however, the politicians who were suspected of vote buying in the first round of polling were returned in later rounds. The exception to this was the last round of Senate elections, held in late April 2001, which saw eight of ten senators accused of electoral graft lose their seats.

One main objective of the new electoral arrangements was to reduce the role of money in politics. This was not only a way to thin the ranks of politicians who had bought their way to power, but also as a means of stopping successfully-elected politicians from using government power to cover the costs of getting elected.[3] At first glance, it seems that there was little improvement during the first elections held under the new election laws. By most accounts, direct cash payments to voters were no less rampant in the constituencies than in the past, although every attempt was made to disguise it out of fear of the Election Commission watchdogs. It would appear that the 'process of reducing the role of money is at best painfully slow,' as it clearly takes time to clean up political processes (*International Herald Tribune*, January 10, 2001). Results are unlikely to be achieved overnight. The Gallup survey results indicate the lack of faith most Thai citizens have in elections, based on responses to the question: 'Do you feel that elections in this country are free and fair?' Of the respondents, 66.3 percent responded 'no;' 31 percent, 'yes;' and 2.7 percent, 'don't know.'

Good governance and government administrative structures

Thailand is divided into seventy-six provinces, approximately 800 districts, 7,000 sub-districts, and 70,000 villages. In addition, urban areas have a special municipal system of administration. Special administrative structures are in place for the municipalities of Bangkok and Pattaya. This system was established around one hundred years ago with the aim of making Thailand a modern nation-state. Although these systems were set up to allow for greater public participation in government policymaking, the history of administration has been one of centralization, hierarchy, and inflexibility. Regional and local diversity was seen to undermine the national consensus, and threaten unity and order. These lower levels of administration were under the responsibility of the powerful Ministry of Interior, which was responsible for the appointment of senior representatives from the province down to the village. Although each level of government had elected assemblies added to the administrative structures, these local assemblies were generally weak and dominated by higher level officials.

At the subnational levels, the assemblies have had little effect to date, although the decentralization plan mandated by the constitution promises a gradual shift in the balance of power to elected bodies. The

Tambon Administration Act of 1999, an organic law required by the constitution, establishes the legal framework for the decentralization plan. In the context of the new constitution, this was an attempt to give each community the opportunity to participate directly in its own development process. It was also an attempt to persuade ministries to transfer budgets, labor, and decisionmaking powers out of Bangkok to local governments (*The Nation*, February 23, 2001). In fact, central government is required under the new constitution to allocate as much as 35 percent of its overall budget to local government in 2006. Therefore, greater emphasis will be placed on the sub-district (*tambon*) levels of administration. It is here that much of the new community-centered development is focused (for example through the Community Development Department, Ministry of Interior, and Department of Agricultural Extension, and Ministry of Agriculture).

If a sub-district has an income of less than 150,000 baht (U.S. $3,750) a year, it is mandated to have a sub-district council composed of appointed local-level representatives. As village heads are supposed to be elected every four years, it would appear that the sub-district councils would be the most basic democratic assemblies in the country. If the sub-district has in excess of 150,000 baht a year, it will have a 'sub-district administrative organization.' This will be made up of appointed representatives (key local people, such as appointed heads of sub-districts, village heads, sub-district and medical practitioners/health officers) and two elected representatives from each village in the sub-district, elected for four years. This gives the balance of power to elected representatives, who also elect the president of the organization. This represents a real grassroots attempt to limit the power of non-elected officials in local administration. It is a recent and continually evolving system, and one that is expected to drive decentralization.

Nongovernmental organizations

One of the most interesting recent developments in the area of good governance has been the increasing role played by nongovernmental organizations (NGOs) in governance (Rathanamongkolmas 2000). In Thailand, welfare services were traditionally centered on monasteries through religious philanthropy, and reinforced by missionary activities and Chinese welfare organizations since the mid-nineteenth century. After 1950, and especially since the 1980s, welfare and development NGOs have appeared and started to expand their activities. By 1989, some 12,000 foundations and associations existed, of which more than 44 percent were in the broad category of welfare (Pongsapich and Kataleeradabhan, 1997).

Much of the early history of Thai NGOs, beginning in the 1960s, was connected with the activities of Puey Unkpakorn (Prasartset 1996; Callahan 1998: 97). Dr. Puey was an eminent Thai intellectual, the former Rector of Thammasat University and Governor of the Bank of Thailand. In 1969, he established the Thailand Rural Reconstruction Movement, the first NGO in the country concerned with issues such as livelihood, education, health, autonomous government, and a social ethics of non-violence.

More recently, NGO involvement in politics and democracy was fuelled by the military coup of 1991, and led by the Campaign for Popular Democracy (CPD). NGOs have formed new relationships with the government and become increasingly involved in policy issues, including participation in the Pollwatch Commission (PWC, also mentioned below). The CPD launched the Forum for Democracy (FFD) in 1992 to promote greater public participation in the democratization process in the period leading up to the election. NGO involvement in the media campaigns (especially television) by PWC and FFD and in their provincial forums had considerable impact on political consciousness-raising among the public.

In terms of rural development, which was perhaps the greatest achievement of the Thai NGOs, the general popular sentiment was that the government had not reached the rural poor. Although NGO activities were limited in scope, they did gain some recognition, and as they were in line with international development best practice, they began to be supported by international agencies, donors, and, eventually, state agencies. The Eighth National Economic and Social Development Plan (1997–2001) reflect these changes and input by NGOs.

The theoretical and practical connections between good governance and human rights are fairly strong, and Thai NGOs have pushed for many years for an increased emphasis on human rights. According to the Gallup survey, only ten percent of respondents feel that human rights are being fully respected, although most (85%) conceded that human rights are being at least partially respected (question 26). Thailand ranks relatively high among the Asian countries in the survey in terms of freedom of speech (question 27). Since the 1980s, the print media, and to a lesser extent the electronic media, have been able to express opinions freely on politics, religion, extra-judicial matters, crimes, etc., with the exception of issues concerning the monarchy.[4]

The establishment of a recognized agency concerned with human rights in Thailand was started when a group of NGOs led by practicing lawyers and legal academics began to lobby to have a clear code of rights instituted into the 1997 Constitution, and to establish the National Human Rights Commission (NHRC). This was not undertaken without considerable resistance from traditional power interests. Indeed, the Council of State tried to emasculate and water down the original proposal. Following a media blitz, however, former Prime Minister Chuan Leekpai eventually supported the original bill with a few modifications (*The Nation*, March 19, 2001).

Without a doubt, the NHRC has proven to be the most publicly contentious agency under the constitution, with debates focused on its independence, jurisdiction, tasks, and powers. Its effectiveness will depend on the general public perception that it is capable of protecting citizens against abuses of power and the impunity of government officials, politicians, and the state (Klein 2002).

Background to rural development in Thailand

Inequalities among rural–urban constituencies remain, and continue to destabilize efforts to improve governance. The rural community in Thailand faces many problems, not least the degradation of natural resources and the environment, a decline of social capital, persistence of poverty, and the implications of the recent economic crisis on alternative income sources.

With regard to the environment, the Gallup survey indicated a fairly even balance between those who feel that the overall state of the environment is satisfactory and those who felt that it is unsatisfactory. When pressed, however, most (70%) feel that the government is not doing enough to address environmental issues. Interestingly, 61 percent view the environment as more important than economic growth (37%). To most respondents (30%), traffic pollution is considered the biggest threat to future generations, followed by loss of rainforests, species, and wildlife (23%) (Gallup survey, questions 1, 3–4).

Rural development emerged as a concern in Thailand as a consequence of the uneven development of the national economy following the launch of the First National Economic and Social Development Plan (1961–1966). From the Fourth Plan (1977–1981) onwards, the need for rural development has been emphasized, including the management and development of natural resources and the expansion of agricultural productivity. The Fifth Plan (1982–1986) specifically mentioned the need to eradicate rural poverty through integrated area development in targeted areas. This was also a period of excessive forest destruction and depletion of natural resources. The Sixth Plan (1987–1991) recognized these problems and aimed to attain the optimal use of natural resources, while also considering social justice and equity, and to achieve the beginnings of a self-reliance strategy. The Seventh Plan (1992–1996) was concerned with stable growth and equitable income distribution, the development of human resources, quality of life, and environmental and natural resources.

The Eighth Plan (1997–2001) elaborated further on the goals set in the preceding five-year plan. Civil society has grown definitely stronger in recent years (Bunbongkarn 1999). For the first time, a national consensus exists among government officials, the private sector, and civil society organizations on the need for a new vision and strategy for rural development. This new approach is an attempt to move Thailand away from the immediate crisis and to provide the foundation for more balanced and equitable growth, increased employment and income for the rural poor, and improved natural resource management in the future.

Nevertheless, problems persist. For instance, in terms of human resource development, the National Economic and Social Development Board (NESDB) estimated in 1997 that only 46.8 percent of children go to high school and 19.3 percent to university—rates much lower than in most neighboring countries. Moreover, the gap between the rich and poor is one of the widest in the region, and is increasing. A number of commentators have suggested that the failure of the current plan to address many of these persistent problems stems from the development of an unsustainable and fragile economy (see, for example, Bello, Cunningham, and Li 1998).

The focus of many current debates on reform and development in Thailand is how to improve the Ninth Plan (2002–2006), by balancing the perceived need for greater self-reliance with the recognition of Thailand's position in the global economy. The Ninth Plan targets employment creation and human resource development. To achieve economic development, many members of NESDB agree that the focus must be on both agriculture (rural needs) and industry (urban needs), and that greater participation in the policymaking process at all levels must be ensured.

Local responses to global events

The recent response to the Asian economic crisis in Thailand was a genuine attempt by some national leaders (led by the King) to reassert the local over the global (or perhaps rather a compromise between the two) through the concept of 'self-reliance' (*pheung-ton-eng*) or 'self-sufficiency' (*setthakit phor-phiang*). Although NGOs have long promoted self-sufficiency in Thailand, since the King's birthday addresses to the nation in 1997 and 1998, the concept has become normalized and known as 'the King's New Theory' (*thrisadii mai*). Even the Ministry of Interior, a bastion of conservatism, has (under top-down direction) now declared a strategy for self-reliance 'in order to solve Thailand's economic crisis by working cooperatively with various sectors.'[6]

As with Ernst Schumacher's philosophy, the concept of self-sufficiency in Buddhist ethics is radically different from the economics of modern Western materialism; and instead 'sees the essence of civilisation not in a multiplication of wants but in the purification of human character' (Schumacher 1973: 50). It focuses on the satisfaction of basic human needs, privileging place-based (local) markets, vernacular tradition (autonomy), and the familiar over the converse: globalization (dependence), internationalization, and the unfamiliar such as the transnational capitalist markets. However, 'opting out' is not, and never was, an option, as self-sufficiency was to be a complementary rather than oppositional ideology.

The notion of a 'Buddhist economics' is an interesting semantic shift from the amoral and disembodying apparatus of international capitalism. The notion was first proposed by the leading modern Buddhist scholar-monk Phra Prayut Payutto, and likewise emerged out of the imagining and reconstruction of national identity and consciousness. Buddhist economics, like similar micro-based ideas and practices, provides an alternative to the domination and control of Western discourse. In terms of resistances, as noted by Amartya Sen, 'the voice of rebellion against the unrestrained market economy...seems to get louder every day' (1999: 8).[7]

As Prime Minister Thaksin Shinawatra stated in 2001, the government's stance of encouraging greater self-reliance and competitive local forces does not imply a turning away from the world or a rejection of macro-concerns and interests, but rather movement toward a form of 'globalisation based on localisation' (*The Nation*, April 25, 2001). Essentially, in Thaksin's view, Thailand must 'think globally, but act locally' to cope with the negative effects of global capitalism. He insists, however, that Thailand will maintain its open-door policy and not turn its back on globalization. In his May 9, 2001 keynote address at the Global Forum in Hong Kong, he was explicit about the merits of his government's rural economic programs: 'to revise and resuscitate the farmers and the village economy in order to generate impetus for domestic demand at the grass roots.' Thaksin plans to reorganize the budget to channel funds to the grassroots level through a revolving fund initiative. This revolving fund will be established in all 70,000 villages throughout the country, and will act as development capital to support local initiatives. Thaksin said that this new development paradigm requires a change in the mindset of both Thai people and foreigners (*The Nation*, May 10, 2001).

Political economy after the 1997 crisis

Thailand's 1997 financial crisis, which was caused by plummeting creditor confidence following a long period of exuberant but increasingly fragile growth, tested not only the country's economic policy, but also its political system (Radelet and Sachs 1998). The frequent changes of government left the country with a fragile political system. In addition, money politics, involving widespread vote buying and the sale and purchase of government concessions, tax, and regulatory assistance, has typified Thai democracy.

A high-level technocracy in key ministries and agencies managed to preserve some level of economic stability through careful macroeconomic management. Yet the crisis was in some sense a signal that the technocratic macroeconomic management regime had failed, mainly because politicians had interfered in these key economic policy institutions.

The government of Chavalit Yongchaiyut (November 1996 – November 1997) failed to deal with or prevent the crisis, and came under strong public pressure to resign in early November 1997. A few days later, Chuan Leekpai's Democrat Party formed a coalition with a small parliamentary majority. This peaceful and legitimate change of government, at a time of great political and economic stress, was almost unprecedented in Thai history. A number of lessons had seemingly been learned from the events of May 1992, especially in terms of broadening the base of democratization, though it remains to be seen how long these will remain in people's memories.

One of the first tasks of the Chuan government was to endorse the program agreed to with the International Monetary Fund (IMF). The main components were the strengthening of economic governance, including commitments to administrative reform and accelerating plans to privatize state enterprises. *However, the government needs to learn how to increase participation in policy and decision making processes*. It must learn how to listen to the people and all relevant stakeholders. The recent cases of the Thai–Malaysian gas pipeline in the south and the Pak Moon Dam in the northeast are cases in point.[8] The constitution (sections 58–62) stipulates that people must have access to information on proposed development projects and mandates the convening of public hearings so that individuals may participate in government decision making.

As the crisis unfolded after 1997, the government and the IMF identified other needed reforms related to developing governance capabilities, improving the competitiveness of Thai industries, developing safety nets, and reforming and rehabilitating the financial sector. The ongoing tasks of corporate restructuring and market opening have also necessitated increased foreign involvement in the financial and, to a lesser extent, the corporate sectors. It is hoped that this will improve corporate culture and governance, modernize business practices, and streamline operations. The sectors most open to competition, such as banking and retailing, are expected to gain the greatest benefits.

Yet unlike the Republic of Korea, which since 1997 has used foreign direct investment to increase the efficiency of local industry, Thailand's post-crisis foreign investment regime remains relatively restrictive. *As a national development strategy emerges, tensions have remained here between local interests and even national identity, and global, transnational market-based interests.* The new government of Thaksin, may have some hard decisions to make, if it wishes to pursue the World Bank/IMF recommendations. Thaksin insists, however, that Thailand remains committed to all its international obligations and will continue its reform efforts to overcome the economic crisis. It appears that the Thai leader is attempting a delicate balancing act between the forces of globalization and localization.

Many still oppose globalization in Thailand, contending that 'the more Thailand opens up to the outside world, the more the poor majority of Thais will suffer' (*The Nation*, May 11, 2001). At the present, as a consequence of the crisis, the emphasis seems to be on economic governance with massive inputs from multilateral programs. The overall emphasis from the World Bank, IMF, and Asian Development Bank (ADB) is on the improvement of economic governance and the strengthening of government finances, public policy formulation, public sector administration, and corporate governance.

The role of international organizations and foreign assistance

At this point, it is useful to review briefly the history of foreign assistance to Thailand. Bilateral and international support for welfare and development programs emerged from the government's counterinsurgency policies in the 1950s. Since the 1960s, the Department of Technical and Economic Cooperation (DTEC) has disbursed nearly all assistance. Volunteer programs, such as the Peace Corps, began in the 1960s (Pongsapich and Kataleeradabhan 1997). Multilateral international assistance has come from United Nations agencies and international financial institutions, and has been active since the 1950s. The IMF, World Bank, and ADB have a long history of involvement, with the World Bank playing the main role in the establishment of the national development strategy in place since 1957. As Thailand's economy developed in the 1990s, a number of countries wound down their development assistance programs to Thailand (e.g., the United States, Canada, and Australia). Events since 1997, however, have caused a rethinking of the nature of development assistance and funding priorities, away from multi-sectoral, integrated development strategies to institutional strengthening and capacity building within selected line agencies, in areas such as governance and democratization, education, fiscal and administrative reform. These are in tune with multilateral financial funding priorities and loans.

The ADB recently noted that although Thailand had made significant strides toward decentralization, it still has work to do in the areas of accountability, participation, predictability, and transparency (*The Nation*, May 10, 2001). The ADB report also stated that although decentralization was a sound idea, if the capacity at the local level is not adequate, it may lead to an increase of problems in terms of corruption and waste of resources. Thailand borrowed approximately US$1 billion from the ADB during 1998–2000.

A new focus since 1997 has been on 'social safety nets' to protect those who have lost the most since the crisis. Despite the rhetoric of the World Bank on social safety nets, the overall emphasis remains on economic management issues (World Bank 1999a, 1999b). Pasuk Phongphaichit and Chris Baker emphasize that social issues are a concern to multilateral financial agencies insofar as social safety nets provide a better means of managing the transition to a more liberalized economy. Taking on the interests and concerns of the poor was simply a means of 'building a moral and political base from which to override opposition to [the World Bank and IMF] reforms' (Phongphaicit and Baker 2000: 103).

Thai values and attitudes toward governance

The 'Asian values' argument indicates that certain pre-determined patterns of development and politics prevail throughout the region, and condition the modes of social and economic organizations (Inoguchi 2000). This culturally deterministic thesis needs to consider the dynamics of cultural variations within the context of changing plural societies. For heuristic purposes, however, it is possible and reasonable to speak here of a 'Thai' as opposed to say a 'Korean' value system, and to identify certain specific (if changing) features of cultural practice. The Gallup survey has shown the variations within Asia in this regard.

Thais have always had positive attitudes toward power, authority and hierarchies, a lesser focus on individual needs than on the collective, unity, social harmony, consensus, and order. It is generally considered that in the traditional Thai way of life, commitment to work and to achieving goals is weak, compared to East Asian and Western nations (Yoshihara 1999). However, enduring cultural characteristics aside, it is clear that the period of Thailand's modernization, from the 1960s onwards, more or less re-centered the individual in an urban milieu and started to hand out rewards for achievements that were inscribed from outside. It also de-emphasized the notions of community, kindred and home, and relegated these values to the nostalgia of tradition.

Perhaps, in the context of modern governance, the most important threatened cultural value is the notion of entourages, or patron–client arrangements. Traditionally, the flavor of politics in Thailand has been personal, as exemplified by the influential role of godfathers (*jao phor*) who operate above and beyond the law without fear of punishment. The conception of *jao phor* began in the early period of modernization and the growth of capital. The new money economy brought with it competition over available resources. It brought a need for the opening up of new territory and the consequent movement of people from one place to another. This took place at a time when land ownership had not been clearly defined and procedures for labor control and recruitment had not been established. Therefore, in areas largely ignored by the state, local-based entrepreneurs functioned as economic and judicial bosses. They emerged into the modern form of the *jao phor* (Chantormvong 2000). In the 1992 elections, certain Bangkok middle-class groups attempted to limit the power of the *jao phor*, based on concerns about the rise of these interests in alignment with the military. These efforts included the setting up of the Pollwatch body to monitor electoral fraud (Pongpaichit and Piriyarangsan 1996).

Currently, the existing structures of the political economy are no longer able to function as they once did. Localized (often non-transparent) places of power and control, the local patronages and the specific loyalties of 'place,' are now becoming increasingly redundant as the country is encouraged to democratize and to open up its institutions. The traditional system and its apparatuses (including local elites) have now come under the gaze of a national politico-judicial 'watchdog,' which in turn is under the ever-widening regulatory gaze of global forces. These days, as a consequence of the intensification of globalization, the entire fabric of relations that define contemporary social life needs rethinking. Localized traditional systems, and especially patron–client relations, may have a great deal to lose by modernity's homogenizing project, yet we should not underestimate the diverse power of local powers to reshape global forces.

Democratization, corruption, and economic development

It may appear that political corruption since the 1980s, particularly rent seeking and clientelism, has had negative implications on economic development, and may hinder Thailand's prospects for future economic development. Rents in this context are characterized as profit opportunities created by government decisions. The notion of clientelism is tied in with the nature of enduring power relationships—so-called patron–client relations. Although these practices do not necessarily involve corruption, certain favors and privileges are extended beyond the call of formal duty. In traditional Thai society, patronage was formalized, defining the nature and obligations inherent in hierarchical social relationships (Laird 2000).

The National Counter Corruption Commission (NCCC) was established under the 1997 Constitution to promote government transparency and accountability, and was given new independent teeth. Attempts to initiate new counter-corruption provisions, combined with increased boldness by the media, made the period of 1998–1999 a crucial one for political scandals. During this time, public pressure forced three ministers to resign. Then, in March 2000, the biggest case to date arose, involving the influential interior minister, Sanan Kachornprasart. This was the 'first time any senior Thai political figure had been brought down by legal process'

(Phongpaichit and Baker 2000: 232–233). Yet even though Sanan lost his formal political power, he continues to use his powerful patronage network to operate behind the scenes.

An even larger case arose in late 2000, when the NCCC ruled that Prime Minister Thaksin had failed to inform the government about the extent of his assets and major transfers to his wife, children, chauffeur, and maid.[9] Facing the threat of a five-year ban from politics, he fought the NCCC's indictment in the Constitutional Court. In an atmosphere rife with populist rhetoric and charges of political interference, the Constitutional Court judges ruled eight to seven that Thaksin was not guilty, overturning the NCCC's decision. Although hailed by many as a chance for Thaksin's government to press ahead with solutions to the country's problems, others bemoaned the return to 'old-style' political influence over supposedly independent organizations.

Over the past few decades, the Thai political system has become more decentralized, although real power remains with the instruments of state in Bangkok. At the grassroots level, most villagers continue to feel that politics is separate from everyday life, a reflection that the patronage system is still strong, at least in rural areas (NDI 2000). But the political system may certainly be seen as less centralized today, in the sense that a growing number of social groups have gained access to the political process and the levers of state power. This is a far cry from the country as a 'bureaucratic polity' in which political struggles occurred within, rather than outside, the state hierarchy (Rigg 1996). Since the 1970s and especially since the 1980s, however, Thailand has witnessed the rise of civic political parties, and the ascent of electoral politics as a means of political contest. The elections of 1988 and 1992 'demonstrated the increasing strength of elected politicians and the further decline of the bureaucratic and military elites' (Bunbongkarn 1996: 190).

In the context of the new Thai politics, the role of the *jao phor* needs analysis, especially with the advent of the new constitution and the most recent House and Senate elections. In the early days of democratization, the various *jao phor* were able to use their traditional prestige and authority to 'secure' rural votes. Now personal ties have been increasingly replaced with economic transactions determined more by market forces (Ockey 1993: 62). Money ensures, however, 'only short-term reinforcement (to patron-client ties) and must be renewed periodically within a competitive environment' to maintain electoral support (Ockey 1996: 358).

Conclusion

I began this chapter with the findings of the Gallup survey that showed, in the period of emergent democratization, that a little over two-thirds of the Thai population considers the political system to be corrupt, and that only six percent of the respondents consider their government to be 'just.' It is a system dominated by money and power, and one that is basically unrepresentative. Political corruption hinders the democratic process by 'undermining efficient economic practices, replacing the formal rule of law with an opaque patronage system, and diminishing the influence of elected representatives' (NDI 2000). Then again, the question of whether democracy helps or hinders economic performance in so-called developing countries is rather uncertain (Ahn and Jaung 1999). Moreover, democratic forms of government do not necessarily ensure 'good governance,' although it seems likely that, compared to other forms of government, 'democracy is likely to produce responsible government' (IIPS 1999).

It can be argued that nothing much has really changed under the surface, despite promises in the new 1997 Constitution, the government's policy of good governance, and the increasing role of civil society organizations and of multilateral organizations such as the World Bank, IMF, and ADB. These international organizations are concerned with the promotion of economic growth and sound democratic governance. At a minimum, these multilateral actors have laid the foundation for a more transparent, representative, accountable, and less corrupt political system, even though, as I have shown in this chapter, more needs to be done before the word 'participation' can become more than mere rhetoric (Klein 2003). Instead, 'participation' needs to become an institutionalized practice of proper and purposeful inclusion, with a strong and sustainable supporting political system that is seen to be working for all Thais, both rural and urban. With the increased involvement of civic groups in domestic politics, it is hoped that institutional corruption will become more constrained and limited in the years to come.

In light of the many obstacles that face Thai democracy, the complacency of its society toward the slow pace of transition to greater democracy needs some explanation, especially given the less complacent politics of other countries in this volume. In this chapter, I can only very briefly review some of the factors involved, leaving the analysis of which variables have greater explanatory power for future consideration. There are substantial debates that this chapter cannot resolve.

First, most Thai people view the monarchy, and especially King Bhumipol Adulyadej, as the major stabilizing force in Thai politics. It is seen as a benevolent insurance that the government cannot overstep its bounds by using inordinate violence or radically unjust policies. This belief in the monarchy's role, along with the deeply-rooted respect of the people for the King, mitigates the emergence of revolutionary movements or calls for radical political change (e.g., changing from a constitutional monarchy to a republic). Second, economic growth has been rapid and consistent enough that people have been willing to overlook some major political problems. For some entrepreneurs, the lack of political influence and opportunities for meaningful political participation are offset by the advantages of financial success. Third, despite the newer strains of socially activist religions, the focus of Thai (Theravada) Buddhism on individual practice and restraint instills many Thai people with an entrenched sense that they should not 'rock the boat.' Although this sense derives in part from Buddhist teachings about separation from worldly matters, it also stems from the rigid hierarchy of the Thai Sangka (monastic order).

Fourth, Thailand was never formally colonized; never had a significant landed aristocracy; and successfully integrated its significant Chinese immigrant population into mainstream society. These all contributed to a lack of any strong, national-level movement capable of recruiting and organizing citizens to initiate a revolution or to otherwise radically transform Thai politics. Fifth, Thai politics has strong elements of 'competitive clientelism,' characterized by rivalries among the elite and a willingness to recruit new people into the elite when deemed appropriate (Doner and Anail 1997). This helps prevent any small group of the elite from consistently monopolizing government power. It may also make people more tolerant of politicians' excesses to see that they may have a chance, however small, to join the ranks of the powerful. Sixth, a long-standing policy among Thailand's leaders to build a sense of national identity based on the 'three pillars' of the nation, religion, and the monarchy, has inculcated many Thais with the notion that the fracture of even one pillar would bring the whole edifice crashing down (Reynolds 1991). This sense, backed by legal sanctions such as *lese majeste* laws, makes most Thais reluctant or unwilling to openly discuss certain aspects of society. Although having open debates on such issues is a critical element of a stable democracy, in Thailand they tend to occur behind closed doors. Lastly, it is important not to ignore the extent to which simple fear of the government's power to punish or make life difficult for people tempers what political actions people will take.

Notes

1 For an overview of the constitutional drafting process and the constitution's main provisions, see Klein (2003).
2 However, a House member must resign his House seat to become a cabinet minister.
3 For example, it is common practice for ministers to use government contracts for supplies and public works projects to direct funds into their personal coffers to offset the high costs of election campaigns.
4 Many people feel this freedom of speech has come under attack from the government of Prime Minister Thaksin Shinawatra. They cite pressure against the news media to show government policies in a favorable light, the withdrawal of advertisements from companies connected with the Prime Minister from certain newspapers (particularly *The Nation*), and the purchase of a TV channel (and subsequent management shakeup) by a company connected with the Prime Minister.
6 Brochure from the Community Development Department, Ministry of Interior, no date.
7 The Gallup survey does not offer any direct measure of people's attitudes about globalization and the value of self-sufficiency. The closest it comes is asking respondents if they agree or disagree with the statement: 'Women in advanced countries must insist more for the rights of women in the developing world' (question 15). Although 83.9 percent of respondents agreed, this is hardly a clear indicator.
8 These are major government infrastructure projects that met with an unusual amount of well-organized local and international resistance.
9 All ministers and their wives must declare their assets on entering and leaving government. Also, see section 209 of the constitution.

Bibliography

Ahn, Chung-si and Hoon Jaung (1999), 'South Korea', in Ian Marsh, Jean Blondel and Takashi Inoguchi (eds.), *Democracy, Governance, and Economic Performance: East and Southeast Asia*, Tokyo: United Nations University Press.

Asian Development Bank (ADB), (1999), '*Governance: sound development management*', policy papers, Asian Development Bank, Manila, Philippines.

Bello, Walden, Shea Cunningham, and Li Kheng Po (1998), *A Siamese Tragedy: Development and Disintegration in Modern Thailand*, London and New York: Zed Books.

Bowornwathana, Bidhya (2000), 'Thailand in 1999: a royal jubilee, economic recovery, and political reform', *Asian Survey* 49 (1), pp. 87–97.

Bunbongkarn, Suchit (1996), 'Elections and democratization in Thailand', in R. H. Taylor (ed.), *The Politics of Elections in Southeast Asia*, Washington, D.C.: Woodrow Wilson Center Press.

Bunbongkarn, Suchit (1999), 'Southeast Asia after the crisis: Thailand's successful reforms', *Journal of Democracy* 10 (4), pp. 54–68.

Bureekul, Thawilwadee (2001), '*Public participation in politics: the senate election 2000*', paper presented at the KPI Congress II, Pattaya, Thailand.

Centre for International Economics (1998), *APEC Economic Governance Capacity Building Survey: An Australian Initiative as Part of APEC's Response to the East Asian Financial Crisis*, Canberra and Sydney: Center for International Economics.

Chantornvong, Sombat (2000), '*Local godfathers in Thai politics*', in R. McVey (ed.),

Money & Power in Provincial Thailand, Singapore/Chiang Mai: ISEAS/ Silkworm Books.

Department of Foreign Affairs and Trade, Canberra (2000), *Transforming Thailand: Choice for the New Millennium*, Canberra: Department of Foreign Affairs and Trade.

Doner, Richard F. and Ansil Ramsay (1997), '*Competitive clientelism and economic governance: the case of Thailand*', in Sylvia Maxfield and Ben Ross Schneider (eds.), *Business and the State in Developing Countries*, Ithaca: Cornell University Press.

Ghosh, Robin, Rony Gabbay and Abu Siddique (1999), *Good Governance Issues and Sustainable Development—The Indian Ocean Region*, New Delhi: Vedams.

Inglehart, Ronald (1997), *Modernization and Postmodernization: Cultural, Economic, and Political Change in 43 Societies*, Princeton: Princeton University Press.

Inoguchi, Takashi (2000), 'Can Asian values be the basis of democratic governance in the Asia–Pacific region?' paper presented at the conference on 'Changing Values and Challenges of Democratic Governance in Asia', Seoul National University, 17–18 November.

Institute for International Policy Studies (1999), *Democracy and Prosperity: Growth, Efficiency, and Fairness*, Tokyo: Institute for International Policy Studies.

Kim Dae Jung and James Wolfensohn (1999), 'Economic growth requires good government', *International Herald Tribune*, 26 February.

King, Daniel and Jim LoGerfo (1996), 'Thailand: toward democratic stability', *Journal of Democracy* 7 (1), pp. 102–117.

Klein, James R. (2002), 'The evolution of Thailand's national human rights commission, 1992–2001', in *Thailand's New Politics: KPI Yearbook 2001*, Michael H. Nelson (ed.), Nonthaburi and Bangkok: King Prajadhipok's Institute and White Lotus Press, pp. 25–65.

Klein, James R. (2003), 'Public participation and hearings in the new Thai political context', in *Legal Foundations for Public Consultation in Government Decision-Making*, in Kenneth J. Haller and Patcharee Siroros (eds.), Bangkok: Executive Public Administration Foundation, and Kobfai Publishing Project, pp. 113–129.

Laird, Jojn. (2000), *Money Politics, Globalization, and Crisis: The Case of Thailand*, Singapore: Graham Brash.

LoGerfo, Jim (1996), 'Attitudes toward democracy among Bangkok and rural northern Thai,' *Asian Survey* 36 (9), pp. 904–923.

LoGerfo, Jim (2000), 'Beyond Bangkok: the provincial middle class in the 1992 protests', in Ruth McVey (ed.), *Money & Power in Provincial Thailand*, Singapore/Chiang Mai: ISEAS/Silkworm Books.

National Democratic Institute for International Affairs (NDI) (2000), *Combating Corruption at the Grassroots: The Thailand Experience 1999–2000*, Washington, D.C.

Ockey, Jim (1993), 'Chaopoh: capital accumulation and social welfare in Thailand', *Crossroads* 8 (1), pp. 48–77.

Office of the Civil Service Commission (1999), *Regulation of the Office of the Prime Minister on Good Governance 1999 [2542]*, Bangkok: Office of the Civil Service Commission.

Phongpaichit, Pasuk and Chris Baker (2000), *Thailand's Crisis*, Chiang Mai: Silkworm Books.

Phongpaichit, Pasuk and Sungsidh Piriyarangsan (1996), *Corruption & Democracy in Thailand*, Chiang Mai: Silkworm Books.

Pierre, Jon and B. Guy Peters (2000), *Governance, Politics and the State*, New York and London: St. Martin's Press and Macmillan.

Pongsapich, Amara and Nitaya Kataleeradabhan (1997), *Thailand's Nonprofit Sector and Social Development*, Bangkok: Chulalongkorn University.

Prasartset, Suthy (1996), 'The rise of NGOs as critical movements in Thailand', in Jayant Lele and Wisdom Tettey (eds.), *Asia—Who Pays for Growth? Women, Environment and Popular Movements*, Aldershot: Dartmouth, pp. 62–75.

Radelet, Steven and Jeffrey Sachs (1998), 'The onset of the East Asian financial crisis', *National Bureau of Economic Research Working Papers*, no. 6680.

Rathanamongkolmas, Abhinya (2001), 'Thailand: a moment of transition', *Southeast Asian Affairs*, pp. 325–336.

Reynolds, Craig J. (ed.), (1991), *National Identity and Its Defenders: Thailand, 1939–1989*, Chiang Mai: Silkworm Books.

Riggs, Fred (1966), *Thailand: The Modernization of a Bureaucratic Polity*, Honolulu: East West Center Press.

Schumacher, Ernst F. (1973), *Small Is Beautiful: A Study of Economics as if People Mattered*, London: Blond and Briggs.

Sen, Amartya (1999), *Development as Freedom*, New York: Alfred A. Knopf.

World Bank Reports (1999a), *Thailand Social Monitor: Challenge for Social Reform*, Bangkok: The World Bank, January 1999.

World Bank Report (1999b), *Thailand Social Monitor: Coping with the Crisis in Education and Health*, Bangkok: The World Bank.

Yoshihara, Kunio (1999), *The Nation and Economic Growth: Korea and Thailand*, Kyoto: Kyoto University Press.

Chapter Seven
Democratic Developments and Changing Values in China
Guo Dingping

Introduction

China has made enormous progress in liberalizing markets and integrating itself into the world economy, and the consequent rapid economic growth has allowed most citizens to enjoy considerable economic freedom, civil liberties, and an increased standard of living. Sinologists around the world have studied and analyzed the last two decades of profound change. Although economic and social achievements attract a great deal of attention and appreciation, political developments are ignored or underestimated. The common belief is that because the Chinese political system has been left untouched by the third wave of global democratization and because the Chinese Communist Party (CCP) maintains a monopoly of power there has been economic but no political reform.

Most studies of Chinese politics focus on elites and on formal institutions and process, very few of them are systematic, empirical studies of mass political culture. As some scholars have noted, the concept of public opinion did not appear in the lexicon of contemporary Sinology until the 1980s (Liu 1996: 2). However, with increased reform and opening to the outside world, Chinese public opinion is becoming more and more indispensable to both foreign and domestic observers in understanding China's politics. That has led to the undertaking of public opinion surveys and studies on changes in the political culture and value system since the late 1980s.

Based on recent surveys conducted in urban China (Beijing and Shanghai), in this chapter I discuss and interpret value changes and analyze the prospect for democratic development in China. In China, the Gallup International Millennium Survey (Gallup survey) interviewed 578 urban residents from major cities. However, the Gallup survey was incomplete, and did not include questions on democracy, human rights, women's rights, crime, and religion. Because of these shortcomings, I use two additional surveys conducted in Shanghai and Beijing. Unlike Beijing, which is the political center and old imperial capital, Shanghai is a commercial metropolis and one of the first coastal port cities to be opened to the Western world.

In June 1999, the Shanghai Committee of the Chinese Communist Youth League in cooperation with scholars from Fudan University and the Shanghai Academy of Social Sciences undertook the Shanghai survey on youth development. The survey interviewed 4279 Shanghai youth between the ages of eighteen and thirty-five on various topics. The only questions of interest to us in this chapter are those about political consciousness and cultural values. Of the respondents, 647 were 'intellectuals,' 726 were 'white collar,' 976 were 'blue collar,' 952 were college students, and 978 were middle school students. I also use the political culture surveys conducted by Yang Zhong in cooperation with the Public Opinion Research Institute of People's University in Beijing from 1995–1997, in which a total of 1287 urban residents were sampled.

In this chapter, I argue that despite the relatively high levels of trust and satisfaction with the CCP regime, the enormous changes in values that have taken place, at least in urban areas, have made it urgent for the government to further its democratic reforms. Since huge regional differences exist between urban and rural China, and between the coastal east and mountainous west, the development of regional democracy continues to be a practical solution to mounting problems such as political corruption. I break down this chapter into four parts. In part one, I present an analysis of the characteristics of Chinese traditional values and of the context for value change. In part two, I deal with selected democratic values. In part three, I discuss the levels of trust and satisfaction with the government and the CCP. Then in part four, I highlight the problems and concerns of the Chinese people, and give their views on political reform and democratization.

Tradition and change

Values in today's China originate from various sources, including traditional Chinese culture, Marxist – Leninist – Mao Zedong ideology, and Western culture. In contrast with the values of post-Mao China, the traditional values referred to here are the mainstream cultural values of ancient and modern China from the early past to the 1970s.

As many scholars have pointed out, great consistency and continuity remains between traditional Confucianism and Chinese Communist ideology, even though anti-traditional political moves were undertaken after the founding of the People's Republic of China (PRC) (Pye 1985: 182–214). In general, the most important similarities in political values are paternalism, moralism, and collectivism.

First, in traditional China, people believed that all power emanated from above and from the center, and culminated in a single supreme ruler. Dong Zhongshu (180–115 B.C.), an eminent Confucian scholar during the Han dynasty, suggested that the emperor was the son of heaven because he had the mandate of heaven, and Dong proposed that Confucianism become ruling orthodoxy. Emperor Wu (156–87 B.C.) of the Han dynasty adopted Dong's proposal and began to promote Confucianism, thereby enabling it to become the dominant value system in China for the next two thousand years. The exaggerated ideal of the great man as leader is an amplification of the Confucian model of father as ultimate authority in the family. Just as the father's word was absolute in the family, so too, was the ruler's.

Second, Confucianism believed that moral cultivation was more effective and lasting than law. 'If people are guided by law, and kept in order by punishment, they may try to avoid crime, but have no sense of shame; if they are guided by virtue, and kept in order by the rules of propriety, they will have a sense of shame, and moreover will come to be good' (Confucius 1993: 10–11). Confucian theorists emphasize moral cultivation because they believe man to be naturally good. This view of the inherent good of man is fundamental to traditional Chinese ideology. It is possible, and necessary, for everyone to cultivate this moral good. Ideally, the ruler has authority because he is morally superior. Ordinary people would naturally follow the example of a virtuous emperor—a patriarch who serves as moral exemplar. Virtue, rather than effective leadership performance, as a qualification for ruling, was emphasized throughout the Maoist years and to a lesser extent during the reform period, with virtue defined in terms of communist ideals. When necessary, 'sacrificing one's own life to complete one's virtue' and 'giving up life to attain righteousness' are considered natural by both Confucian and Communist ideology (Liu 1981: 134). For the past two thousand years, governance has hinged entirely on the moral quality of the rulers and officials.

Third, although collectives differ in form and size, both ideologies have advocated and appreciated personal sacrifice for the sake of the collective. Chinese culture recognizes only those who live and work for the collective interest. No individual will be accepted who openly and single-mindedly pursues personal fame and status. In a famous tract entitled 'On the Training of a Communist Party Member,' Liu Shaoqi said, 'The test of a Communist Party member's loyalty to the Party and to the task of the revolution and Communism is his ability, regardless of the situation, to subordinate his individual interests unconditionally and absolutely to those of the Party' (Brandt 1967: 336). This tract is selected even now as one of the most important readings for political education. Collectivism is a central concept in Chinese traditional values, which is not confined to the CCP but permeate all kinds of organizations that supersede the individual.

Confucian and Communist values may be desirable ideals, but in a closed agrarian society with no foundations in the rule of law, traditional values based on personal moral cultivation and aimed at harmonious relationships in big families proved utopian. Very few rulers during the past two thousand years were exemplars of Confucian values; they were more than likely despots. Everyday life showed great discrepancies between moral requirement and personal behavior. Even Confucius admitted that he could not meet his own standards for a man of virtue. Behind the scenes, people tended to disregard the moral requirements of Confucianism and, later on, Communism. The project to build 'a new socialist man' during the Maoist era was carried out with great thoroughness and zeal, but its attempts at political education failed to change values.

The great gap between traditional values and individual behavior has led to many different interpretations of Chinese character and Chinese culture. Although there was much praise, there was also a great deal of criticism both at home and abroad. Debates raged over the relationships between Confucianism, development, and democracy. For example, in the early twentieth century, Max Weber stated that the salient feature of Confucianism was the way it adapted to the world, rather than transformed it, and that Confucian values were inappropriate to economic development. Subsequently, most scholars have believed that it was Confucianism that contributed to hindering China's modernization. However, Yu Yingshi, Tu Weiming, and other scholars believe that rapid economic development in Japan, South Korea, Taiwan, Hong Kong and Singapore indicate that Confucian values do not intrinsically clash with development. They suggest that the successes of these countries are good examples of 'Confucian capitalism' (Han 1999: 32–33).

Similarly, it is widely believed that traditional Confucianism was either undemocratic or antidemocratic. As Samuel Huntington argues:

> Classic Chinese Confucianism and its derivatives in Korea, Vietnam, Singapore, Taiwan, and, in diluted fashion, Japan, emphasized the group over the individual, authority over liberty, duty over rights.... Harmony and cooperation were preferred over disagreement and competition. The maintenance of order and respect for hierarchy were central values. A conflict of ideas, groups, and parties was viewed as dangerous and illegitimate. Most important, Confucianism merged society and the state and provided no legitimacy for autonomous social institutions to balance the state at the national level (1991: 300–301).

The great progress toward democratization in East Asia in recent years has made scholars rethink the relationship between Confucianism and democracy. 'Asian-style democracy' and 'Confucian democracy' are examples, in which harmony, stability, and consensus are emphasized as supportive elements for democracy (Neher 1994: 949–961).

In fact, for many years, scholars and political leaders have considered the lack of democratic values and the immaturity of Chinese political culture as important reasons for why there was no democracy or should be no democracy in China (Mori 1993: 262–263). But democratic activists and radical scholars ridicule those arguments, advocating instead that the superannuated traditional culture, which is unsuitable to modern political development, must be discarded and Western cultural values adopted wholesale.

Behind the debates is 'a stereotype of political culture theory' that argues that political culture more or less predetermines both political structure and political behavior and that the elements of political culture are resistant to change (Diamond 1999: 164). For example, Lucian Pye's treatment of Asian political culture approaches the stereotype in its assumptions that political culture is 'remarkably durable and persistent;' that political culture is essentially a priori causality, and that 'cultural variations are decisive in determining the course of political development' (Pye 1985: 20, VII). Empirical research over the past decades shows, however, that political culture is 'plastic and malleable over time. Political culture is not destiny.' 'Cultural patterns and beliefs do change in response to new institutional incentives, socioeconomic development, and historical experience' (Diamond 1995: 21). Although there are few empirical studies on political culture in China, there is no doubt that values have changed during the past two decades of drastic transformation from a closed, planned economy to an open, market one.

Since the Opium War in the 1840s, Western culture has affected China enormously precisely because of the yawning gap between traditional Confucianism and Western culture. Yet China's acceptance and absorption of Western culture has been selective and intermittent. Since the 1840s, China's learning from the West has undergone a process that began with the learning of Western technology and then moved to politics and culture, embracing concepts such as the freedom, democracy, and equality. However, the Chinese have always been suspicious of Western political philosophy, social theories, and values. As Mao Zedong commented, 'Imperialist aggression shattered the Chinese dream of learning from the West. They wondered why the teachers were always aggressive toward the pupils. The Chinese learned much from the West, but what they learned could not be put into effect. Their ideals could not be realized' (Brandt 1967: 451). In fact, Chinese values had changed little prior to the late 1970s, even though China had witnessed a century and a half of tremendous political change.

In contrast, the reform and open-door policies of the past almost three decades have caused rapid socioeconomic development and increased foreign exchanges, which in turn have caused a fundamental change in values. A new historic era in China began in December 1978. The signpost of this new era was the third plenum of the Eleventh Central Committee of the CCP. It marked not only a decisive break with those ideological and political lines of Mao Zedong, which culminated in the Cultural Revolution, but also signaled the end of nearly three-quarters of a century of revolutionary ferment and upheaval. Even more significant historically, this termination of the revolutionary period was accompanied by a retreat of political power (i.e., the party-state) from an increasingly deep penetration into civil society and the economy, and a reverse of the fundamental trend of political development since the May Fourth period, 1915–1921 (Tsou 1986: 219).

Deng Xiaoping took over as China's preeminent leader in 1978, and publicly declared his commitment to accelerating the long-delayed process of political institutionalization in China. In a landmark speech entitled 'On the Reform of the System of Party and State Leadership'

(Deng 1984: 320–343), Deng called for political reforms that would democratize political and social life and establish a system governed by rules, clear lines of authority, and collective decisionmaking institutions, and would replace the over-concentration of power and patriarchal rule that had characterized China under Mao.

Because the political system was responsible for the poor economic performance of the previous thirty years, the first step in the reform process had to be political. The reformers began by repudiating Mao's obsession with class struggle and ideological transformation and proclaiming that henceforth, the 'central task' of the country would be the 'four modernizations' of agriculture, industry, science and technology, and national defense.

To secure acceptance of the new political line by the country's vast cadre and to accelerate the modernization drive, the reformers undertook a set of political reforms that eventually resulted in political changes. First, the reformers publicly exposed the mistakes of past years to discredit those policies and make change possible. Second, ideological transformation was put aside and political pragmatism was adopted as a reform tactic. The precepts of Deng Xiaoping such as 'practice is the sole criterion of truth' and 'seek truth from facts' sanctioned a much more pragmatic approach to policies. The boundaries of permissible discussion were widened greatly. Third, the experts and intellectuals, wrongly criticized in past political movements, were rehabilitated. Deng declared them to be part of the 'productive forces,' and hence indispensable to the modernization effort. Fourth, rule by law was promoted and improved. The rule of law has been a goal that Chinese leaders have striven for since 1978. The fifth political reform, designed to increase the level of competence in party and government, was to promote the technically trained to leadership positions (Morley 1993: 46–48).

These political reforms, although incomplete, have provided a basic framework for economic reform. They sought to enliven the economy by introducing market relations and using profit to motive, thereby unleashing the initiative, energy, and drive so lacking in the previous system. The politicoeconomic reform policies brought remarkable success.

Intensified rural reform has given new motivation to hundreds of millions of Chinese farmers and has helped develop the rural economy. Urban reforms, which began in 1984, promoted the integration of the domestic market, and contributed to a better standard of living for urban residents. During the last two decades, per capita income of city dwellers rose by 1630 percent, from 316 yuan in 1978 to 5160 yuan in 1997. Prior to 1978, the state set 97 percent of all prices. At the end of the twentieth century, however, over 93 percent of prices are market determined. The market mechanism plays a decisive role in the economy (Song 1998: 11–13). As a result, most traditional values have changed in response to political, economic, and social developments.

Democratic values

It is generally assumed that 'the development of a stable and effective democratic government depends upon the orientation that people have to the political process—upon the political culture' (Almond 1963: 498). But what kind of political culture is considered necessary for the development and maintenance of liberal democracy?

According to studies on the evolution of Western democracy, a democratic culture encompasses tolerance of differences, acceptance of others, pragmatism and flexibility, trust, efficacy, openness to new ideas and experience, willingness to compromise, and civility of political discourse. At the level of mass culture, citizens have to be involved in politics, seek relevant information and knowledge, evaluate their leaders intelligently, and participate in elections and other political activities to improve their government's performance. That means citizens have to maintain attitudes toward authority that are neither blindly submissive nor completely hostile, but rather responsible and always watchful (Diamond 1999: 166–167).

In contrast with the above democratic values, Chinese political culture is often described as authoritarian. Before the 1949 Communist ascendancy over China, most Chinese seemed to be politically apathetic and ignorant. Between the 1950s and the 1970s, the CCP launched a series of mass political movements that led to a Chinese populace who exhibited extreme enthusiasm about public and political affairs. Especially during the years of the Cultural Revolution (1966–1976), almost all Chinese people were concerned about, and participated in politics. Since reforms were first implemented, Chinese people have been perceived to be obsessed about money-making and material goods with no interest in public affairs. In a word, Chinese culture has had no democratic personality for a long time.

However, recent surveys show a substantial amount of change toward democratic values in Chinese political culture, at least in modern cities. Chinese people are often said to be dependent on, and obedient and respectful toward their parents, leaders, and rulers.

A survey in Shanghai indicates that the young people are not as dependent and sometimes would like to defy their leaders if possible.

As Table 7.1 shows, young people in Shanghai have become fairly independent in everyday life. Few discrepancies appeared in regard to independent consciousness when the Shanghai youth were analyzed

Table 7.1: How Shanghai youth view independence (%)

Respondents	Yes	Sometimes	No	No answer
Whatever I do, I hope to get help from others				
'White collar' youth	6.6	49.9	42.4	1.1
'Blue collar' youth	7.9	54.8	36.2	1.1
Young intellectual	7.1	52.7	39.4	0.8
I make decisions by myself and do not rely on others				
'White collar' youth	61.8	35.4	2.2	0.6
'Blue collar' youth	61.2	35.5	2.0	1.3
Young intellectual	63.8	33.8	1.9	0.5
I can not do anything without parents' help				
'White collar' youth	7.2	30.6	61.0	1.2
'Blue collar' youth	6.5	35.2	56.9	1.4
Young intellectual	7.3	29.5	62.4	0.8
I rely on the unit to resolve my difficulties				
'White collar' youth	5.0	39.7	54.3	1.0
'Blue collar' youth	6.5	39.4	53.0	1.1
Young intellectual	5.3	46.2	47.6	0.9
I dare to insist on my own opinion even in the face of leaders				
'White collar' youth	26.6	59.9	12.1	1.4
'Blue collar' youth	24.2	63.8	11.2	0.8
Young intellectual	25.8	63.4	9.9	0.9
My way of life is different from others				
'White collar' youth	15.3	43.8	39.1	1.8
'Blue collar' youth	16.5	43.1	39.7	0.7
Young intellectual	11.1	43.0	44.9	1.0
All depend on myself, others are undependable				
'White collar' youth	37.7	41.6	19.7	1.0
'Blue collar' youth	40.1	43.0	15.8	1.1
Young intellectual	36.2	44.7	18.4	0.7

Source: SCCYL (1999: 260–261).

Note: Sample of 'white collar' youth = 726; 'blue collar' youth = 976; young intellectual = 647. Actual text of question in Shanghai is 'Are you the type of person described in the following statements?'

according to income, education, and occupation. More than 95 percent thought that they always or sometimes made decisions by themselves and did not rely on others. In traditional China, people were connected by family ties. The young were required to pay respect to their parents and to obey them, and the parents in turn were expected to nourish, protect, and help their offspring. This was the foundation and essence of a paternalism that connected citizens to the state in a hierarchical relationship. Yet in the Shanghai survey, approximately 60 percent of respondents decline the help offered by their parents; more than 30 percent believe that they sometimes need such help; and less than 10 percent said that they always need their parents' help. Similarly, about half of the respondents indicated that they do not need the help provided by their work unit even in difficulty, which in the planned economy of the past controlled all aspects of everyday life—including job, house, and salary. Only about 5 percent of respondents expressed the need for help.

More importantly, young people in Shanghai are more assertive in public affairs. In the past, people, especially the young, were taught to be submissive and obedient to their leaders. The survey, however, shows a different picture of Shanghai youth. Of the three groups of 'white collar,' 'blue collar,' and intellectual youth, respondents who say that they always or sometimes insist on their own opinions in opposition to leaders accounted for 86.5 percent, 88 percent, and 88.2 percent, respectively.

In fact, those value changes are congruent with the market-oriented reforms that began nearly three decades ago. The introduction of the market mechanism and the curtailment of party-state intervention has made everyone a more independent, autonomous and responsible individual. The public has been thrown from a sweeping socialist welfare system into a free but unsafe market economy. They have gained the freedom to make decisions for themselves, but they also have become responsible for their actions. No doubt, the market mechanism has fostered independence and individualism, both of which are believed to be indispensable to democracy.

Market-oriented reforms are blamed also for moral degeneration. For example, the reforms, epitomized by Deng Xiaoping's dictum, 'let a part of the people get rich first,' has produced many money worshipers. Increased levels of selfishness and mistrust have also accompanied the social transition from a central planned economy to a market economy. The results of the 1999 Shanghai survey, displayed in Table 7.1, show that approximately 80 percent of respondents said that they rely only on themselves and that others are undependable.

Political enthusiasm during the 1980s was strong as reflected in the student movements for political reform and freedom. But with the intensification of market-oriented reforms since the early 1990s, business and money-making have become the most important concerns. People, especially the young, have become indifferent to, or have lost interest in political propaganda, political movements, and political struggles. Of course, professional political operatives are the exception. Although the Fifteenth CCP National Congress adopted Deng Xiaoping Theory (socialism with Chinese characteristics) as China's guiding ideology in tandem with Marxist-Leninist-Mao Zedong Thought, a 1998 national survey indicated that only 12.6 percent of Chinese youth consider Deng Xiaoping Theory as the most important piece of knowledge. Instead, practical skills such as computers and human relations are deemed the most important (CYCRC 1999: 344).

Indeed, Chinese people have lost interest in political ideology since the adoption of a more pragmatic reform strategy in the late 1970s. Many surveys, however, show that because their lives were influenced every day by politics during the transitional reform years, Chinese are very interested in all kinds of political information and political discussions.

As Table 7.2 shows, about two-thirds of the respondents are interested or very interested in politics in general or national affairs. Not surprisingly, a higher percentage of respondents in Beijing showed interest in Beijing public affairs. Although many residents are interested in national and local affairs, few people discuss politics with others. The survey led by Zhong shows that less than half of the respondents talk often about politics with family members, relatives, colleagues and friends. The level of interest in politics is relatively high in Beijing.

In China, Beijing may be a special case in which residents show a higher level of interest in politics for several reasons. Beijing is the capital and has always been among the most political cities in China, because it has been the stage for such events as the May Fourth Movement of 1919, the start of the Cultural Revolution, and the Tiananmen Democracy Movement of 1989.

Whether the level of interest in politics in Beijing is high enough for democratic transition cannot be judged because comparative data does

Table 7.2: Level of political interest among Beijing urban residents (%)

	Very much Interested	Interested	Not very interested	Not interested
Politics in general	12.0	60.9	25.1	2.0
National affairs	14.1	65.0	19.5	1.4
Beijing affairs	22.1	64.9	11.9	1.1

	Whenever we meet	Very often	Occasional	Never	Cannot tell
Discussion of politics with others	2.4	42.9	51.1	2.9	0.7

Source: Zhong (1998: 767).
Note: Sample equals 1265 respondents.

not exist, as in Table 7.2, with other countries. However, according to a comparative empirical study based on a 1993 nation-wide survey of political culture and political participation, the percentage (44.4%) of people in mainland China who talked about politics with others falls between the high level (60%) for Germany and the low level (32% and 38%) for Italy and Mexico in the 1960s (Shi 2000: 545–546). As is well known, Italy has been a democracy for many years, and Mexico has recently succeeded in its shift from authoritarianism to democracy.

The 'rule of law' is a principle traditionally associated with liberal democracy. During the first thirty years after the founding of the PRC, most Chinese were ignorant of the law and mistrustful of legal channels, a reasonable position in an environment where politics routinely superseded law. In 1978, however, Chinese leaders began to develop legal ideas and institutions. The new Chinese legality is a depoliticized view of law as opposed to a political one in which law is seen to be part of politics, a weapon of the state to be used in class struggle. China has acknowledged the *rule of law*, which means that everyone is subject equally to the law. The principle of the *rule of law* has advanced since the mid-1990s with the passage or amendment of many laws and the substantial progress of legal reforms.

Along with the legal reform, China has launched a number of campaigns from the early 1980s to educate ordinary citizens about the content of important laws and about ideas such as equality before the law. Now, many citizens believe that the law is indispensable to their lives and are able to use the law to protect their rights and interests.

One indicator of the effect of legal education is the increase in lawsuits against government agencies and officials through the use of the administrative litigation law, an act unthinkable to past Chinese. Before the enactment of the Administrative Litigation Law in October 1990, Chinese citizens victimized by miscarriages of justice and abuse of state power had no legal recourse. Although a considerable number of citizens challenged administrative acts by filing suit in China's courts, their claims had no legal basis and their chances of winning were extremely small. The passage of this law immediately unleashed a flood of new lawsuits against the government, the number of which has increased steadily from 9934 in 1989 to 98,000 in 1998. Official data for 1992 shows that of the cases filed, the courts upheld the government's administrative decisions in 28 percent of them; dismissed the government's decisions in 19 percent; forced changes in original government's decisions in 1.8 percent; and dismissed the plaintiffs' complaints in 7.8 percent. Plaintiffs withdrew their lawsuits in 37.8 percent of the cases. The marked increase in lawsuits against the government reflects the upsurge of Chinese legal consciousness, on the one hand, and the huge gap between citizen demands and government performance on the other.

Although the ideas of democracy were introduced to China one hundred years ago, war, revolution, and other factors prevented progress in democratization. Even after the reform and open-door policies of the late 1970s and despite the increased demands for democratization, the political transition from totalitarianism/ authoritarianism to democracy did not begin until the end of the twentieth century. The CCP has been established as the sole ruling party and it cracks down harshly on any opposition party or political dissidents.

Although some China scholars predict that development of the Chinese market economy will trigger a gradual process of political democratization, others believe that, despite substantial changes in its economy, China is not likely to become a 'liberal democracy' due to its 'inherently authoritarian political culture' (Goldman 1994: 1). The introduction of the market mechanism and the opening up to the outside world (mainly Western) brought the dissemination of Western ideas and values to Chinese society. Some intellectuals and college students became infatuated with Western democratic ideas—such as a multi-party system, bicameral constitutions, federalism, freedom, equality, and human rights—and in the 1980s repeated ideological struggles also occurred within the CCP. Those struggles included the anti-spiritual pollution campaign of the early 1980s, the anti-bourgeois liberalism movement of the mid-1980s, and the anti-

Western, imperialist peaceful evolution (*Fan Heping Yanbian*) of the late 1980s and early 1990s.

In an effort to solve the increasing economic and political problems that threatened political order and stability, ideas directly contrary to democracy began to garner attention in the late 1980s. Labeled 'neo-authoritarianism,' these ideas advocated a strong, dictatorial but technocratic government to solve Chinese problems, such as the regimes in the 1960s and 1970s of Park Chung-Hee in South Korea and Lee Kuan Yew in Singapore.

After Deng Xiaoping's inspection tour of southern China in early 1992, the Beijing government accelerated market reforms, even though the decentralizing reforms of the 1980s had brought a loss of central authority and all the serious consequences associated with such a loss. In response, neo-conservatism, a continuation of neo-authoritarian ideas, became prevalent. This set of ideas also called for political stability, central authority, tight social control, and a role for both ideology and nationalism (Chen 1997: 593).

To a large extent, neo-conservative thoughts reflected a deep suspicion about liberal democracy as a way of governing China. This suspicion, initially raised by neo-authoritarian thinkers, was apparently reinforced and even 'justified' by two important developments in the 1990s. First, the domestic chaos and instability brought about by the dissolution of the Soviet Union and the changes in Eastern Europe regimes forced Chinese intellectuals, including those who had been pro-democratic, to question the validity of democracy. Chinese intellectuals began to ask if China could stand or, indeed, needed the kind of democratic change occurring in the former Soviet bloc that incurred state dissolution, ethnic strife, civil disorder, and mass unemployment. Second, China's mounting domestic problems, which resulted from accelerated market reforms after 1992, caused deep concern among intellectuals. China's weakness was alarming: extraordinarily rapid economic growth was occurring very unevenly in a society with only limited rule and under a central government whose authority was crumbling. Corruption, crime, a floating population, unemployment, and income disparity all had a destabilizing effect on the social order. Grave domestic concerns and uncertainties not only strengthened the position of those who consistently supported neo-authoritarian politics, but also converted to neo-conservatism many who previously had favored liberal democratic ideas.

Despite departures from the official line, as Feng Chen puts it, 'neo-conservatism can be seen as a tacit consensus between leadership and intellectuals on how reform should be carried out' (Chen 1997: 612). Most of China's economic and political reforms have been put into practice according to the vision of neo-conservative scholars.

Those developments, however, do not necessarily mean there is no support or demand for democracy. Ideally, a belief in the legitimacy of democracy should be held at two levels. First, as a general principle, democracy is considered the best (or, at a minimum, the least bad) form of government possible. Second, as an evaluation of one's own country's democratic regime, in spite of its failures and shortcomings, it is regarded as better than any non-democratic regimes that might be established (Diamond 1999: 168–169). Undoubtedly, on the first level, democracy has the extensive support of the political and academic elite and the masses in China. But on the second level, the belief in democratic legitimacy in China is not deeply rooted and is conditional, depending on effective performance. Therefore, Chinese people, political leaders, and intellectuals in particular, tend to embrace authoritarianism at the first sign of trouble. This may explain why political conservatism, including neo-authoritarianism and neo-conservatism, repeatedly appears as a solution to crises throughout the twentieth century in China (Jiang 2000: 57–73). This gap between abstract principles and behavioral norms was also observed in the political culture survey in Beijing.

As Table 7.3 shows, Beijing's urban residents have complex public attitudes toward democracy and civil liberties. Over 85 percent seem tolerant of people with differing political views and 93.2 percent favor wider press freedom. An overwhelming majority voiced support for more democratic ways of choosing local government officials. However, the responses to the last three statements in Table 7.3 indicate a low level of political efficacy and to some extent the remains of authoritarian personality among these residents. Over 70 percent of respondents believe that the well-being of the country is dependent mainly on government leaders, not the people. The table also shows that the majority surveyed do not want to challenge authority, even when they believe their ideas are correct. An overwhelming majority of the respondents prefer stability and order to freedom.

Table 7.1 shows that over 85 percent of respondents in the 1999 Shanghai youth survey believe that they would dare to insist on their own opinions even if it meant confronting the leadership. Here, the discrepancy between Beijing and Shanghai is huge. The following three points may account for the difference. First, historically, Shanghai is a modern and highly-westernized commercial city and

Table 7.3: Selected democratic values (%)

	Strongly agree	Agree	Disagree	Strongly disagree	N
Regardless of one's political beliefs, he or she is entitled to the same legal rights as anyone else	40.8	45.5	11.9	1.8	1256
The press should be given more freedom to expose corruption and other wrongdoing	66.7	26.5	6.0	0.7	1259
Elections to local government positions should be conducted in such a way that there is more than one candidate for each post	53.0	41.5	4.5	1.0	1254
The well-being of the country is mainly dependent upon state leaders, not the masses	31.8	39.4	23.9	4.9	1257
In general, I don't think I should argue with the authorities even though I believe my idea is correct	26.6	42.1	24.5	6.9	1258
I would rather live in an orderly society than in a freer society prone to disruption	55.8	38.5	3.8	1.9	1255

Source: Zhong (1998: 771).
Note: N = number of respondents.

Beijing is an imperial capital. Second, the respondents surveyed in Shanghai are young people. Third, the wording of the questions is different. For example, in the Shanghai survey, it is unclear whether there would be a conflict between the leader and the respondent if the respondent insisted on his or her own opinions. In general, most Chinese people do not like to challenge authority.

The desire for stability and order has been extensive during the last two decades. Chinese people are afraid of chaos (*luan*), a fear that is rooted in their political culture. It is also rooted in the experience of the pre-1949 period, and especially in that of the Cultural Revolution. Furthermore, many Chinese believe that there is a conflict between order and freedom, in other words, liberalization may cause instability. Indeed, both the elite and the masses associate instability with free societies, particularly after what happened in the former Soviet Union and Eastern European countries as they liberalized during the late 1980s and early 1990s. In the Chinese language, especially in CCP ideology, liberalism (*ziyou zhuyi*) and liberalization (*ziyouhua*) are pejorative words, although more and more Chinese are embracing the notion of freedom or liberty (*ziyou*). It is this emphasis on order and stability that forms the psychological foundation of the authoritarian regime in China.

Identity and trust

Findings from recent surveys taken in Beijing and Shanghai indicate that enormous value changes have taken place during the last two decades, although traditional Confucianism remains to an extent. Foreign cultural values have been actively and widely absorbed and assimilated in contemporary China as international exchanges grow and globalization intensifies. The traditional values of paternalism, moralism, and collectivism have eroded. For example, in the West, individualism is universally recognized as respect for an individual's own interests and rights and for those of others. But in China, where collectivism had often been overemphasized, individualism was condemned as being synonymous with selfishness, something that neglected overall interests and benefited the individual at the expense of others. However, a national survey that interviewed 6534 urban youth between 14 and 28 years of age in 1998 revealed that 49.1 percent of the respondents endorsed the proposition that everyone subjectively serves himself and objectively serves others. In the same survey, only 22.6 percent of the respondents rejected that idea, and 28.4 percent of the respondents said that they could not decide (CYCRC 1999: 352). The difference between Chinese and Western values is diminishing as they become more similar. As mentioned above, recent surveys show that democratic values are extensively supported, especially in urban China.

Since value changes have taken place and democratic values have been embraced to some extent in China, what, then, are the public attitudes toward the nation and government of China, the CCP leadership, and the Marxist–Leninist ideology during this era of globalization and democratization?

Historically, China regarded itself as the Middle Kingdom (*Zhongguo*) and for centuries adhered to that conceit. But then the West began its expansionist efforts into China supported by the strength of its modern industrialization and technology. First, Britain went to war in 1839, and then one country after another pushed China around, plundering it and carving it up. The People's Republic of China (PRC), founded after the CCP came to power in 1949, ended the semi-colonial history of modern China and declared the beginning of the new socialist China. Two years after Mao's death, the subsequent leadership group with Deng Xiaoping at the center took the initiative to open China to the outside world. Not surprisingly, Chinese were ashamed and chagrined that thirty years of socialism had produced only meager results compared to the other nations of East Asia. Chinese were aware of the extent to which China had fallen behind internationally. Not only Japan, which had forged ahead with stunning speed, but also the 'four tigers'—Korea, Taiwan, Hong Kong, and Singapore—had outpaced China by rapidly modernizing.

One result of the open-door policy is a sharply increased foreign presence. Academic and cultural exchange between China and other countries continue to grow. The government has sent thousands of scholars and students abroad, particularly to Japan and the United States, thereby giving them intense exposure to foreign values and ideas. As a result, in contrast to erstwhile self-conceit, a sense of self-humility has spread over the whole country. Socialism and Marxism were doubted, and the CCP was blamed for the country's backwardness. Even patriotism, which is taken for granted almost all over the world, was challenged. Some people criticized unfairly during the Anti-rightist Movements or the Cultural Revolution asked why we must love the motherland when we were forsaken and not loved by it (Tsou 1986: 228).

Since as early as 1982, the CCP has taken a series of measures to resolve the credibility crisis faced by it and socialist ideologies. At the Twelfth Party Congress of 1982, the CCP tasked itself with creating a 'socialist spiritual civilization' that would offer CCP members effective moral protection against the corrosive effects of 'bourgeois liberalization' and other unwanted by-products of structural reforms and opening to the outside world. In his report delivered to the Congress, General Secretary Hu Yaobang asserted, 'capitalist and other forces hostile to our socialist cause will seek to corrupt us and harm our country.' Confronted with such a challenge, Hu called on all CCP members to hold firmly to the party's established ideals, moral values, and organizational discipline (MacFarquhar 1997: 348–349).

The CCP and Chinese government faced pressure from abroad and at home in the aftermath of the 1989 crackdown on the Tiananmen student democracy movement. Cognizant of the inadequacies of Communist ideology, Chinese leaders consciously cultivated nationalism as a new glue for bonding the country together. Communism was discredited as a result of the Tiananmen Incident and the Soviet

Union's collapse. Jiang Zemin and others, therefore, used the education system and propaganda to nurture a national pride in response to foreign pressure.

In August 1994, the CCP promulgated 'An Outline for Implementing Patriotic Education,' in which the trinity of patriotism, collectivism, and socialism was emphasized, so that the overriding priority became the patriotic education of the youth. Meanwhile, some scholars suggested that Chinese leaders use nationalism to enhance and consolidate political legitimacy. For example, defining nationalism as a precious, 'natural' political resource that could be exploited to maintain and strengthen the unity and consensus of a political community, Xiao Gongqing said that the time had come for Chinese leaders to use nationalism to fortify the legitimate basis and restructure the moral values of the CCP regime (Xiao 1994).

Chinese leaders have used patriotism instead of communism to educate the young people, in particular students. Consequently, nationalism has become much stronger since the 1990s. The 1999 Shanghai survey shows a very high level of national identity among young people, which is evidence contrary to the 'identity crisis' theory.

More than 90 percent of the respondents feel proud to be Chinese, and over 80 percent said that there is congruity between patriotism and socialism, thus endorsing the proposition that loving the motherland is to love socialist China.

In fact, in a 1993 national survey on youth social consciousness, the results were far more serious than the responses of college students in 1999. According to that survey, only 37 percent of the respondents correlated patriotism with socialism and agreed to the proposition that loving the motherland is to love socialism; 38.2 percent believed that loving the motherland did not necessarily mean loving socialism; and 24.8 percent indicated that loving the motherland meant at least being 'not anti-socialist' (SCCYL 1999: 181). By contrast, the results of the 1999 survey are very promising and favorable, especially from the perspective of the CCP's huge effort in patriotic education during the last decade.

The Gallup survey provides complementary data for the high level of national identity in China. The survey does not have any questions that directly relate to national identity, but we can observe consistency between respondents' choices and China's official stance and foreign policy. Table 7.4 shows a sharp contrast between eight other Asian countries with an average of 38 percent of respondents saying that

Table 7.4: The United Nations' most important future aim (%)

	China	8 Asian countries	Lowest	Highest
Improve human health	25	19	13	27
Give humanitarian aid in times of natural disasters	15	30	14	44
Give humanitarian aid in times of war/conflict	10	28	10	34
Prevent war by intervention	34	31	27	43
Maintain peace by armed forces	5	21	5	37
Develop into a world government	10	11	8	22
Protect human rights	0	38	0	52

Source: Gallup survey, question 25.
Note: The eight Asian countries are China, Korea, Japan, Taiwan, Singapore, Malaysia, Thailand, and the Philippines.

the protection of human rights should be the most important aim for the United Nations (UN) in the future, whereas none of the Chinese respondents shared this belief. In contrast to the average 21 percent among eight Asian countries that said that the maintenance of peace by armed forces should be the most important aim for the UN, only 5 percent of Chinese respondents, less than one-fourth the Asian average, chose this answer. It is also noteworthy that 34 percent of Chinese respondents thought that the prevention of war through intervention should be the most important future aim of the UN, the second highest among the Asian countries surveyed, following Taiwan at 43 percent, and certainly higher than the average for the countries in this study.

The Gallup survey was conducted five months after the U. S. bombing of the Chinese Embassy in Belgrade, which provoked outrage and indignation and caused massive student demonstrations in China. Considering that background, the results shown in Table 7.4 are very understandable, and to a great extent, logical. Chinese people display a great national cohesiveness when faced with foreign challenge.

While Chinese people show a high level of national identity, support is also high for the market-oriented reforms and open-door policies that the CCP and the government have adopted since the late 1970s. A series of local surveys that interviewed approximately two thousand college students in Shanghai from 1992–1997, indicated increasing support for government policies. In 1997, 85 percent of college students agreed to the proposition that establishing a socialist market economic system was the only correct road to prosperity and greatness and 92 percent thought the policies of the central government were effective. Moreover, a high percentage (96%) was optimistic about political and economic development.

The 1999 Shanghai survey had some questions about political attitudes toward three of the four cardinal principles in the reform period of China: the CCP leadership, Deng Xiaoping Theory, and the socialist system. Table 7.5 shows the results to this set of questions.

In 1979, Deng Xiaoping put forward the four cardinal principles that were reaffirmed in the preamble to the 1982 Constitution stating that 'Under the leadership of the CCP and the guidance of Marxism-Leninist-Mao Zedong Thought, the Chinese people will…continue to adhere to the people's democratic dictatorship and follow the socialist

Table 7.5: Level of trust in political principles among Shanghai youth (%)

Respondents	Agree	Disagree	Don't know
China can modernize only under CCP leadership			
Young intellectuals	83.4	4.4	12.2
'White collar' youth	78.8	4.2	17.0
'Blue collar' youth	84.5	4.1	11.4
College students	76.0	16.8	7.1
Middle-school students	77.9	16.2	5.8
Deng Xiaoping Theory is the fundamental guarantee of modernization in China			
Young intellectuals	90.1	1.9	8.0
'White collar' youth	86.5	1.9	11.6
'Blue collar' youth	91.1	1.0	7.9
College students	88.8	6.2	5.1
Middle-school students	92.6	4.0	3.3
Socialist system will have stronger survival power in the twenty-one century			
Young intellectuals	71.1	6.0	22.9
'White collar' youth	67.6	6.0	26.4
'Blue collar' youth	78.0	3.9	18.1
College students	72.7	16.4	10.9
Middle-school students	81.3	11.7	7.0

Source: SCCYL (1999: 178–179)
Note: Sample of young intellectuals = 647; 'white collar' youth = 726; 'blue collar' youth = 976; college students = 952; and middle-school students = 978.

road.' After the collapse of the Soviet Union and the end of the Cold War, many radical scholars and democratic activists considered the four cardinal principles to be outdated, especially when China had experienced two decades of rapid economic growth and had become increasingly involved in the wave of globalization. So, what are the public attitudes toward those principles?

The 1999 Shanghai survey shows that on average, 80.1 percent of respondents believe that the CCP leadership is important and indispensable to China's modernization; 89.8 percent agree with the proposition that Deng Xiaoping Theory, namely, Marxism in contemporary China, is the fundamental guarantee for the realization of modernization; and 74.1 percent feel that the socialist system has a stronger survival power in the twenty first century. The high percentage in support of Deng Xiaoping Theory may be the result of the education campaign conducted since 1993 and of the elevation of the theory to the level of a guiding ideology together with Marxism-Leninist-Mao Zedong Thought at the Fifteenth CCP Congress in 1997.

In contrast, Shanghai youth do not favor socialism. A rate as high as 26.4 percent of 'white collar' respondents have reservations about the proposition that socialism would be stronger in the future. Of the college student respondents, 16.4 percent responded negatively to the proposition. Many people were shocked by the failure of socialism in the former Soviet Union and Eastern Europe and, consequently, lost confidence in socialism. A larger proportion of people believe in the Deng Xiaoping Theory because socialism with Chinese characteristics is not an original notion. In a 1993 Shanghai survey, as many as 19.8 percent of college students and 14.1 percent of college teachers believed that socialism with Chinese characteristics was essentially capitalism under CCP leadership.

The 1999 survey on Shanghai had a few questions about public attitudes toward political development, in particular democratization in China. Table 7.6 shows that Shanghai youth are somewhat satisfied with achievements in politics. Approximately 60 percent of respondents believe that Chinese citizens will be to participate more directly in national and local political affairs. Furthermore, they are cautiously optimistic about the future of democratization in China. On average, over 60 percent endorsed the proposition that Chinese society will become more and more democratic. But a national survey in 1987 showed that only 32.4 percent of respondents were optimistic about democratization in China, which stands in sharp contrast to the

Table 7.6: Attitudes toward democratization among Shanghai youth (%)

Respondents	Agree	Disagree	Don't know
Citizens can participate more directly in national and local political affairs			
Young intellectuals	60.7	26.2	13.1
'White collar' youth	61.1	25.9	13.1
'Blue collar' youth	53.5	29.6	16.8
Citizens' opinions can influence government decision making			
Young intellectuals	27.0	62.8	9.2
'White collar' youth	30.0	58.7	11.3
'Blue collar' youth	30.7	53.1	16.2
Chinese society will become more and more democratic			
Young intellectuals	62.6	20.1	17.3
'White collar' youth	64.3	17.3	18.4
'Blue collar' youth	58.2	21.9	19.9

Source: SCCYL (1999: 183).
Note: Sample of young intellectuals = 647; 'white collar' youth = 726; and 'blue collar' youth = 976.

46.2 percent who were not optimistic (Ming 1989: 97). Yet when asked whether citizens' opinions influenced government decision making, most respondents show a sense of frustration with a high average of 58.2 percent believing that citizens' opinions have no influence on policy-making. Similarly, in a Beijing survey, 72.2 percent of respondents believe that suggestions and complaints the public makes to government are often ignored (Zhong 1998: 779).

Empirical studies have shown that even in advanced democracies and third-wave democracies, citizens tend to be cynical about the responsiveness of the political system to their concerns. For example, a comparative study showed that 65 percent of the respondents in Taiwan and 71 percent in South Korea do not believe that the government takes the interests and opinions of people like themselves into account when making important decisions (Chu 2001: 122–136). We have also found similar results in the Gallup survey. According to the Gallup survey results based on the seven Asian countries of South Korea, Japan, Taiwan, Singapore, Malaysia, Thailand, and the

Philippines, only a 20 percent average of respondents believe that their government responds to the will of the people.

I have presented some trends in political support and trust in China, but am unable to systematically compare them with other Asian or Western countries. However, generally speaking, Chinese respondents show a relatively high level of support and trust in politics in contrast with the declining political support and spreading public skepticism seen in the advanced industrial democracies (Pharr 2000: 7–13). Remnants of the Chinese deferential political and cultural tradition may partly account for this difference. But as shown earlier, enormous value changes have taken place since China adopted market-oriented reform policies and opened up to the outside world in the late 1970s. Hence, the discrepancy may be explained by the following perspective.

Robert D. Putnam and his colleagues have presented a model for explaining declining public trust: 'Public satisfaction with representative institutions is a function of the information to which citizens are exposed, the criteria by which the public evaluates government and politics, and the actual performance of those institutions' (Pharr 2000: 23). This model can be applied, with some modification, to explain the high levels of public trust and satisfaction in China. Concretely, public trust in China is evaluated based on the performance of government, criteria of evaluation, information, and political experience.

First, government performance has been ameliorated. Although measuring performance objectively is a challenging task, one obvious approach is to measure macroeconomic outcomes. As shown above, China has experienced amazingly rapid growth, especially along coastal areas such as Shanghai. Consequently, the living standard of Chinese citizens has been raised many times. In the Beijing survey, 88.4 percent of respondents agree that 'my living conditions have noticeably improved since the reforms in 1978;' 65.2 percent believe that 'my social status has noticeably improved during the last two decades;' and 90.1 percent say that 'I am confident that China will become an economic power in the twenty-one century' (Zhong 1998: 779). This good feeling contributed very much to the high scores for the Communist regime.

Second, the criteria of evaluation are geared toward a developmentalist and materialist direction in contrast to the post-materialist direction in the industrialized democracies. Of course, this does not mean that Chinese people have no political demands and that China has no political issues, but as Deng Xiaoping put it, 'Economic works are the biggest political works at present; economic issues are the overriding political issues' (Deng 1994: 194). The CCP gave priority to economic affairs and regarded economic development as the fundamental criterion to judge all policies and measures. Considering China's past experiences as a semi-colonial and semi-feudal society, and that its productive forces lag far behind those of industrialized societies, this developmental backwardness has restricted the Chinese people's political demands. The people are more concerned with living conditions and are, consequently, more easily satisfied with rapid growth and economic betterment.

Third, a lack of information inhibits public demonstrations of discontent with government and politics. Although Chinese citizens show more interest in political affairs and are more knowledgeable about these matters, and the mass media is more and more available to the public, the fact that there is no true freedom of the press is important. Any public criticism of the CCP regime, Chinese leaders, or the four cardinal principles is not permitted. The past two decades have seen a ten-fold increase in the number of mass media outlets, but no one can challenge CCP authority or a publish severe criticism of the supreme leaders or the CCP. Most new periodicals do not touch on politics, offering instead the latest perspectives on sports, fashion, music and movies. Chinese leaders reserve the right to shut down publications that in their view promote opposition to CCP rule. Although the revolution in global information technology—for instance, e-mail, the Internet and cell phones—is said to have broken through these walls, the Chinese government has strengthened its restrictions on information available on the Internet. Moreover, according to a 1998 national survey of 14- to 28-year-old urban youth, 69.1 percent say that they do not have access to the Internet or online websites (CYCRC 1999: 339). Therefore, Chinese citizens are fed the official view every day by government-controlled mass media. Stories in the Chinese media show only one side of the story, with the result that the public has been indoctrinated so much by constantly repeated official views that these views gradually transform themselves into public attitudes.

Fourth, political experience strengthens confidence in government and politics. Political experience with democracy and alternative regimes has a sizable independent effect on political attitudes and values, often overpowering the national level of socioeconomic development, individual socioeconomic status, and the regime's economic performance (Diamond 1999: 162). China has no experience with democracy. From the 1912–1913 transitory experiments with democracy, including multi-party politics, to the failed attempt of Yuan Shikai to restore the imperial system, most Chinese people, in particular the CCP, drew the lesson that Western-style democracy is not suitable to China. After the political turmoil of war and revolution, Chinese have a high appreciation for national independence, political stability, social order, and the economic prosperity of the last two decades. Because the Chinese have no experience with democracy but still admire the concept, albeit not on Western terms, they tend to be satisfied with recent achievements in democratization, especially when compared with the cult of personality, dictatorship, and brutal class struggles of the past, particularly the Cultural Revolution. As some scholars have observed, little has been achieved thus far in the way of actual democratization, but the institutional foundations for genuine democracy are slowly taking shape. For example, the maturation of the rule of law, the emergence of the National People's Congress and local People's Congress as power players, and the development of village self-government and grassroot democratization are important components of this evolutionary process (Diamond 1997: 224–225). These components also explain why a majority of respondents are satisfied with past political development and optimistic about democratization in the future.

Problems and prospects

As analyzed above, although there may be some influence from political manipulation, it is obvious that the majority of ordinary urban citizens support and trust both Chinese government policies and the CCP regime. That strong support is based mainly on economic achievements and social progress. Even though political development has not been as rapid as economic development and surveys show a sense of frustration over political efficacy, most Chinese people are optimistic about future democratization in their homeland. For the time being, we can conclude that China is not on the verge of collapse owing to a putative legitimacy crisis, but this does not mean that China practices good governance.

For the most part, in this chapter, I have examined value changes based on survey data collected in Shanghai and Beijing. Yet both these urban centers are not representative of the rest of China because huge regional differences exist between urban and rural areas and between the coastal east and mountainous west.

Although reforms began in rural areas twenty years ago and changes occurred with the implementation of responsibility system, today, farmers' incomes are growing almost three times more slowly than urban incomes. Yet taxes on rural communities are growing faster than those in the cities, leading to an increasing gap between the 'haves' in the urban areas and the 'have nots' on the farm. The income ratio between urban and rural residents was 2.4 in 1978 before decreasing to 2.1 in 1985 and then increasing to 2.4 in 1987, 2.8 in 1995, and 3.2 in 2000 (Ru 2001: 198). A silent battle has raged for several decades between farmers and local government officials who are squeezing the farmers to maximize tax revenue. Through that battle, the autonomous village committee has been established and experiments in grassroot democracy as an institutional innovation are being conducted, which are reportedly contributing to easing tensions between rural cadres and farmers.

In fact, grassroot democracy did not work as well as expected in some rural areas. In some parts, China's tax and land battles have reached a boiling point. A number of riots have erupted in the heartland of rice- and wheat-growing villages in recent years. For example, security forces killed two farmers and wounded twenty others during a clash on April 15, 2001 in the village of Yuntang in Jiangxi province. A similar incident took place in Guangdong province in 2005.

Under such circumstances, local government is not expected to enjoy a strong level of public support and trust. A survey conducted in 1989 showed huge discrepancies of trust in government between metropolitan and agrarian areas. Of the metropolitan respondents, 80.9 percent said that they trust government compared to 53.5 percent of rural respondents (Ming 1989: 69). The same survey also showed that trust in government decreased as city size decreased.

But this does not necessarily mean that Chinese peasants are going to revolt against the CCP regime; their discontent lies mostly with local government and officials. Just as peasants in feudal society rebelled against only corrupt officials but not emperors, most peasants still have faith in Beijing to solve their problems. To ease regional differences, the Chinese government has promoted many projects, such as the Great West development that is expected to bring hope to the poor western Chinese peasants, and the abolishment of agricultural tax, which is highly appreciated throughout the country.

The most serious threat to governance in China is political corruption. Despite claims of great success against corruption, perennial abuse continues to emerge and become more and more serious. President Jiang Zemin and other leaders have routinely issued calls to fight corruption regardless of what and who it involves. Although only one politburo member (Chen Xitong) was convicted of corruption to date, allegations have been made about the vice-chairman of the Standing Committee of the National People's Congress (Cheng Kejie). Also, at the vice-minister and vice-governor level, one governor (Hu Changqing) was sentenced to death in March 2000. The level of corruption is unprecedented in the history of the PRC, and it has further undermined the legitimacy of the regime and has become one of the biggest sources of political instability and economic disorder. Surveys show repeatedly that corruption is the biggest concern in today's China.

In many cases, CCP members have been implicated in all kinds of scandals, seriously damaging the reputation and image of the party. When asked 'what do you think of the Communist party member for your area,' 44.7 percent of respondents say that most CCP members are no different from the masses; 10.1 percent believe that most CCP members are not as good as the masses (CYCRC 1999: 352).

A more serious concern for the Chinese government is that some people have begun to doubt whether the Party can succeed in the anti-corruption struggle without fundamental political reforms such as the introduction of a multi-party system. In a 1992 survey of college teachers' attitudes in Shanghai, 23.5 percent did not reject the proposition that corruption cannot be properly addressed without the introduction of a multi-party system.

In the wake of the Cultural Revolution, Chinese leaders and political activists alike emphasized democratic political reform. Up to the late 1980s, political reform aimed at building socialist democracy with Chinese characteristics was discussed widely and experimented with to some extent. However, as socioeconomic problems such as inflation, disorder, corruption, and instability appeared and worsened in the late 1980s, political order, centralization, efficiency, and stability became the ultimate targets that Chinese leaders pursued for economic and political development. The political reforms introduced since the early 1990s have been cautious to a fault.

As in other East Asian countries, the developmental state in China has been strengthened, government capacity improved, and political systems institutionalized to a great extent. Although the political institutions of the PRC remain essentially Leninist in that the CCP continues to enjoy a monopoly of power, with independent media and autonomous trade unions almost wholly absent, it is obvious that the Chinese political system has partly adapted to a changing environment.

Unlike the 1950s, the CCP is more 'middle class,' its leaders better educated and more highly differentiated. Able public officials are performing new functions in an environment in which the law has become increasingly important. Government decisionmaking is increasingly based on rational considerations as authorities struggle to develop the market economy (Burns 1999: 593–594). Several years ago, the former general secretary of the CCP, Jiang Zemin, raised the so-called theory of the three represents—that the CCP must represent the most advanced production forces, the most advanced culture, and the comprehensive interests of the people. Obviously, Chinese leaders want the party to absorb a wider range of people, including intellectuals, professionals, hi-tech personnel, and even private entrepreneurs, who are seen as the embodiment of advanced production forces and culture in the new century. This is also an indication that Chinese are ready to jettison Lenin's and Mao's obsolete idea of the CCP being the party of workers, the vanguard of the proletariat.

Sooner or later, successful developmental states must face crises caused by the extreme tension inherent between an advanced economy and an authoritarian regime. Authoritarian regimes have a mixed efficacy, in that their performance is sometimes creditable. Such regimes, however, cannot translate that efficacy into political legitimacy in the way democracies can (Pridham 1995: 146).

China has made great strides since the early 1980s with its market-oriented economic reforms and limited political reforms, that is, through a state-led development strategy. As market-oriented reforms have intensified since the mid-1990s, China is pushed to consider further political reform and democratization within a changing environment, especially when it is faced with the impact of rapid economic development and social change—under the pressure of globalization and its entrance to the World Trade Organization (WTO)—and in order to prevent a social and economic crisis, strengthen the legitimacy of the CCP, and maintain political stability (Liu 1999: 35–36). Indeed, at the plenary session of the policy-setting CCP Central Committee in October 2000, the political leadership decided that the Party should 'strengthen the construction of democracy' and encourage 'citizens to participate in politics in an orderly manner.' Recently, political civilization has been emphasized as an integral part of socialism with Chinese characteristics. At the same time, a survey on attitudes of the political elite shows that political reform was the biggest concern among CCP cadres. As Baogang He points out, the preconditions for democracy already exist to some extent in China with a democratic culture, civil society, and reform factions within the party who will play the democratic card (He 1996: 225). The question is how these factors will interact at a favorable time so as to expedite the transition from authoritarianism to democracy in China. Whether the transition succeeds depends on the choice of a democratizing strategy from which regional democracy may be an important alternative.

As the CCP has repeatedly said, China is a socialist country, and without democracy there can be no socialism or socialist modernization. Although democratization is a gradual process that cannot be accomplished overnight, advancing this process in an orderly and steady way has become a task of exigency for China scholars as well as Chinese leaders.

Taking into consideration the huge regional differences in economic development and cultural values, we may predict the high probability of imbalances across the country in the transition from authoritarianism to democracy. In fact, rapid economic and political decentralization is creating a nascent federalist structure in China, which augurs well for future regional democratic breakthroughs (Diamond 1997: 226). In other words, a decentralized political system allows every region to experiment with democratic reforms with characteristics particular to that region. That means that democratization may proceed at a faster pace in the outlying regions, especially those with socioeconomic and cultural conditions more hospitable to it.

During the last two decades, local people's congresses have made more progress toward democratization than has the national congress. The central leadership has allowed more political contests at subnational people's congresses than at the national level because those contests are less threatening to the state, and they also serve to control bureaucratism and to promote local incentives (Xia 2000: 214). Regional democracy could trigger a transition at the national level if the process continues and political contests at the local level spread to more and more regions and eventually feed back to the national level.

The expansion of direct elections in rural areas also shows that China is making steady progress toward regional democracy. Direct elections in villages and townships are one of the most encouraging political reforms of recent years, and they have helped, in part, to prevent corruption and maintain stability in the countryside. These elections indicate that popular participation can be constructive to, and supportive of government legitimacy and, consequently, helpful to economic and political development.

Bibliography

Almond, Gabriel A, and Sidney Verba (1963), *The Civic Culture: Political Attitudes and Democracy in Five Nations*, Princeton: Princeton University Press.

Brandt, Conrad, Benjamin Schwartz and John K. Fairbank (eds.) (1967), *A Documentary History of Chinese Communism*, 2nd edition, New York: Atheneum.

Burns, John P (1999), 'The People's Republic of China at 50: national political reform,' *The China Quarterly*, no. 159, pp. 580–593.

Chen, Feng (1997), 'Order and stability in social transition: neoconservative political thought in post-1989 China', *The China Quarterly*, no. 151, pp. 593–613.

CYCRC or *Zhongguo Qingshaonian Yanjiu Zhongxin* (China Youth and Children Research Center) (1999), *Xing zhuangtai: dangdai chengshi qingnian baogao* (New trends: report of contemporary urban youth), Beijing: *Zhongguo Qingnian Chubanshe* (China Youth Publishing House).

Confucius (1993), *The Analects of Confucius*, Chinese–English bilingual edition, Jinan: Qi Lu Press.

Deng, Xiaoping (1994), *Deng Xiaoping Wenxuan, Di Er Juan* (Selected Works of Deng Xiaoping, Volume II), Beijing: *Renmin Chubanshe* (People's Publishing House).

Diamond, Larry (1999), *Developing Democracy: Toward Consolidation*, Baltimore and London: The Johns Hopkins University Press.

Diamond, Larry, Juan Linz, and Seymour Martin Lipset (eds.) (1995), *Politics in Developing Countries: Comparing Experiences with Democracy*, Boulder: Lynne Rienner Publishers.

Diamond, Larry, Marc Platter, Yun-han Chu, and Hung-mao Tien (eds.) (1997), *Consolidating the Third Wave Democracies: Regional Challenges*, Baltimore and London: The Johns Hopkins University Press.

Goldman, Merle (1994), *Sowing the Seeds of Democracy in China*, Cambridge: Harvard University Press.

Han, Sung-Joo (ed.) (1999), *Changing Values in Asia: Their Impact on Governance and Development*, Tokyo: Japan Center for International Exchange.

He, Baogang (1996), *The Democratization of China*, New York: Routledge.

Huntington, Samuel P. (1991), *The Third Wave: Democratization in the Late Twentieth Century*, Norman: University of Oklahoma Press.

Jiang, Yihua (2000), '*Ershi shiji zhongguo sixiang shiahang de zhengzhi baoshu zhuyi*' (Political conservatism in the history of thoughts of twentieth century China), in Li Shitao (ed.), *Zhishi fengzi lichang: jijing yu baoshu zhijian de dongdang* (The stances of intellectuals: fluctuations between radicalism and conservatism), Shidai Wenyi Publishing House.

Liu, Allan (1996), *Mass Politics in the People's Republic: State and Society in Contemporary China*, Boulder: Westview Press.

Liu, Shaoqi (1981), *Selected Works of Liu Shaoqi*, Beijing: *Renmin Chubanshe* (People's Press).

Liu, Zhifeng (ed.) (1999), *Zhongguo zhengzhi tizhi gaige wenti baogao* (Reports on the Political Reforms in China), Beijing: Zhonguo Dianying Chubanshe.

MacFarquhar, Roderick (ed.) (1997), *The Politics of China: the Eras of Mao and Deng*, 2nd edition, New York: Cambridge University Press.

Ming, Qi (1989), *Zhongguo zhengzhi wenhua: minzhu zhengzhi nanchan de shehui xinli yinsu* (Political culture in China: elements of social-psychological difficulties in democratic politics), Yunnan: Yunnan People's Publishing House.

Morley, James W. (ed.) (1993), *Driven by Growth: Political Change in the Asia–Pacific Region*, New York: M.E. Sharpe.

Mori, Kazuko (1993), *Gendai chugoku seiji* (Politics in contemporary China), Nagoya University Press.

Neher, Clark (1994), 'Asian style democracy,' *Asian Survey*, 34 (11), pp. 949–961.

Pharr, Susan and Robert Putnam (eds.) (2000), *Disaffected Democracies: What's Troubling the Trilateral Countries?* Princeton: Princeton University Press.

Pridham, Geoffrey (ed.) (1995), *Transitions to Democracy: Comparative Perspectives from Southern Europe, Latin America and Eastern Europe*, Aldershot: Dartmouth Publishing Company.

Pye, Lucian (1985), *Asian Power and Politics: The Cultural Dimensions of Authority*, Cambridge: Belknap Press.

Ru, Xing, Xueyi Lu, and Tianlu Chan (2001), *Zhongguo shehui xingshi fengxi yu yuce* (The year 2001: analysis and prediction of social situations in China), Beijing: *Shehui Kexue Wenxian Chubanshe* (Social Sciences Documentation Publishing House).

SCCYL or *Gongqingtuan Shanghaishi Weiyuanhui* (Shanghai Committee of Communist Youth League) (1999), *Shiji zhijiao de Shanghai qingnian: Shanghai qingnian fazhan baogao* (Shanghai Youth at the turn of century: Shanghai youth development report), Shanghai: Xuelin Publishing House.

Shi, Tianjian (2000), 'Cultural values and democracy in the People's Republic of China', *The China Quarterly*, no. 162, pp. 540–559.

Song, Tingming (1998), 'Two decades of economic reform', *China Today*, 47, pp. 10–13.

Tang, Liang. '*Kaikakki no chugoku ni okeru kokka-shakai kankei no henyo*' (Change in relations between state and society in China during the reform years), *Ajia Kenkyu* (Asian Studies), 46 (2).

Tsou, Tang (1986), *The Cultural Revolution and Post-Mao Reforms: A Historical Perspective*, Chicago: University of Chicago Press.

Xia, Ming (2000), 'Political contestation and the emergence of the provincial people's congress as power player in Chinese politics: a network explanation', *Journal of Contemporary China*, 9 (24), pp. 185–214.

Xiao, Gongqing (1994), '*Minzu zhuyi yu Zhongguo zhuanxing shiqi de yishi xingtai*' (Nationalism and ideology during the transitional period in China), *Zhanlue yu Guanli* (Strategy and Management), Beijing, no. 4.

Zhong, Yang, Jie Chen, and John Scheb (1998), 'Mass political culture in Beijing', *Asian Survey*, 38 (8), pp. 763–83.

Chapter Eight

India's Maturing Democracy

Sanjay Kumar

Introduction

India is a unique country among all its Asian neighbors. The uniqueness of India is reflected in its geography, its people, its diversities, its complexities, and, more so, in its political system. In geographical terms, India is the seventh largest country in the world and the second in Asia. With a population of just over 1 billion, it is the second most populous country in the world after China. India uses a federal system of government that divides the country into twenty-eight smaller politico-administrative units called states, where government is popularly elected by the people.[1]

India is marked by diversities—in particular, differences of language, culture, caste, ethnicity, and religion (Smith 1981; Nehru 1983). Among the Indian population, hundreds of languages and many dialects are spoken. India has also multiple religions that have varying sizes of communities, with Hindus, Muslims, Christians, Sikhs, Buddhists, and Jains composing the largest groups.[2] In addition to adhering to different religious beliefs, Indians also identify themselves through the caste system—a traditional, hereditary system of social stratification in India. Although castes number in the thousands, they are very different from each other in terms of socioeconomic status and their traditional occupational structure. The upper castes are socially and ritually higher in status than other castes. Given the multidimensional character and diversities found in India, one of my major focuses in this chapter is to examine how Indians identify themselves.

India is also experiencing rapid changes in economic structure (Jeffery and Bajpai 1997). The process of liberalization began in the early 1990s, and with it a loosening of absolute government control in the economic sphere. Subsequently, foreign investment has rapidly grown in India. Whereas new foreign companies have started economic activities in India, some existing government companies have been privatized. All this was done with a view to overall economic development that would benefit all—the rich and the poor. But these changes have failed to alleviate poverty to the desired levels, leaving over one-quarter of the population living below the poverty line. In this chapter, I am also interested to look at how the Indian people feel about the changing economic scenery and what their response has been to India's new economic order.

In a country of multiple identities where economic progress has not reached all the segments of the population, the political system may be expected to be somewhat unstable. Since the much-hyped democratic system has failed to raise the masses to, or at least near the desired levels of economic self-sufficiency (i.e. above the poverty line) and literacy, the expected outcome is that Indians would have very little support, if any at all, for democracy.[3] But what makes India's case somewhat unique is that in spite of multiple identities, which most often act as centrifugal forces, democracy as a form of government survives and has deepened its roots over the years. As the world's largest democracy, India has experienced fourteen national elections, which have elected many national governments with a considerable degree of success. Why has India's democracy been stable when many other Asian countries have yet to democratize? In this chapter, I examine some of the factors that may have possibly contributed to the strengthening of democracy in India.[4]

Participation in political process

A distinct feature of Indian democracy is the relatively high level of political participation. After India became independent in 1947, it held its first national elections (Lok Sabha elections) in 1952 to elect the political representatives of parliament. Since this was the first national election, people were very enthusiastic about exercising their right to vote for the first time in an independent India. Despite high levels of enthusiasm, the voter turnout was very low: only 46 percent of eligible voters cast their vote.

Figures released by the Election Commission of India suggest that voter turnout has significantly increased over the years from just under 50 percent in the second national election (1957) to well above 50 percent in later elections. The fourth national election (1967) saw a turnout of 61 percent and since then most elections have had generally

Figure 8.1: Turnout rates in India's lower house, 1952–2004

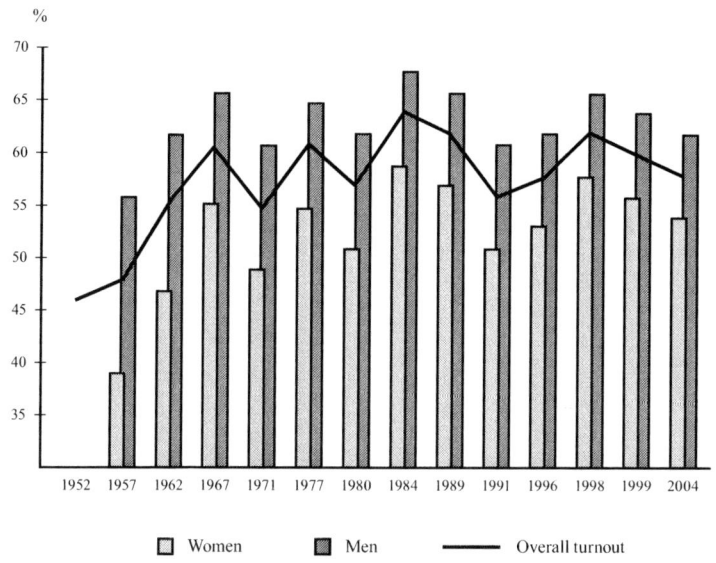

Source: Official results, Election Commission of India, available at: *http://www.eci.gov.in/*.

above 60-percent turnout rate. The 1984 national elections held after the assassination of Indira Gandhi, the then Prime Minister, witnessed the highest voter turnout at 64 percent. Figure 8.1 shows the rates of voter participation from 1952–2004.

Significantly, the number of women voters has increased dramatically over the last couple of decades. In the 1957 national election, only 39 percent of women voted, but in more recent elections the gap between the voting rates of women and men has narrowed considerably. Again, the highest turnout among women voters thus far occurred in the 1984 election, which also had the highest overall turnout on record. Although the level of political participation of women (based on their voting habits) has had ups and downs, the current voter participation rates of women continue to remain somewhat lower than those of their male counterparts.

In the past fifty years of elections, the political participation of the rural electorate has increased—not only has the percentage of rural voter turnout increased, but more importantly, during the last few decades, the turnout among the rural voters has surpassed their urban equivalents (see Figure 8.2). Although statistics for elections

Figure 8.2: Voting rates in rural and urban areas

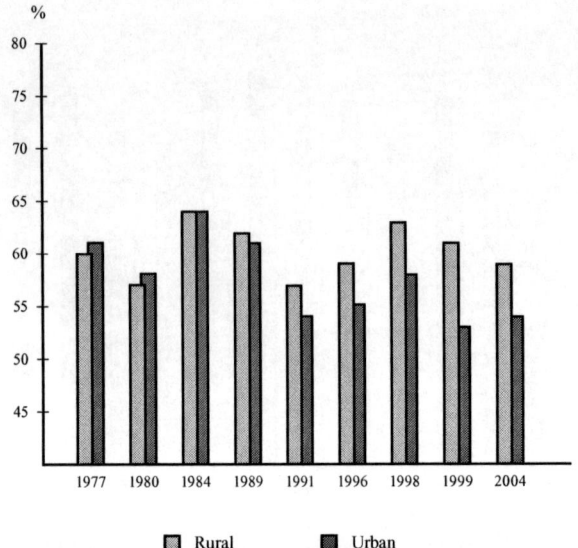

Source: Center for the Study of Developing Societies (CSDS) Data Unit (http://www.lokniti.org/dataunit.htm).

Note: Rural-urban classification is based on census data.

held prior to 1977 are unavailable, it is generally believed that elections held before that year witnessed much lower voter turnout in rural constituencies. Statistics indicate that voter turnout in the 1977 national elections in both rural and urban constituencies were approximately the same, and that change started in the 1990s. The first time that the percentage of rural voters exceeded those of urban voters was in the 1991 Lok Sabha (lower house parliamentary) elections, when rural constituencies witnessed 57 percent turnout, compared to 54 percent for urban constituencies. Since that election, rural Indian voters have consistently shown greater participation in exercising their right to vote.

The turnout in political participation should not be seen only in terms of increasing voter participation in rural India, but also in terms of increasing political participation from underprivileged communities. The official figures for the turnout among different communities are not available, but findings of surveys conducted by Centre for the Study of Developing Societies (CSDS) suggest that compared to past elections, in recent years, voters belonging to the

Table 8.1: Turnout among social communities, 1996–2004 (%)

Social Communities	Lok Sabha				Average
	1996	1998	1999	2004	
Dalits	62.2	67.3	62.9	60.2	63.2
Adivasi	56.1	61.5	51.7	61.3	57.6
Lower caste	60.0	60.7	58.6	58.4	59.4
Upper caste	54.0	61.5	61.8	56.3	58.4
Muslims	55.7	65.2	66.9	46.4	58.5
All	57.9	62.1	60.0	58.4	59.6

Source: National Election Study, various years.
Note: The turnout figures for the survey have been weighted by the actual turnout figures for all elections.

Scheduled Castes (SC) communities (former untouchables) and those from the Scheduled Tribe (ST) communities have started to vote in greater numbers (Palshikar and Kumar 2004). (See Table 8.1.)

Democracy is based on the principles of 'one man, one vote.' It is reasonable to assume that people from the underprivileged, lower-caste communities who outnumber people from the affluent communities (referred to as upper castes) should have a greater say in Indian democracy. Yet the political history of the last four decades indicates otherwise—that a large section of society has remained on the fringes of the political process. In some parts of the country, many of the underprivileged have not been allowed to exercise their right to vote. But the greatest change that Indian democracy has witnessed over the years has been the increasing political participation of people from underprivileged communities.

The participation of all Indian people in the political process has grown from voting in elections to an increased level of public interest in election campaigns in the last decade. (See Figure 8.3.) Whereas in 1996 nearly 33 percent of voters expressed a keen interest in the election campaign, 40 percent of the electorate indicated that they took an interest in the 2004 election campaign. The extensive community-wide analysis of people's interest in election campaign suggests that this growing trend is occurring also among the marginalized segments of society.

Moreover, as the level of interest in election campaigns grows, a greater involvement of the public in campaign-related activities is also evident in the last decade.[5] In the 1996 national election, only 8 percent of voters indicated that they took part in campaign activities compared

Figure 8.3: Interest in election campaigns (%)

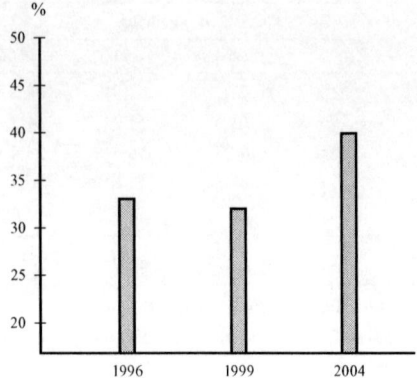

Source: National Election Study (1996, 1998, and 2004) and CSDS Data Unit.

to 32 percent of voters in the 2004 national election who confirmed participating in the election campaign. The National Elections Study survey indicates a steady increase in the participation of the public in election campaign activities.

Increased faith in democracy

A possible explanation for the increasing political participation of the Indian people over the last few decades may be their strong faith in the political system. Among the people living in South Asia, Indians have the longest experience with a democratic government, and this in turn has convinced people that democracy is the best form of government. Findings of the data collected through the National Election Study 2004, suggest that most Indians strongly endorse democracy as the form of government in India. (See Figure 8.4.) People appear to be highly satisfied with their democratic government. This is evident from the fact that about 70 percent of people believe that democracy is better than any other form of government, whereas only 4 percent of people hold the contrary view. Another 6 percent say that it makes no difference between having a democratic government and another form of government, and 20 percent of people have no opinion on this issue.

This opinion is shared by people across the social spectrum. To begin with, one might have expected older people to be more supportive of democracy than their younger counterparts. But the

Figure 8.4: Preference for political system

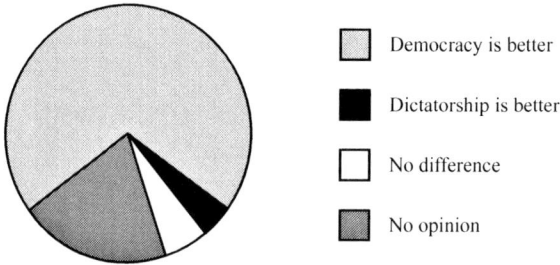

Source: National Election Study 2004 and CSDS Data Unit.
Note: Sample size is 27,184. 'Don't know' responses are excluded.

findings of the survey show hardly any difference of opinion among the varying age groups on this issue. Similarly, the difference of opinion among people with different levels of educational attainment is marginal on this issue. The illiterate and those with a high level of education all seem to be equally committed to a democratic form of government. A large majority of the Indian public firmly believe that democracy is better than any other form of government.

Democracy is generally understood as the rule of the majority of the people. Whosoever wins the largest support gets elected and forms the government. It is generally believed that a democratically elected government would cater to the needs of those who had voted the government to power. India has always had large numbers of poor people. In a democracy when it comes to voting, it is only the number that matters. Since the number of poor people is large, they matter to every political party during elections. The victory or the defeat of any political party is dependent on which party receives the vote of the poor people. It was expected that since the votes of the poor matter to every political party, whichever government came to power would take care of the needs of the poor. The expectation was if poverty could not be alleviated, that at least it could be minimized to some extent after more than fifty years of Indian democracy. The reality is that there are hardly any positive signs of the benefits of democracy going to the poor. The expectation was that the long experience of democracy would have helped the poor to fight poverty. Yet this has not happened in India. Nevertheless, the poor still have great faith in democracy, just as the financially better off and better educated electorate do. (See Table 8.2.)

Table 8.2: Preference for political system by age, education, and class (%)

	Democracy is better	Dictatorship is better	No difference
Age Group			
Below 25 years	88	5	7
26–35 years	88	5	7
36–45 years	88	4	7
46–55 years	89	4	7
56 years and above	86	5	9
Education Level			
Illiterate	84	5	11
Primary	87	5	7
Secondary	90	4	6
Above secondary	92	4	4
Economic Class			
Very poor	86	5	9
Poor	87	5	8
Lower	89	4	7
Middle	90	5	5
Rich	88	6	6

Source: National Election Study (2004) and CSDS Data Unit.
Note: Sample size is 27,184. 'Don't know' responses are excluded.

What seems to have strengthened the roots of democracy in India is the enormous level of faith in the political system and belief in the legitimacy of the individual vote. In such a huge democracy with millions of voters, where the electoral system is based on the principle of 'one man, one vote,' one might think that people do not place a great deal of importance on the single vote that they are allowed to cast at election time. But this fails to accurately capture how Indians feel about their right to vote. People do not only have great faith in democracy, but they also have a strong belief in the democratic system. For a large majority of people, their vote matters.

Data collected over time suggest that faith in the democratic system has increased over the years among Indian voters. Three decades ago, only 48 percent of the Indian people believed that their vote mattered, but, in 2004, that number grew to 67 percent. (See Figure 8.5.) The belief that the individual vote makes a difference is growing stronger by the decade, and clearly indicates that the confidence of voters to exercise their franchise has strengthened in last few years.

Figure 8.5: Believe that the individual vote matters (%)

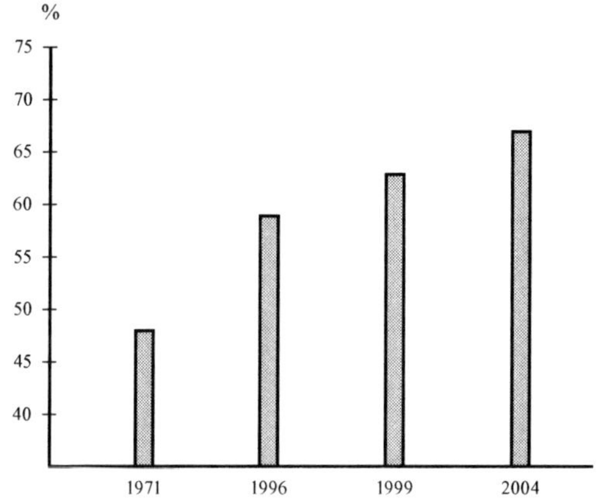

[Bar chart showing: 1971 ≈ 48%, 1996 ≈ 59%, 1999 ≈ 63%, 2004 ≈ 67%]

Source: National Election Study, various years and CSDS Data Unit.

Similarly, the recognition of the importance of political parties in Indian democracy has become stronger and stronger over the last few decades. Whether the voters like or dislike a political party is a separate issue that does not alter the fact that the majority of the electorate view political parties as an integral part to democracy. A large majority of Indian voters believe that democracy in India cannot operate without political parties and legislative assemblies. Recently, public support for political parties has become more pronounced than in the early days of Indian democracy. According to the results of the National Election Study, in 1971, only 43 percent of the people believed that political parties were important in India. This number, however, jumps to nearly 72 percent in 2004. Whereas the percentages for those who hold a negative opinion on political parties have not changed, overall, people have become more definite about their opinions.

Rural India is very different from urban India in terms of economic prosperity, educational and employment opportunities, and standard of living.[6] In general, the rural population is at the lower end of these socioeconomic indicators and the city dwellers on the higher end. Yet despite these differences, the rural people hardly differ from their educated urban counterparts when it comes to expressing their views on politics and other related issues. Both seem to have a firm faith in the democratic system and political parties. (See Table 8.3.)

The general assumption is that differences of opinion should exist between people of two different generations, and that the opinions

Figure 8.6: Increasing belief that political parties are important (%)

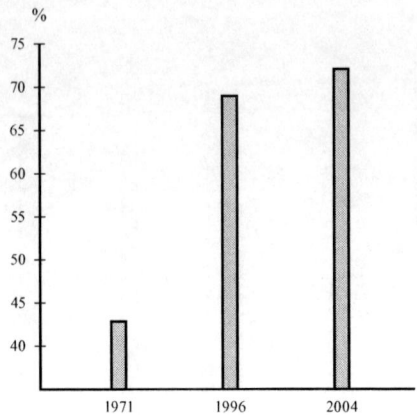

Source: National Election Study (1971, 1996, 1999 and 2004) and CSDS Data Unit.

of younger people might stand in sharp contrast to those of an older generation. This is what sociologists term cultural lag. Although my focus does not include examining generational differences on various social issues, the findings of the National Election Study survey indicate that on political issues, the difference of opinions between the generations is negligible. Voters of all generations, more or less, have equal faith in democratic institutions and in the importance of their vote. People of all ages shared the view that political parties and legislative assemblies are essential to the functioning of Indian democracy.

Another potential source for differences of political opinion among people may be differences in education levels, especially between those who are illiterate and those who are educated. But this does not hold true for the Indian. Those who are illiterate or who have a lower level of education may not be as knowledgeable, but among those who express their views, the opinions of the illiterate segment of the population and those of the highly educated barely differ on political issues. Irrespective of their educational attainment, people firmly believe that political parties and legislative assemblies are important for the functioning of democracy, and that, without these political institutions, government cannot run. Whether illiterate or educated, all believe that their vote is important. Hence, to some extent, this explains the increasing participation of people in political processes, both directly and indirectly.

Table 8.3: Importance of vote and parties (%)

	Those who think their vote matters	Those who believe that India cannot be run without parties and assemblies
Locality		
Urban voters	81	89
Rural voters	79	89
Age Group		
Below 25 years	81	88
26–35 years	81	90
36–45 years	79	89
46–55 years	78	87
56 years and above	76	89
Education		
Illiterate	72	88
Primary	79	88
Secondary	83	89
College educated	87	90
Social Class		
Very poor	75	89
Poor	77	89
Lower	81	89
Middle	83	90
Rich	85	90

Source: National Election Study (2004) and CSDS Data Unit.
Note: Sample size is 27,184. 'Don't know' responses are excluded.

India is a country with a large number of poor people, of which a quarter still live below the poverty line. After independence and the adoption of a democratic form of government, the expectation was that a democracy would respond better to the needs of the poor who form the majority. Although some progress has been made, democracy has failed to meet the expectation of poverty relief held in the formative years. Under these circumstances, one would expect the poor to be greatly dissatisfied and to be critical of the existing political system, but the findings of the National Election Study survey indicate that both the poor and the rich express the same level of faith in the democratic system.

Similar proportions of people from all economic classes share the view that the government cannot be run successfully without political parties and legislative assemblies. These two are key to the functioning of Indian democracy. Yet not everything is fine: despair permeates the lives of the poor. Although the poor vote in most elections, compared to the rich they seem to be somewhat subdued in expressing their belief that their vote matters in democracy and that it plays an important part in Indian democracy.

The snapshot of Indian democracy is not all gloomy: findings of the National Election Study survey conducted during the last decade suggest that a growing proportion of the poor believe that their vote matters. During the 1996 national elections, approximately 68 percent of the very poor believed that their vote was important, with this figure growing to 75 percent in 2004. In the last decade, all economic classes have experienced an increased awareness about the significance of the individual vote; interestingly, the proportional increase is higher among the very poor than in other socioeconomic classes.

Belief in democracy

Among the Indian public, the passage of time has brought a strengthening of political faith in democracy. A democratic system represents the will of the majority, and it is expected to respond to the needs and demands of this majority. Five decades of democratically elected governments is an accomplishment, but the sad reality is that after fifty years of democracy at work, immense poverty still plagues the majority of the Indian electorate. Even with the continuation of abject poverty, the public participation rates in the political process have risen along with public trust in the political system and institutions. The question that begs to be asked is: what makes the poor support a system that has been unable to deliver on key issues for them?

The economic data indicate that large numbers of people still live below the poverty line in India, but the same data also indicate that the national economy has undergone considerable change recently (National Sample Survey, NSS, 1999–2000). During the last decade, the Indian economy has experienced tremendous structural changes (Singh 1993; Sachs and Bajpai 1997; Jenkins 1999). One of the most important changes has been increasing privatization and the opening up of various foreign and multinational companies in India, which impacts profoundly the occupational structure of the country. On the one hand, new employment opportunities are growing in the private sector, and on the other hand, the government is undertaking a process of downsizing and retrenchment of public employees. All these changes in the occupational structure affect the financial well-being of households. Currently, debates rage over whether Indians have become more prosperous or have become poorer.

The findings of the National Election Study survey indicate that people hold both kinds of opinions. On balance, however, it seems that the proportion of those who believe that they have become economically more prosperous outnumber those who believe that they have become much poorer. About 28 percent of people believe that their economic conditions have improved in the past few years, whereas only about 19 percent feel that their economic conditions have become much worse. Thus, it appears that the balance is tilted in favor of positive opinions. Although, at the national level, positive assessments of the changing economy exceed negative ones, differences of opinion exist between socioeconomic classes.

Figure 8.7: Change in economic conditions among different segments of population

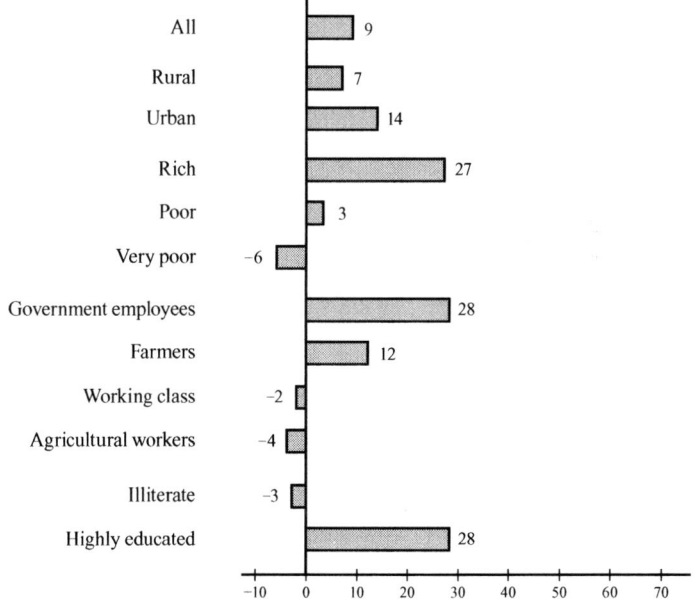

Source: National Election Study (2004) and CSDS Data Unit.
Note: Sample size is 26,215. Figures calculated only among those who held an opinion on this issue. The net figure reported is calculated by subtracting those who mentioned that the economic situation has become worse from those who felt their economic situation has improved.

A large percentage of the rich, or those employed in the government sector, or those highly educated note a significant improvement in their economic conditions over the past few years. On the reverse side of the changing economic structure are those who evaluate their economic condition as becoming much worse, and they include the very poor, the illiterate, manual workers, and agricultural laborers. Between these two opposing assessments are those who feel that their economic conditions have improved but not to a great extent—the improvement is just satisfactory. This group of people includes generally those who live in villages and are engaged in farming for their livelihood.

The changes in economic conditions are also reflected in that the Indian public has a general feeling of being more prosperous today than in the past. Although the rich and affluent segments of society may have benefited the most from economic development, it cannot be denied that some benefits of economic progress have also reached those in the lower social strata of society. Hence, the sense in the country is that overall economic progress has been achieved. It is this development that has made many Indians feel that their lives have progressed and have become more dignified life compared to the past. The percentage of people who believe that they live a less dignified life than their parents is 22 percent for urban and rural Indians. It is not surprising that urban dwellers (44%) feel that their dignity has improved more than those in rural areas (37%).

Although more people feel that they live a more dignified life than their parents, this feeling is not shared equally among different economic groups. (See Table 8.4.) The majority of the rich (58%) and large numbers of the middle class (48%) believe that they live a more dignified life, but among the poor (33%) and very poor (30%) the numbers are much lower. The majority of the poor and very poor believe that their life is not much different from that of their father. The dalits (the 'backward' caste) also believe that their life has changed very little in comparison to that of their father. The level of development may not have taken place to the desired extent, but the Indian public is satisfied generally about the level of development reached thus far. It is this satisfaction that makes people in India maintain their faith in democracy.

Satisfaction with economic development

It is noteworthy that the scope of discontentment about development is class based. Thus, it is probable that regional disparity and class

Table 8.4: Present living conditions (%)

	Living a more dignified life	Less dignified life	No difference
Locality			
Rural	37	22	41
Urban	44	22	34
Religion			
Hindu	39	23	38
Muslim	41	24	35
Christian	57	22	21
Sikh	35	28	37
Other minorities	45	23	32
Caste/Tribe			
Upper caste	44	24	32
Middle caste (Backward castes)	38	23	39
Dalits (Lower caste, S.C.)	33	23	44
Adivasis (Primitive tribes, S.T.)	43	23	34
Social Class			
Rich	58	17	25
Middle	48	19	33
Lower	38	20	42
Poor	33	24	44
Very poor	30	28	42
All	39	22	39

Source: CSDS South Asia Survey (India) and CSDS Data Unit.
Note: Sample size is 5041.

disparity within each region exist, because not all regions of a country and all segments of society within a region can benefit equally in the ongoing processes of development. This is true of the Indian situation (Kurian 2000; Datt and Ravallion 2002; Deaton and Dreze 2002; Dholakia 2003; Bhattacharya and Sakthivel 2004). Economic development is not enough to meet the daily needs of all the people, and, as a result, many experience hardships in their lives. Conversely, some economist point to the results of another national-level survey that show that in spite of some recent improvement in the income of the people, the majority do not earn a sufficient amount and that their life is full of hardships. Even with recent economic development, only one-quarter of the population earns enough to meet their daily needs.

More surprisingly, a very tiny section of population earns more than what they need to meet their needs. Only a small percentage of people are in a position to save after meeting their family needs.

Furthermore, nearly one-quarter of the Indian people indicated that they led a life of extreme economic hardships, and another 40 percent people said that they also do not earn enough to meet their daily needs and that their life is one of economic hardships. Although the rich seem to be relatively well-off, the poor and the very poor appear to struggle with their low income. Among the very poor and the poor, about 89 percent and nearly 80 percent, respectively, either live their life in great difficulty or with hardships. Naturally, the life of the rich and the middle class are the reverse of the poor and very poor. In terms of differences between the cities and villages, life is generally harder for those in rural settings. When comparing the percentages of those who suffer daily hardships, have barely enough income, or are able to save, the rural counterparts always fare less well than urban dwellers. (See Table 8.5.)

Undoubtedly, India still has a large proportion of poor people, the majority of which live a difficult life, but what distinguishes Indians from people in other developing/developed countries is their high level of satisfaction with their economic life. Indians hold different opinions about their present economic condition, but, on balance, more people are satisfied than dissatisfied. Of the population, nearly one-third feels satisfied with their present economic condition.

The level of satisfaction about economic conditions also varies according to different social groups. People who live in the cities are

Table 8.5: Sufficiency of income by economic class (%)

Economic class	Income not sufficient, live life in great difficulty	Income not sufficient, live life in difficulty	Income just all right	Income covers the needs, can make little savings
Rich	3	17	51	29
Middle	7	36	43	14
Lower	19	46	30	5
Poor	32	48	17	3
Very poor	49	40	10	1
Rural people	26	42	26	6
Urban people	15	33	36	16
All	23	40	28	9

Source: South Asia Survey (India) and CSDS Data Unit.
Note: Sample size is 5041.

more economically affluent, and it is, therefore, not surprising to note that urban people feel more satisfied with their economic situation than those who live in villages. The rich also feel more satisfied with their economic condition than the poor and very poor. Moreover, the nature of occupational structure has changed. Gone are the days when people used to only look for employment in the government sector. Now the trend has somewhat reversed. The younger generation prefers to work in the private sector rather than for the government. Attitudes of the young have changed due to the new salary structure where most of the young and talented are paid large, private-sector salaries. With this change in workplace preference, it is normal that the younger people are more satisfied with their present economic condition than those of the older generation. Despite being poor, the great degree of satisfaction among the people helps to sustain the people's faith in democracy. (See Figure 8.8.)

Figure 8.8: Overall satisfaction of people with their present economic conditions

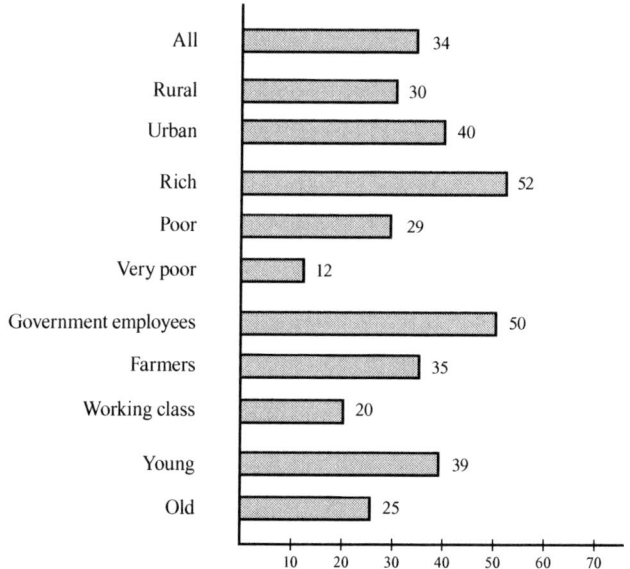

Source: National Elections Study (2004) and CSDS Data Unit.
Note: Sample size is 26,232. Figures calculated only among those who held an opinion on this issue. The net figure reported is calculated by subtracting those who are dissatisfied from those who feel satisfied.

Satisfaction with future economic conditions

More than anything else, what holds people's faith in democracy is a positive attitude about the future. Although economic development has reached different groups of people, large proportions of people have been left out of the process of economic development. Yet these large segments of the population believe that their economic conditions will improve in the months and years to come.

Of this 'have not' group, 66 percent think that their economic conditions will improve; 8 percent believe that their economic conditions will become much worse; and 26 percent feel that their economic conditions will barely change. In general, Indians are optimistic about their economic future. Whereas the rich and the well-off are more positive about their economic future, this optimistic view cuts across all social groups, with the exception of those engaged in manual and agricultural labor. It is only among those who are engaged in manual work, either in the organized sector or in the unorganized sector like agriculture, are the opinions more negative than positive. This group does not believe that their economic condition will improve in the coming years.

If we look at the opinions of the people about their future economic expectations, we find that those who are high on the socioeconomic ladder hold more positive opinions than those near the bottom of the ladder. (See Figure 8.9.) For example, the upper castes are relatively much more positive about the economic conditions of their children compared to those who belong to the dalit community. Similarly, among those who are already prosperous, the overwhelming majority of them believe that their children will have a much better life than the present life they lead. As we go down the socioeconomic ladder, the intensity of a bright economic future deems. Although the majority of people, even among the poor and very poor, believe that the life of their children will be much better than their life, a significant proportion of them feel that the economic well-being of their children will not change substantially from that of their life and that they may have, more or less, the same quality of life.

Even though opinions may differ about the comparative economic well-being of the present compared to the past, opinions about the future appear to be much more optimistic. More than two-thirds of the Indians feel that their children will have a better life compared to the life that they have lived or expect to live. The proportion of people who think that the life of their children will be worse than their life

Figure 8.9: Future expectations about economic conditions

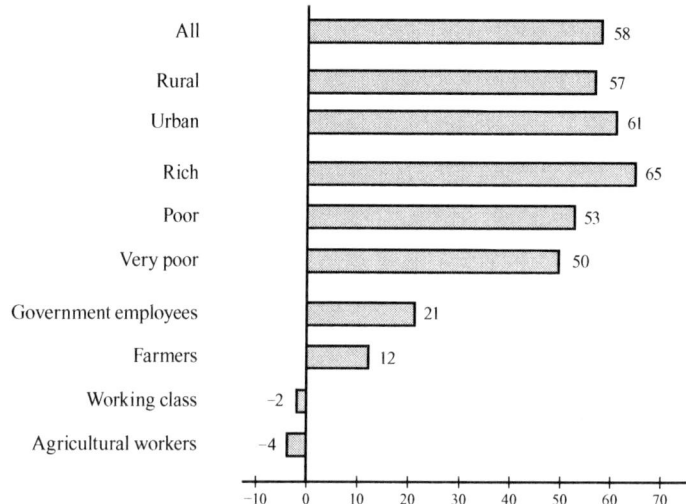

Source: National Elections Study (2004) and CSDS Data Unit.
Note: Sample size is 20,345. Figures calculated only among those who held an opinion on this issue. The net figure reported for all is calculated by subtracting those who believe that their economic condition will become worse in future from those who feel that their economic condition will improve.

at present is very small. Nearly one-fourth of the people think that their children will experience no difference in the quality of their life in the coming years. The increasing urban affluence is reflected also in opinions about the future. Compared to the people living in villages, people living in the cities are more positive about their future economic prospects. (See Table 8.6.)

Although opinions on the economic future do not differ greatly among religious communities, Christians tend to be more positive about the future of their children. A large proportion of Christians believe that their children will have a better life than their parents.

Conclusion

The unfolding socioeconomic and political story of India in the past decade suggests that large-scale changes are occurring in Indian society. Some of these changes are moving in different directions, and are at times even contradictory to each other. Yet the core sociopolitical structure remains unaffected.

Table 8.6: Perception of future economic conditions (%)

Background of respondents	Children's life would be better	Children's life may be worse	No difference
Locality			
Rural	66	10	24
Urban	74	7	19
Religion			
Hindu	68	11	21
Muslim	68	9	23
Christian	78	11	11
Sikh	63	14	24
Other minorities	63	16	21
Caste/Tribe			
Upper caste	72	11	17
Middle caste (Backward castes)	68	10	22
Dalits (Lower caste, S.C.)	64	11	25
Adivasis (Primitive tribes, S.T.)	64	14	22
Social Class			
Rich	79	9	12
Middle	72	9	19
Lower	70	7	23
Poor	65	9	26
Very poor	58	14	28
All	68	10	22

Source: South Asia Survey (India) and CSDS Data Unit.
Note: Sample size is 5041.

As in many parts of the world, the Indian economy is changing rapidly with an increasing trend toward privatization. In the early 1990s, Indians did not readily accept the government's privatization initiative, but over the years, more and more people have come to support the policy of privatization. While the debate continues over whether the policy of economic liberalization has led to economic prosperity or not, and whether it has benefited the poor or not, the attitude of Indians toward democracy and politics has not been negatively affected by this national discussion. If anything, the faith in democracy has increased over the years.

Three factors appear to have contributed to an increasing level of faith in democracy: relative economic prosperity among certain segments of the population; a fair degree of satisfaction about current economic conditions; and optimistic expectations about future economic prospects. These three areas of positive assessment appear to have greatly strengthened Indian democracy. The increased support for Indian democracy is reflected in growing public participation in the political process. Increased voter turnout and growing public interest and participation in different election campaign-related activities is evidence of the faith of the Indian electorate in the democratic process. In sum, ever since independence, India represents a picture of a maturing democracy—a democracy that is becoming stronger and stronger with each passing decade. Indeed, it is fair to say that India presents a unique picture of unity among tremendous diversities.

Notes

1 Until 1999, there were 25 states. In 2000, three new states were created. Uttranchal, Jharkhand, and Chhatisgarh were carved out of Uttar Pradesh, Bihar, and Madhya Pradesh, respectively.
2 According to 2001 Census, Hindus accounted for about 80.5 percent and Muslims about 13.4 percent, together constituting 94 percent of the total population. Christians and Sikhs accounted for about 2.3 and 1.9 percent, respectively.
3 According to the National Sample Survey (NSS) 1999–2000 (55th round) report, approximately 27 percent of people live below the poverty line. The poverty ratio is higher in rural areas (26%) than in urban areas (24%).
4 The findings of the surveys reported in the chapter draw from the National Election Studies (NES) and other surveys conducted by the Centre for the Study of Developing Societies (CSDS). The survey during the NES 1996–1999 was a panel study that consisted of about 9,000 voters from 432 locations, randomly selected across all the major states of India. The NES 2004 consisted of about 27,189 respondents. The interviews were conducted at 2,380 locations across all 29 states of India. For more details, see *www.epw.org.in*. For more information about CSDS including information about the data handbooks used in this chapter, see *http://www.csdsdelhi.org/intro.htm*.
5 Activities include attending meetings regarding the election campaign; participating in political processions and election rallies; participating in door-to-door campaigns; making political donations or contributions; collecting campaign funds; and distributing election pamphlets and posters.
6 Although India is becoming more and more urban, just under three-quarters of its population still lives in villages. In the 2001 Census, about 28 percent of India's population lives in urban centers. The pace at which urbanization is taking place, it is expected that by the year 2021 half of India's population will be living in urban centers.

Bibliography

Bhattacharya, B. B. and S. Sakthivel (2004), 'Regional growth and disparity in India: comparison of pre- and post-reform decades', *Economic and Political Weekly*, 29 (10).
Deaton, Angus and Jean Dreze (2002), 'Poverty and inequality in India', *Economic and Political Weekly*, September 27, pp. 3729–3748.
Dholkia, R. (2003), 'Regional disparity and economic and human development', *Economic and Political Weekly*, September 27, pp. 4166–4172.
Frankel, Francine (2005), *India's Political Economy: 1947–2004*, New Delhi: Oxford University Press.
Jafferlot, Christophe (2003), *India's Silent Revolution: The Rise of the Lower Castes in North India*, London: C. Hurst & Co.
Jenkins, Rob (1999), *Democratic Politics and Economic Reform in India*, Cambridge: Cambridge University Press.
Krueger, Anne (2002), 'The Indian economy in global context', in Anne Krueger (ed.), *Economic Policy Reforms and Indian Economy*, New Delhi: Oxford University Press.
Kurian, N.J. (2000), 'Widening regional disparities in India—some indicators', *Economic and Political Weekly*, 35 (7), pp. 538–550.
Nehru, Jawaharlal (1983), *The Discovery of India*, New Delhi: Oxford University Press.
Palshikar, S. and Sanjay Kumar (2004), 'Participatory norm: how broad-based is it?' *Economic and Political Weekly*, 34 (51), pp. 5412–5417.
Sachs, Jeffery D. and Nirupam Bajpai (1997), 'India's economic reform—the steps ahead', *Journal of International Trade and Economic Development*, 6 (2).
Singh, Manmohan (1993), 'New economic Policy, Poverty and self-reliance' in Siddheswar Prasad and Jagdish Prasad (eds.), *New Economic Policy: Reforms and Development*, New Delhi: Mittal Publication, pp. 1324.
Smith, Vincent (1981), *Oxford History of India*, Oxford: Oxford University Press.
Yadav, Yogendra (2000), 'Understanding the second democratic upsurge: trends of Bahujan participation in electoral politics in the 1990s', in Francine R. Frankel et al. (eds.), *Transforming India: Social and Political Dynamics of Democracy*, New Delhi: Oxford University Press, pp. 120–145.

Appendix

Gallup International Millennium Survey (1999)

Research scope

- Respondents: General public aged 18 or over (97%)
- Total sample size: 53,800+
- Sampling area: National/Urban
- Interview method: Face-to-face/Telephone
- Fieldwork period: August 1999 – October 1999
- Surveyed countries and sample size: Argentina (1,513); Armenia (800); Australia (780); Austria (780); Belarus (1,009); Belgium (1,001); Bolivia (1,326); Bosnia (500); Bulgaria (1,104); Cameroon (1,001); Canada (1,038); Chile (605); China (578); Colombia (1,000); Croatia (998); Czech Rep (500); Denmark (1,001); Dominican Republic (500); Ecuador (660); Estonia (487); Finland (1,049); France (1,006); Georgia (1,013); Germany (1,004); Ghana (1,002); Hong Kong (509); Hungary (1,000); Iceland (619); Ireland (1,395); Italy (1,001); Japan (1,321); Kazakhstan (500); Korea (1,509); Latvia (504); Lithuania (1,003); Luxembourg (500); Macedonia (820); Malaysia (1,014); Mexico (515); Netherlands (902); Nigeria (1,030); Norway (552); Pakistan (462); Paraguay (500); Peru (1,001); Philippines (1,000); Poland (968); Romania (1,350); Russia (2,000); Singapore (506); Slovakia (1,000); Spain (602); Sweden (1,000); Switzerland (502); Taiwan (526); Thailand (510); Turkey (2,001); United Kingdom (1,022); Ukraine (1,200); Uruguay (527); USA (1,005)

Questionnaire

Hello my name is ____ from ____. We are conducting a global opinion poll in relation to the Millennium and we would very much like you to participate. The same questions are being put to thousands of people like you in more than sixty countries around the world.

It will be the largest survey ever of global opinion at the steps of the new Millennium. The results will be widely published around the globe. The survey covers a number of very important issues in understanding the situation today and what the people of the world expect from the future. Would you like to participate? The interview takes approximately 20 minutes.

The first subject is the environment.

The environment

Q1. How satisfactory do you find the overall state of the environment in *[this country]*? Do you find it...
- Very satisfactory
- Mainly satisfactory
- Mainly unsatisfactory
- Very unsatisfactory
- DO NOT READ OUT: Don't know

Q2. In your opinion, has the government done too little, too much or the right amount to address the environmental issues in *[this country]*?
- Too little
- Too much
- The right amount
- Don't know

Q3. Which of the following statements do you tend to agree with more?
- It is more important to protect the environment than to ensure economic growth
- It is more important to ensure economic growth than to protect the environment
- DO NOT READ OUT: Don't know

Q4. I am going to read a list of environmental issues currently facing many countries. Please tell me which two you consider to be the biggest threat to future generations not only in *[this country]* but in the whole world as well.
- Traffic pollution
- Pollution of drinking water
- Global warming

- Holes in the ozone layer
- Accidents with nuclear energy
- Industrial pollution
- Pollution from farming
- Loss of rainforests, species and wildlife
- DO NOT READ OUT: None
- DO NOT READ OUT: Don't know

Now we change the subject and move to a different topic.

Democracy

Q5. Would you say that *[this country]* is governed by the will of the people?
- Yes
- No
- Don't know

Q6. Do you feel that elections in *[this country]* are free and fair?
- Yes
- No
- Don't know

Q7. Which of the following words describes you perception of the government of *[this country]*?
- Efficient
- Bureaucratic
- Corrupt
- Just
- Responds to the will of the people
- DO NOT READ OUT: None
- DO NOT READ OUT: Don't know

And once again, moving to a new topic.

Religion

Q8. Apart from weddings, funerals and christenings, about how often do you attend religious services these days?
- More than once a week
- Once a week

- Once a month
- Only on special holidays
- Once a year
- Less often
- Never, practically never
- Not answered

Q9. What is your religious denomination?
- Roman Catholic
- Protestant
- Other Christian
- Jew
- Muslim
- Hindu
- Buddhist
- Other
- None
- Refused to answer

Q10. Would you say that there exists one and only one true religion, that there is truth in many religions or that there is no essential truth in any religion?
- One and only one true religion
- Many true religions
- No true religion
- Don't know
- Not answered

Q11. How important in God in your life? Please use this scale to indicate. 10 means very important and 1 means not at all important

Q12. Do you take some moments of prayer, meditation or something like that?
- Yes
- No
- Don't know
- Not answered

Q13. Which of these statements comes closest to your beliefs?
- There is a personal God

- There is some sort of spirit or life force
- I don't know what to think
- I don't really think there is any sort of spirit, God or life force
- DO NOT READ OUT LOUD: Not answered

I'd now like to change the subject again and ask you about another topic.

Womens' rights

Q14. Would you say that in *[your country]* women have equal rights with men or not?
- Yes, women have equal rights
- No, women do not have equal rights
- Don't know

Q15. I'm going to read out some statements and I'd like you to tell me for each one whether you agree or disagree?
- Education is more important for boys than for girls
- Both the husband and the wife should contribute to the household income
- On the whole, men make better political leaders than women do.
- When jobs are scarce, men should have more rights to a job than women
- A woman needs to have children in order to be really fulfilled
- Sometimes when a women says no to sex, she doesn't always mean it
- Women in advanced countries must insist more for the rights of women in the developing world

Again, we change the subject.

Crime

Q16. How concerned are you personally about the level of crime in *[this country]*?
- A great deal
- A fair amount

- Not very much
- Not at all
- DO NOT READ OUT: Don't know

Q17. To what extent would you say your concern about crime has increased or decreased in the past five years?
- Increased a lot
- Increased a little
- Stayed the same
- Decreased a little
- Decreased a lot
- DO NOT READ OUT: Don't know

Q18. How well do you think the government is handling the issue of crime?
- Very well
- Fairly well
- Not very well
- Not well at all
- DO NOT READ OUT: Don't know

Q19. In some countries, private citizens are allowed to own guns, whilst in other countries they are banned completely. Thinking of this country, do you think there is too much control of guns, too little control or about the right amount of gun control?
- Too much
- Too little
- About right
- Don't know

Q20. When a person is sentenced by a court of law, what should be the main aim of imprisonment?
- To re-educate the prisoner
- To make those who have done wrong pay for it
- To protect other citizens
- To act as a deterrent to others
- DO NOT READ OUT: Don't know

Q21. Are you personally in favor or against the use of the death penalty?
- In favor

- Against
- Don't know

The next topic is what matters most in life.

What matters most in life

Q22. I would now like to ask you, what you would say matters most in life. I will read out a list and ask to tell me only two things that matters the very most in life?
- To have a good job
- To have a good education
- To be faithful to my religion
- To have a good standard of living
- To live in a country where there is not war
- To have a happy family life
- To live in freedom
- To live in a country without violence and corruption
- To have a good health
- DO NOT READ OUT: Don't know

Q23. I will now read out the list again, but this time I would like to ask you, which are the two things that you would say matters least in life?
- To have a good job
- To have a good education
- To be faithful to my religion
- To have a good standard of living
- To live in a country where there is not war
- To have a happy family life
- To live in freedom
- To live in a country without violence and corruption
- To have a good health
- DO NOT READ OUT: Don't know

We now turn to a different subject, namely the United Nations.

The UN

Q24. How satisfactory do you find the results achieved by the UN up until now?

- Very satisfactory
- Somewhat satisfactory
- Somewhat unsatisfactory
- Very unsatisfactory
- DO NOT READ OUT: Don't know

Q25. What would you say should be the most two important aims for the United Nations in the future?
- To improve the health of human beings
- To give humanitarian aid in times of natural disasters
- To give humanitarian aid in times of war/conflict
- To prevent war by intervention
- To maintain peace by armed forces
- To develop into a world government
- To protect human rights
- DO NOT READ OUT: Don't know

The next subject is human rights.

Human rights

Q26. I am now going to read out to you some of the rights mentioned in the Universal Declaration of Human Rights and I want you to tell me whether you think that this right is being fully respected, partially respected or not respected in *[your country]*
- No one shall be subject to torture
- All are equal before the law
- Marriage shall be entered into only with the free and full consent of the partners
- Everyone has the right to freedom of religion
- Everyone has the right to freedom of speech
- Everyone has the right to equal pay for equal work

Q27. In general do you think that human rights are being fully respected, partially respected or not being respected at all in *[your country]*.
- Fully respected
- Partially respected
- Not respected
- Don't know

Q28. In 1948, The United Nations proclaim the Universal Declaration of Human Rights which states that all human beings are entitled to human rights irrespective of race, color, sex, language, religion or political opinion. Please tell me for each of the following whether discrimination is taking place frequently, sometimes, rarely or whether such discrimination never takes place in *[your country]*.
- Discrimination on the basis of sex
- Discrimination on the basis of color
- Discrimination on the basis of language
- Discrimination on the basis of religion
- Discrimination on the basis of political opinion

Q29. Article 5 of the Declaration states: 'No-one shall be subjected to torture or to cruel, inhuman or degrading treatment or punishment'. This was re-affirmed in 1993 by most of the 185 countries in the world. In how many of them do you think the use of torture is currently documented?
- Don't know
- None
- Less than 20
- 20–50
- 51–100
- 101–150
- 150+

Q30. Do you think that any use of torture is documented in *[this country]*?
- Yes
- No
- Don't know

Q31. How effective do you think each of the following would be in reducing or eliminating torture? For each: is that very effective, quite effective or not at all effective?
- Stricter control of police/law enforcement officers
- Stricter international laws against the use of torture
- More prosecutions of those suspected of torture
- Greater public awareness of the incidence of torture
- Grassroots campaign to ban torture

Q32–35. On the topic of the Year 2000-problem that computers may suffer (omitted).

Demographics/classification

Sex:
- Male
- Female

May I have your age please?
- Under 18
- 18–24
- 25–34
- 35–44
- 45–54
- 55–64
- 65+

What is your current education?
- No education
- Primary education
- Secondary education (High School)
- University degree
- Don't know/No response

What is you current occupation?
  <NOT WORKING>
  - No current occupation
  - Housewife/looking after home
  - Student/Military Services
  - Part time employed
  - Unemployed
  - Retired/Unable to work
  <SELF EMPLOYED>
  - Farmer/Fisherman
  - Owner of shop or company
  - Business owner/Partner
  <EMPLOYED>
  - Professional (lawyer, medical practitioner, consultant, architect, etc)

- Employed in service sector (hospital, police, school, restaurant, etc)
- General Management (any type of director etc)
- Middle Management (unit head, project manager etc)
- Working mainly at desk (clerical type of job etc)
- Traveling type of job (salesman, driver etc)
- Manual worker (skilled and unskilled)
- Never Worked
- Other
- No response

Could you please tell me your marital status?
- Single
- Married/living together
- Separated/Divorced/Widow
- Don't know/No response

Are there any children under 15 living in your house?
- Yes
- No
- Don't know

Index

9/11 8, 33

accountability 16, 64–5, 67, 70–1, 92, 95, 104, 110–11, 122, 124
administrative guidance 22
Adulyadejm Thai (Theravada) Buddhism 127
Anti-nuclear power movement 79
Anti-pollution and protests 79
Asia 1–10, 14, 18–19, 22, 31, 34–5, 38–9, 40, 43–4, 47, 49, 51, 59, 67–9, 71, 73, 84, 106, 111, 123, 128–30, 135, 148, 161–3, 168, 177–8, 182
Asia in Japan's embrace 5
Asian Development Bank 110, 121, 128
Asian financial crisis 18–19, 129
Asian politics 2, 66
Asian values 2, 4–5, 7–9, 18–19, 31–2, 42–3, 59–60, 68–9, 84, 87, 105–6, 123, 129
Asian values offensive 4–5
Asian-style democracy 18, 135
authoritarian regime 57, 61, 65–6, 147, 159

Barisan Alternatif 86, 93
Barisan National 86, 88
Buddhist economics 119
Buddhists 99, 163
Bumiputera 87, 89–90, 92
Bush, George W. 33, 35

cable television 102
capitalism 2–3, 119, 135, 152
Chinese Communist Party 3, 131
Christian 87, 163, 177, 181–3, 188
citizens 1–2, 6, 9, 13, 15–16, 20–1, 28, 30, 33, 42, 44–7, 49, 51–3, 56, 58–1, 65–9, 72–5, 81–2, 84, 94, 101–2, 109–10, 114, 117, 127, 131, 138, 140, 142–3, 152–6, 159, 190
citizenship 46, 71, 89, 106
civic mindedness 46
civil liberties 7, 9–10, 13–15, 23, 25, 41, 56, 71, 75, 83, 96, 131, 145
civil society 7, 45–6, 65, 72, 78, 80, 83, 86, 88, 97, 102, 108, 113, 118, 126, 136, 160
classical democracy 6
Cold War 2, 4–5, 8, 44, 152
collective action 58, 80
collectivism 133–4, 147, 149
collectivist 4
colonialism 1
communism 5, 134, 148–9
communitarian values 4
communities 105, 110, 157, 163, 166–7, 181
comparative democratization 66
competitive clientelism 127
confidence in government 45, 58
Confucian capitalism 135
Confucianism 4, 31, 133–6, 147
corruption 28, 30, 45–6, 50, 64–6, 92, 96, 108, 111–2,

122, 124, 126, 130, 132, 144, 146, 157–8, 160, 191
Corruption Perceptions Index 65
coups 107
creditor confidence 120
critical citizenry 15, 68
cultural liberalization 93, 101–2, 104
Cultural Revolution 136, 138, 141, 146, 148, 156, 158
cynicism 21, 26, 28, 45, 64, 73–4, 83

democracy 1–2, 4–10, 13–22, 24–5, 28, 35, 44–5, 47, 49, 51, 56, 59–61, 64–8, 70–6, 78–9, 82–4, 86, 92–5, 97–8, 101–2, 104–5, 107–8, 112, 116, 120, 126–7, 132, 134–6, 138, 140–5, 148, 153–60, 163–4, 167–74, 176, 179–80, 182–3, 187
democratic consolidation 56, 66, 70
democratic governance 16, 20–1, 41, 46, 55–6, 67–8, 70–2, 75, 83–4, 96, 108, 126
democratic opening 70
democratic representation 47–8
democratic transition 3, 61, 64, 68, 70–1, 73–4, 141
democratization 2–3, 5–8, 16, 18, 48, 57, 60–1, 64–6, 73–4, 87, 100, 105, 107–9, 116, 120, 122, 124–6, 131–2, 135, 143, 147, 152–3, 156, 159–60
Deng Xiaoping 136–7, 140–1, 144, 148, 151–2, 155
developmental authoritarianism 5

developmental state 2, 4–9, 15, 20–2, 87, 101, 105, 158–9
developmentalism 16, 87, 100–5
dictatorship 1, 7–8, 15, 107, 151, 156, 169–70
direct elections 160
dirigiste developmental state 87, 101, 105
disaffected citizenry 44, 55
disaffected democracy 21
discrimination 33, 54–5, 76–7, 83, 89, 193
disparities 2, 14
divergence 1, 3, 12
do not know responses 11–12, 24–5, 27, 48, 72, 114

East Asia 4–8, 16, 22, 31, 49, 51, 59, 67, 87, 104, 123, 135, 148, 158
East Asian miracle 4
economic globalization 60
education 21–2, 24, 26, 30–3, 36–42, 60–1, 71, 77, 89, 91, 97–9, 101–3, 112, 116, 122, 134, 140, 142, 149, 152, 169–73, 189, 191, 194
efficacy of government 49, 96
elections 1, 7, 9–13, 31–2, 40, 60, 62–4, 70–2, 86–8, 92–4, 96–9, 104, 107–8, 112–14, 123, 125, 138, 146, 160, 164–9, 174, 179, 181, 187
electoral democracy 64, 66–7
English 41, 101–2
environmental movement 79
equal pay for equal work 52–4, 75–6
equality 51–5, 67, 71, 75, 77–8, 83, 136, 142–3

equality before the law 52–4, 142
export-oriented industrialization 90

family 4, 15, 21, 30–1, 40, 133–4, 140–1, 178, 191
financial crisis 91, 100
foreign direct investment 90, 121
free and fair elections 7, 10, 13, 71, 96–8
free and full consent of the partners for marriage 76
free market economy 60
freedom from being subjected to torture 76
Freedom House 2, 9–16, 18, 23–4, 32, 40–1, 56, 71, 96
freedom of religion 75–6, 192
freedom of speech 52–3, 56, 59, 64, 75–7, 116, 128, 192
Fukuyama, Francis 2

Gallup International Millennium Survey 1, 20, 46, 71, 86, 96, 131, 185
gender equality 54, 78
global capitalism 119
globalization 5, 8, 60, 101, 119, 121, 124, 128, 147, 152, 159
governance 1–2, 4–10, 14, 16, 20–2, 25, 27–9, 41, 46–7, 49, 55–6, 60–1, 67–8, 70–2, 75, 83–4, 96, 107–17, 119–23, 126, 133, 156–7
government 1–5, 7, 10, 15–17, 20–2, 25–6, 28–9, 32–3, 36, 40, 44–51, 56–68, 72–6, 78–9, 81–4, 86–92, 95–105, 107–22, 124–8, 132, 137–8, 142–8, 150–1, 153–9, 161, 163–4, 168–9, 172–6, 179, 181–2, 186–7, 190, 192
government by the will of people 21
government efficacy and performance 29, 45, 49, 60–1, 67, 72, 82, 138, 143, 154, 159
gun control and the death penalty 82

health 9, 15, 30–1, 40, 45, 61, 73, 94, 112, 115–16, 150, 191–2
hierarchy 114, 125, 127, 135
high costs 45, 128
Hindus 99, 163, 183
Hu Yaobang 148
human rights 1, 9–13, 15–17, 22, 32, 41, 51–3, 60–1, 67, 71, 75–8, 83, 98–9, 109, 116–17, 132, 143, 150, 192–3
Huntington, Samuel 71, 135

ideological vacuum 4
illiberalism 7
industrialization 3, 21–2, 90, 147
inefficiency 45
information revolution 6
institutional checks 64
integration of global markets 2
International Monetary Fund 56, 92, 120

Jains 163
Jiang Zemin 149, 158–9
job 30–1, 41, 58, 78, 82, 90, 100, 140, 189, 191, 195

Kim Dae Jung 56–7, 59, 66, 109

King Bhumipol 108, 118-9, 127
Kuomintang 5

Lee Denghui 5
Lee Kuan Yew 4, 59–60, 144
Liberal Democratic Party (LDP) 28
Liberalism 6–7, 45, 71, 143, 146
Liberalization 3, 56, 70, 93, 100–2, 104, 146, 148, 163, 182
Liu Shaoqi 134
localization 121
Lockheed scandal 26–8, 40

Malaysia Chinese Association (MCA) 87, 103
Malaysian Indian Congress (MIC) 87
Mao Zedong 132, 136, 141, 151–2
mass political culture 66, 131
May Fourth Movement of 1919 141
middle class 17, 93, 95, 100–2, 107, 123, 159, 176, 178
modernization 17, 20, 123, 134, 137, 151–2, 160
Mohamad, Mahathir bin 4
monarchy 107, 110–11, 113, 116, 127
money politics 90, 107–8, 112, 120
moral cultivation 133–4
moral obligation 75
Muslims 87, 99, 163, 167, 183

nature conservation movement 79
negativism in politics 67
no violence 30–1, 40

non-bumiputera 87, 89
non-governmental organizations (NGOs) 64, 91, 93–4, 99, 115–17, 119

organized protests 72, 79, 107, 111

participation 7, 45–6, 57, 64–5, 71, 86, 104, 107–12, 114, 116, 118, 120, 122, 126–7, 142, 160, 164–8, 172, 174, 183
participatory democracy 92–3, 95, 97, 104–105
patriotism 148–9
patron-client relations 45, 107, 124
patronage 89, 108, 124–126
peace 21, 30–1, 150, 192
per capita GDP 23–25, 29, 32, 34–5, 40
pluralization of mass media 102
political culture 66–7, 86, 100, 131–2, 135–6, 138, 142–3, 145–6
political democracy 6, 107
political institutionalization 136
political interest and involvement 46
political parties 16, 62, 64, 67, 90, 102–4, 107, 113, 125, 171–3
political reform 16, 74, 108, 131–2, 137, 141, 145, 158–60
political rights 9–10, 13–15, 23, 25, 41, 56, 71, 96, 108
political tolerance 46
political transparency 64
poor 17, 45, 61, 67, 116, 118, 121–2, 137, 157, 164, 169–70, 173–82

populist rhetoric bureaucratic polity 125
public commitment to democracy 67, 70
public good 45–6
public opinion surveys 1, 10, 14, 17, 131
public safety 78, 80–3
public satisfaction 44, 46, 82, 154
public works and services 101–3
Pye, Lucian 135

quasi democracy 86, 96, 100

reformasi 86, 91, 93, 95, 99, 104
regional federal system 163
regional governance 8
religion 17, 21, 30–1, 33, 40, 75–7, 87, 89, 97–8, 116, 127, 132, 163, 177, 182, 187–8, 191–3
rent-seeking 124
responsible governance 47, 49
resurgence of Islam 102
Ruggeiro, Renato 2
rule of accountability 110
rule of integrity 109
rule of law 7, 16, 67, 71, 86, 92, 95, 97, 109, 126, 134, 137, 142, 156
rule of participation 110
rule of transparency 109
rule of value for money 110
rural 17, 89, 116–19, 125–6, 132, 137, 156–7, 160, 165–6, 171, 173, 175–9, 181–3
rural development 116–18

Sartori, Giovanni 62
Scheduled castes 167

Scheduled Tribe communities 167
self-reliance 118–19
self-sufficiency 119
semi–democracy 59
Sen, Amartya 109, 119
Shinawatra, Thaksin 108, 119, 128
Sikhs 87, 163, 183
social capital 45–6, 71, 117
social liberalism 71
social movements 72
societal liberalism 6–7
South Asia 1–2, 168, 177–8, 182
Southeast Asia 5–7, 22, 49, 51, 67, 87
standard of living 9–13, 16, 30–2, 40–1, 131, 137, 171, 191
syncretic state 86

technological innovation 6
third-wave democracy 2, 4, 6–9, 15
Tiananmen 141
trade unionism 58
traditional liberalism 45
trust 44–7, 49, 51, 55–6, 59, 62, 68, 71–5, 96–7, 109, 132, 138, 147, 151, 154, 156–7, 174
Tu Weiming 134

U.S. Presidential system 62
U.S.-led military actions in Afghanistan and Iraq 8
United Malays National Organization (UMNO) 87–8, 90–3, 95, 101
Universal Declaration of Human Rights 10, 52, 76, 192–3

vote buying 107–8, 111, 113, 120

war 1–2, 4–6, 8, 25, 28, 30, 36, 38, 40, 44, 136, 143, 147, 150, 152, 156, 191–2
war on terrorism 8
Weber, Max 134
Western-style democracy 59–60, 156
white-collar trade unions 64
World Bank 4, 121–2, 126
World Trade Organization 2, 159

Yu Yingshi 134